For Rupprecht Scherff,
who got me to thinking about the
Kronprinzessin Cecilie,
and for Marjolein Leopold,
who helped me to learn more about her

Acknowledgments

Other than those to whom this book is dedicated, my thanks are due to many. First of all to Kitty, my devoted helpmate, my joyful wife and my patient partner of half a century. Then to a whole bunch of others who have not had to put up with the attention-absorbing devotion to the research that has gone into this endeavor. Ken Gaulin, who knows more about steamships than I, by far, who provided critical input at the start and along the way. Paul Nicolai, my occasional lawyer, produced the court record of our heroine, the *Kronprinzessin*; Marty Hecht, the volunteer archivist at Lowell Observatory ransacked "the web" for countless esoterica; Larry Wasserman of Lowell Observatory, worked out the phases of the moon as pertinent to several episodes; Otto Franz, also of Lowell Observatory, performed sterling feats of translation from original German texts; Helmut Microys read the entire manuscript at an early stage of its completion and saw to it that I used correct Germanic grammar; Elizabeth Kariel corrected my syntax while her husband split my cordwood; and John Boyle, my associate in alpine politics, generously offered numerous insightful additions from his excellent library.

Many of the photographs used in this book are taken from the library of the Steamship Society of America in Baltimore, where Giselle Haitsuka has been most gracious in answering questions and preparing photographs. Other illustrations and immense help in improving the text came from the gracious Klaus Keidel, manager of the Deutsches Shiffarts Museum in Bremerhaven, and from Hans-Jürgen Kapell, archivist for HAPAG/Lloyd in Hamburg. The maps that accompany the text were painstakingly prepared by Cynthia Webster, also of Lowell Observatory.

As I was almost finishing the manuscript, I visited with a former associate in the 10th Mountain Division in World War II. Bob Gess had been assigned as my personal messenger in 1944, when I was charged with the Weapons Platoon of Company "L" of the 85th Mountain Infantry, and to him I owe my survival in combat. On this later occasion, however, he presented me with some papers, photographs and books that he had inherited from his father, who had served in the U.S. Navy during the Great War. These items were most helpful in completing the text — and once again I am enormously in his debt.

I have made frequent use of public sources in this endeavor, most often the Cline Library of Northern Arizona University, and, of course, the aging pages of the *New York Times*.

THE KAISER'S MERCHANT SHIPS IN WORLD WAR I

Launching the *Imperator*, 23 May 1912. HAPAG/Lloyd.

THE KAISER'S
MERCHANT SHIPS
IN WORLD WAR I

by William Lowell Putnam

McFarland & Company, Inc., Publishers
Jefferson, North Carolina, and London

ALSO BY WILLIAM LOWELL PUTNAM

John Peter Zenger and the Fundamental Freedom
(McFarland, 1997)

Library of Congress Cataloguing-in-Publication Data

Putnam, William Lowell.
    The Kaiser's merchant ships in World War I / by William
Lowell Putnam.
        p.   cm.
    Includes bibliographical references and index.

    ISBN 978-0-7864-0923-5
    softcover : 50# alkaline paper ∞

    1. Merchant ships— Germany — History — 20th century.
2. World War, 1914–1918 — Naval operations, German.
3. Passenger ships— United States— History — 20th century.
4. World War, 1914–1918 — Naval operations, American.

D581 .P68 2001
940.4'5943 — dc21

                                    2001031221

British Library cataloguing data are available

Manufactured in the United States of America

Cover image: Cunard liner *Carmania*, built in 1905 (Steam Ship
Historical Society of America)

McFarland & Company, Inc., Publishers
  Box 611, Jefferson, North Carolina 28640
    www.mcfarlandpub.com

Contents

Preface

The thesis of this book is that the merchant marine of Germany played an unintended but decisive role in that nation's defeat in the Great War of 1914–18.

The internal resources of Germany were still intact in 1918, though her export trade had all but ceased. Her manpower reserves became the limiting factor in continuing the war. With the delivery of a million American fighting men — occupying one quarter of the Western Front by the fall of 1918 — Germany's hopes were clearly doomed: a fact that had become obvious to everyone, even finally, to the Kaiser himself.

The mechanism which delivered this army to Europe did not exist in America before the war began. When the Kaiser's armies were mobilized for war, everyone in his high command knew it would only be a short campaign. The troops would be home "before the leaves fall" and certainly no later than Christmas. The wrongness of this calculation led the German rulers into complacency regarding the whereabouts of their large merchant fleet when the war began. It was assumed that the English enemy would control the seas, so instructions were issued to seek shelter in a neutral port. As soon as the French were knocked out of the war, Britain would make peace and the German merchant marine, second in size in the world and now carrying much more prestige, would be free to go about its business once more. In the meantime, America was the biggest and best neutral nation and the liners would be safe there.

After these very ships delivered the American army, the crowning irony of the Kaiser's misguided assumption occurred late in 1918 when the American president arrived in France to take his place at the Versailles peace table. Escorted by a retinue of battleships and other small naval craft Woodrow Wilson debarked at Brest from one of the world's finest luxury ships, the American liner *George Washington*. To many people, this was a most appropriately named ship. What better name could be borne by a ship bringing the American president to take the leading place in settling the affairs of Europe? Little appreciated by many was the bitter fact that the name had been bestowed on the ship at the time of her launching by its prewar owner, the North German Lloyd.

The luxury liners of North German Lloyd and its friendly competitor, the Hamburg-American line, brought first the American army and then the American president to Europe. Without those vessels, the war might well have dragged on much longer — as the elder von Moltke had predicted — and perhaps have ended differently. These vessels were the biggest — if not always the fastest — and surely the most trusted ships of the transatlantic trade. With others that carried the German flag, they represented the ultimate perfection of the Hanseatic maritime tradition.

At the start of the Great War of 1914–18, there were 11 German-owned shipping firms whose vessels plowed the North Atlantic Ocean and beyond. Operating out of Gydnia was the small Gydnia-Amerika Line. From Hamburg, Germany's largest port, sailed seven lines— German-Australian, German East Afrika, Hamburg-Amerika (HAPAG), Hamburg-Süd Amerika, F. Laeisz, Oldenburg-Portuguese and Woermann. From Bremen sailed three — Atlas Levant, Hansa and North German Lloyd (hereinafter often called NDL). The narratives that follow are largely concerned with the passenger ships operated by HAPAG and NDL, owners of by far the largest and best-known fleets, but they were all good ships that earned good profits for their owners and sailed the oceans with pride and purpose until the political egos of Europe, in a last gasp of vainglorious royal prerogative, destroyed their livelihoods and drove all but a minuscule handful of them into foreign ownership.

Thrilling histories of ships— for war and peace —fill many a shelf in many a library, but only a few of those described below went out in a literal blaze of debatable glory. Most of these ocean liners finished their days in ignominious obscurity, their halcyon eras of bright bunting, shrieking whistles and cheering crowds, even their original builders and names, long forgotten. They deserved better. This book, therefore, contains only a few tales of heroism at sea, and equally little of human conflict against the forces of nature. These ships won their glory in peace and only accidentally in war. But some of them — even close to half a century after the last of them went to the breakers' yards—remain known as among the greatest seagoing vessels of all time.

This book could have easily been a story of men, rather than ships, for the men who built and ran the two major steamship companies of Germany, as well as the skippers of their ships, were extraordinary. Not only did they build their peacetime enterprises to world leadership in the years prior to 1914, but they had to start almost from scratch to rebuild them in 1919. Then, having regained their status as leaders among the maritime transportation industry, a generation later Germany's political leadership forced their successors to go through the same process of destruction, and the Hanseatic entrepreneurs had to rebuild their enterprises a third time. Such feats of human persistence have seldom been equaled and they deserve recognition. This narrative is basically concerned with the wartime careers of these entrepreneurs, and though an outline of critical events in their lives follows, their full personal stories must be told by others. The basic part of this narrative concludes with the settlement of the Great War of 1914–18.

Other than references specifically cited in the text, the interested reader may find helpful background information in the following volumes:

- *Atlantic Highway*, by Warren Armstrong; John Day; New York, 1962.
- *Graf Spee's Raiders*, by Keith Yates; U.S. Naval Institute Press; Annapolis, 1995.
- *Building the Kaiser's Navy*, by Gary E. Weir; U.S. Naval Institute Press; Annapolis, 1992.

PART ONE

1

Background

Most Americans at the start of the 21st century have little personal recollection of what their history texts refer to as World War I, but it became known in England as "The Great War" (a term we shall use throughout this book in order to avoid confusion) and in Germany as "Der Erste Weltkrieg." It is not our intention to recite in detail the countless small, large and age-old factors that entered into the causes of this conflict; dozens of skilled historians in dozens of countries have already analyzed these matters from all their various angles and viewpoints. However, it might be well to recapitulate a few salient facts.

In 1914, the countries of Europe were linked by a complex series of overlapping treaties and traditions of mutual support. Though by 1911, it was clear that all the major participants had already chosen sides. Part of what held off the inevitable conflict was the uncertainty connected with the very complication of these varied more recent agreements and longer-standing traditional relationships. They simply could not all be implemented without considerable disappointment or severe breakage. Of all these understandings and formal commitments, two were most significant:

The economically vigorous and newly consolidated German Empire — run by the Hohenzollerns — was closely linked culturally and commercially with its sometimes friendly Teutonic neighbor, the somnolent remnant of the ancient Holy Roman Empire, run by the Habsburgs and reconstituted as the Dual Monarchy of Austria-Hungary. The Habsburg family, originally of Swiss origin, controlled the kingdom of Hungary after 1438 when Albert V of Austria was elected as king Albert II of Hungary. Despite lingering Italian resentment over Austrian retention of land south of the more easily defended Danube-Adriatic divide that the Risorgimento movement felt should be Italian territory, since 1882 the two German-speaking entities had been linked with Italy in a supposedly secret treaty known as the "Triple Alliance." To this day, however, despite the postwar settlement in Italy's favor, the natives of South Tyrol resent the partition that followed the Great War and retain their native German language and culture. Meanwhile, the Austrian fortifications that had been built to dominate the Italian valleys of Venezia and Friuli remain impressive landmarks. As a seriously complicating sidebar to this Italo-Teutonic linkage, in 1902, the Kingdom of Italy entered into an agreement with the Republic of France whereby each promised to remain neutral in the event of an attack on the other.

Czarist Russia and republican France had been bound since 1893 by a mutual defense agreement that was basically aimed at forestalling future German aggression against either country. And in 1904, highly stimulated by the rapidity and quality of German naval construction, Great Britain abandoned its traditional "Balance of Power" foreign policy, overcame the remnants of a centuries' old enmity, and took the first tentative steps into an "Entente Cordiale" with France. This agreement was strengthened in 1907 by an Anglo-Russian treaty of mutual support that brought into being a "Triple Entente." The existence of this alliance, despite a long Anglo-German relationship, was an almost direct response to Kaiser Wilhelm II's continual saber-rattling and, of course, increased the German paranoia about being "encircled by enemies."

These were the two main camps, but other less well-known agreements covered the obligations in time of war of almost every nation of consequence in Europe, with the exception of treatyless Switzerland, which everyone respected as a safe haven of neutrality. Thus, it was widely held within the soon-to-be "Central Powers" of Germany, Austria, Bulgaria and Turkey as a "stab in the back" when premier Salandra's Italy declared war against Austria on 23 May 1915; just as it was regarded as another stab in the back a generation later when dictator Mussolini's Italy jumped on a practically prostrate France in June of 1940. Italy's entry into the Great War was followed two weeks later by a declaration of war on the part of San Marino. Italy, however, did not declare war on Germany until three months later. Italian entry on the side of the Entente was stimulated by a recognition that in the long run Allied resources would prevail and more immediately by British promises of attractive territorial readjustments after the war at the expense of Austria — which came to include the ancient Venetian possessions of Trieste and Istria.

Little appreciated at the time in many important circles were a number of considerations that affected the fighting abilities of some of the belligerent powers. Of these, the major four were:

(1) The very strong feeling of Slavic "big brotherhood" held by the Czars of Russia toward the kings of Servia (more frequently known three generations later as Serbia.) Any reader of the society pages would have known that Czar Nicholas II had been best man at the wedding of Serbian King Alexander I on 5 August 1900.

(2) The inherent military weakness in the Dual Monarchy due to so few of its heterogeneous subject peoples feeling nationalistic loyalty enough to fight and die on behalf of Emperor Franz Josef. For most of them, their native land was neither Austria nor Hungary. This condition was proven in the subsequent conflict when the Austro-Hungarian casualty rate was almost exactly half that of Germany's.

(3) The "certainty" felt by the German High Command that Russia could not mobilize enough of its huge manpower potential to do anything serious in less than six weeks, and likely twice as long. Right in so much else, the Oberkommando was wrong in this assumption by a factor of almost ten, resulting indirectly in the saving of France during the opening weeks of the war.

(4) The German misjudgment about the bulldog determination of England — when pushed too far — to uphold its treaty obligations. In this case it was the London Treaty of 1839 dealing with the territorial integrity of Belgium, which had also been signed by Austria-Hungary, France, Prussia and Russia. This colossal misjudgment of national character was to be repeated 25 years later when Germany invaded Poland. One might observe that the brief "Falkland's War" of 1982 was a misjudgment of the same nature, but by a different nation.

While the proximate causes, the lengthy build-up and the critical land actions of the Great War were, of course, important to the deployment of naval vessels and more particularly the auxiliaries that are the topic of this narrative, we do not make any attempt to redo herein the work of distinguished historians such as the more contemporary Sir Winston Churchill and the scholarly Barbara Wertheim Tuchman. Serious students of these matters are referred to Churchill's five volume series and Mrs. Tuchman's *Proud Tower* and *Guns of August*.

Contrary to a commonly understood American nonfact, the Great War did not come to an end with unexpected suddenness on the 11th hour of the 11th day of the 11th month of 1918. Except on the brutally bloody western front, it petered out over many months in stages.

(1) Despite a pact not to conclude a separate peace with the Central Powers, the first revolution took Russia out of the war by the end of 1917, an event formalized in the Treaty of Brest-Litovsk, signed by Germany and the Kerensky (Menshivik) government on 3 March 1918. This document, however, was later abrogated in its entirety by Article 116 of the subsequent Treaty of Versailles.

(2) Other than recurrent feelers toward a negotiated settlement, the first crack in the seeming solidity of the Central Powers came on 29 September 1918, with an armistice agreement signed in the northern Greek city of Thessalonica (modern Salonika) that took the horribly war-ravaged Bulgaria out of the conflict.

(3) Two major breaches in the crumbling walls of Europe's aggressor belligerents appeared a month later on 30 October 1918. Turkey — never a really forceful belligerent — reached an armistice accord with the Allies that was signed at Mudros on the Aegean island of Limnos. In addition, while Germany had been slowly starving to death economically, as predicted and planned by the policymakers of Great Britain, Austria Hungary — humiliated by the battle of Vittorio Veneto — left the Kaiser's side on the same date, in a cease-fire accord signed at the Villa Guisti in Verona.

(4) The famous armistice for the "Western Front" that was signed in the railway car on a siding at Rethondes (some 50 kilometers northwest of Château-Thierry) pertained only to Germany and was not a peace agreement at all; it was merely an agreement whereby everyone ceased firing and the Germans, finally exhausted by the "distant blockade," laid down their weapons.

All these "cease-fire agreements" were later formalized in a series of treaties that reestablished normal diplomacy and recolored the political maps of Europe and the World. There were four of them, of which the most remembered was also the most important.

(1) The Treaty of Versailles — never ratified by the United States, which executed its own separate accord in 1921 — was signed under protest by Dr. Johannes Bell and Hermann Müller as representatives of the new German Reichstag.[1] It contained 440 Articles, of which 28 dealt with Alsace-Lorraine and nine with Danzig. It also completely abrogated the 10 May 1871 Treaty of Frankfort which brought an end to the French-instigated Franco-Prussian War.

(2) A further treaty ending "the war to end all wars" was signed at Neuilly (just west of Paris on the right bank) on 27 November 1919. It

settled the future fate of Bulgaria, a small-time player, but big-time sufferer, in the recent war.

(3) The dismemberment of Austria-Hungary — whose self-centered leadership had caused the spark that ignited the late conflict[2] — came in two bites: an Austrian treaty was signed at St. Germain (some 15 kilometers west of Paris) on 10 September 1919; and a separate treaty with Hungary was executed in the Trianon Palace of Versailles on 4 June 1920. Together these treaties gave national "freedom of choice" to much of central Europe, reviving the existence of Poland and producing the new nations of Czechoslovakia and Yugoslavia, as well as greatly enhancing the territory of Rumania and somewhat that of Greece.

(4) At Sèvres, just south of Paris, on 10 August 1920, a never to be fully executed treaty was signed confining Turkey to its present dimensions. This agreement was substantially modified by the subsequent Treaty of Lausanne on 24 July 1924.

The fact that all these agreements, reallocating the world's geography, politics, and economy, were negotiated in the French language and signed on French turf indicates the strength of French influence in reaching what turned out to be a series of unfortunate, if not disastrous, accords. Despite the enormous human losses suffered by France, when the Germans — thanks to burgeoning American intervention — were finally disarmed (for their land was never invaded and fought over as in World War II) the French retained the largest army in the world and were riding high. Their understandable desire to totally suppress the German nation, regardless of economic reality, was only prevented by an insightful measure of British realism and the momentarily strong influence of Woodrow Wilson, who represented, even if few Europeans wished to admit it at the time, the real world power of the day.

The enormous losses suffered during the Great War carried forward a major legacy of bitterness, and were themselves bred of prior bitternesses dating back to the beginning of time. But it is worth understanding the nature of those losses, in order to appreciate the immediate motives of those trying to put the world back together at those Parisian conferences. The following statistics do not include the irreparably wounded, thousands and thousands of whom lingered as national burdens for decades.

In the Europe of NATO, the EU and the euro, where anyone can cross the Franco-German border at 100 kph, it is difficult to envisage the nature and number of the events of late 1914 which evoked the long-lasting and passionate hatreds that materialized at the negotiating tables of Versailles five years later. In the minds of the Kaiser's Oberkommando, Belgium was not expected to resist a German transgression of her soil; much less were her civilians expected to feel themselves transgressed. When the second of these suppositions also proved to be false, the invaders professed themselves shocked by the sullen and occasionally active hatred shown by Belgian noncombatants. This, in turn, brought on German overreactions and reprisals that shocked the world. The burning of the city of Louvain might have been understood, perhaps even explained and forgiven, harsh though it was; but not the deliberate torching of Louvain's globally esteemed library — an international treasure. The execution of civilians caught in an act of war could have been understood, if not admired. But there was no way to pass off as civilized the invader's mass slaughter of Dinant's 384 civilians — the aged, the infirm and even infants only a few weeks old, who could hardly be construed as a threat to the invaders. That could neither be forgiven nor forgotten during the lifetimes of those affected, however vicariously.

Russia, out of the war in early 1917, lost one in every 105 of its people as direct war-related fatalities. Japan, on the other hand, lost a total of only 300 men and garnered immense new territory for its picayune fatality rate of one in 180,000.[3] The United States, late coming into the conflict, lost but one in 800. The British Empire lost one in 503.[4] Italy, no more enthusiastic in this war than its sequel, lost one in 72. But France lost one in every 15 of its males, all those who were physically strong, a national bloodletting of epic proportions that was due, at least in some part, to the dogmatism and incompetence of its military leadership. Serbia, where the war started, and which was totally overwhelmed by Austro-Hungarian and German armies, also lost heavily — one out of every ten persons. Small wonder there are some residual hard feelings among neighbors in that part of the world.

On the losing side, the fatality rates were equally impressive. The German Empire lost one in 40 (Germany itself 1 in 32); the Austrian, one in 76; the Ottoman, one in 71; but tiny Bulgaria took the worst beating with the killing of one in 22 of its entire population.

For the purposes of this book, the most important provisions of the Versailles Treaty were those starting with Article 231 that dealt with reparations. These were both punitive and very detailed, even down to stating the precise number and quality of sows, heifers, rams, and so on to be supplied gratis by Germany to France and Belgium over the next seven years.

Reparations, payable by the losers and generally running into the billions of francs (or marks), were the Victorian equivalent of war crimes trials. To every victor has always belonged the spoils of combat — a convention that only the United States and only in the 20th century failed to emulate and enjoy. By contrast, in 1871, the victorious Germans imposed a three billion franc "ransom" on French independence from occupation. After the conclusion of the Great War, the French were in no mood to overlook that item, among numerous others, and Germany's assets, the more portable the better, were seen as eminently fair game. After the Second World War, Germany had no assets—only war criminals.

The crucial phrase of Article 231 began: "Germany recognizes the right of the Allies and Associated Powers to the replacement, ton for ton (gross tonnage) and class for class, of all merchant ships and fishing boats lost or damaged owing to the war." Following from this provision, every German merchant ship of 1,600 tons or greater was to be handed over to the Allies; one half of all ships between 1,600 and 1,000 tons; and one quarter of all ships less than 1,000 tons. This pretty much wiped out everything still afloat except river craft. Furthermore, this amount of existing German shipping was recognized as being insufficient to compensate all the Allies for all their losses. Therefore, Germany was also required to use its undamaged shipyard capacity for construction of new vessels which would then be turned over gratis to the Allies over the next three years.

Germany's widely feared High Seas Fleet, the very construction of which had frightened England into its alliances with Russia and France, had already been surrendered to the victorious Allies, only a token force being retained. Germany was ultimately allowed to keep six small battleships, six light cruisers, 12 destroyers and 12 torpedo boats. All of the U-boats, which had so terrified the western belligerents, were to be handed over. Despite the wartime loss of 61 such vessels—over half of all that put to sea—there were still dozens of them at large or all but completed in German ports. Within a month of the armistice, many of them went to Scapa Flow, where—on 21 June 1919—they and much of the German High Seas Fleet were scuttled by belatedly loyal seamen in furtherance of the Kaiser's wartime order that no German ship was ever to be allowed to fall into British hands.

Despite the fact that many of these ships were subsequently refloated, Article 185 took specific cognizance of this event, and as punishment for it Germany was required to turn over an additional eight battleships. (Three of these were subsequently sunk by Billy Mitchell's land-based bombers off the Virginia Capes in a largely ignored demonstration of the effectiveness of air power over sea power.) The eight were: *Oldenburg, Thüringen, Ostfriesland, Helgoland, Posen, Westfalen, Rheinland,* and *Nassau.* Along with them went eight more light cruisers, 42 "modern" destroyers and 50 "modern" torpedo boats—all to be selected by the Allies.

Germany was no longer to be a naval power; the British negotiators saw to that.

Interestingly, no mention was made in the Versailles Treaty of the German optical industry—then far and away the world's leader. It might have been advisable to have. In mid–1915, the British had been obliged to purchase, through a Swiss intermediary, 32,000 binoculars from German manufacturers to supply the needs of their troops fighting the Germans in Flanders.

Future security issues aside, war reparations, to be exacted mostly from Germany and paid mostly to France, were the major element of the Versailles Treaty. Compounded with European war debts—almost entirely due the United States—these obligations were far too great for anyone to realistically hope they might be fully met. In fact, other than those of tiny Finland, a country that was only a dream before 1917, most of them never were repaid. That portion which was collected came about mostly because of a complex daisy chain of financing: American "loans" to Germany enabled Germany to pay *some* of the reparations, in turn enabling the victorious Allies to pay *some* of their war debts to America.

The costs of the war and its immediate aftermath can be noted from the changes in the national debts of the major contestants (expressed in millions of U.S.$):

	1913	1918	1920
France	6,346	30,000	46,000
Britain	3,485	36,391	39,218
USA	1,028	17,005	24,974
Italy	2,921	12,000	18,102
Germany	5,048	44,341	53,052
Austria	2,152	16,475	17,668
Hungary	1,731	8,513	9,412

All debts of czarist Russia were abrogated by the Bolshevik regime, which did not believe in capitalism at all.

Within a very few years, the repayment and reparations process was understood to be unsatisfactory to all parties. The French, in particular, while ignoring the warlike rampages of Napoleon and others, felt that they had suffered so much in human terms that it wasn't right to require them to pay for the war economically as well. The British, who had been the world's richest people before the war, had lost enormously in both sterling terms and national prestige, despite being on the winning side. The Germans—who had seen massive casualties but no war on their home turf—felt they had been suckered into the whole humiliating and expensive peace process. The Russians went through several years of internal turmoil, abrogating all obligations of the prior regime and finally coming out not far from where they had started: with a despotic ruler, with central control of the economy, suspicious of all foreigners and deathly opposed to any liberty of thought. The Russian people were subjected, both before the Menshevik revolution of early 1917 and after that of the Bolsheviks in October, to a process of governance described in the words of Count Sergey Yulyevich Witte: "... this insane regime ... this tangle of cowardice, blindness, craftiness and stupidity...."[5] Witte, who, at age 56 had been the first prime minister to serve under the Czar's "liberalized" constitution of 1905, had opposed Russia's entry into the war on behalf of Serbia and was that nation's most farsighted statesman in generations. He, however, died in 1915 and was writing about the Czar's governance, but he might just as well have been describing that which followed.

The Austrians were reduced to a national "basket case" that could see a future only in a close economic alliance with Germany. The Serbians, whose feistiness had sparked it all, ended up winners, if such a term can be used; their new territory included the once Austrian provinces of Bosnia, Croatia, Slovenia and Montenegro. The Americans felt that they had somehow been forced to pay for the sins and greed of everyone in Europe, which they and their ancestors had crossed the ocean to escape from. As everyone found out a generation later, the settlement of the "War to End all Wars" just bred another and even worse global conflict during the course of which at least *some* of the mistakes made by both sides earlier were not repeated.

Finally, it should be recognized that long before Adolf Hitler denounced the Versailles Treaty as a mere "scrap of paper," many of its terms had expired or already been fulfilled. Many others had been ignored, altered or adulterated in a belated, if never truly acknowledged, acceptance of the reality that—warlike or peaceful, on the make or on its knees—Germany was the economic engine of all Europe. Without peaceful German prosperity, there would be no peaceful European prosperity. It was the wisdom to comprehend this reality and deal with it appropriately that gives the unsophisticated Missouri farmer, Harry Truman, who went overseas to war in 1917, a much higher place in history than the college professor, Woodrow Wilson, who sent him off to the Great War.

2

Overview

At the end of July 1914, the German merchant marine was on a par with the Kaiser's High Seas Fleet — both seagoing elements were of high quality and fast catching up with the still much larger flotillas of British merchantmen and the Kaiser's Britannic cousin's Royal Navy. In addition, the major German merchant fleet — HAPAG, operating out of Hamburg — was the largest such entity in the world. By the end of 1918, less than five years later, the once-vaunted passenger liners of Germany's merchant fleet and the equally fearsome Kaiserliche Marine were fast-fading memories. The one had been sunk, taken over or captured almost to a ship, and then used against Germany in war and later for profit by the enemies of the Fatherland; the other, having played an all but insignificant part in the conflict, was surrendered and partly scuttled in disgrace.[6]

The much touted High Seas Fleet had been Kaiser Wilhelm II's ill-considered attempt to achieve a maritime power and glory to equal if not exceed that of his royal uncle, Edward VII, and after 1910, his cousin George V.[7] Indeed, this fleet's very construction was the major factor in forcing Great Britain to alter a centuries-old policy and close ranks with France — albeit a second rank naval power — in a common defense. When war actually arrived, however, the High Seas Fleet never made it far into the "high" seas, being confined, for fear of defeat by King George's much larger Home Fleet, to its main base of Wilhelmshaven, except for a brief foray to take part in the inconclusive battle off Denmark's Cape Jutland.

In this confusing and mismanaged battle, originally planned as a foray to lead the Home Fleet into an ambush of U-boats, the vastly outnumbered and outgunned High Seas Fleet acquitted itself far better than the Royal Navy's Home Fleet. Its losses in personnel were half those of the British and its comparable losses in ships, even fewer. When it was over, however, the German fleet fled the scene of action and was ordered never to put to sea again.

Other elements of the German Navy, its Far East Squadron in particular, caused great consternation and more than a few highly distressing episodes for the Royal Navy during the early months of the Great War, but their part in the global conflict was nonetheless swiftly eliminated. Soon thereafter, Admiral Reinhard Scheer, realizing the great probability of ineffectiveness at naval conflict of Grand Admiral Tirpitz's enormously expensive capital ships, endorsed the construction of a different concept in surface raiders and of numerous Unterseeboote to prey on the enemy's warships and merchant marine in an alternative attempt to bring the Kaiser's rivals to their knees. Alfred von Tirpitz (1849–1930), who had more of the Kaiser's ear than others, had been recalled from command of the German Far East Squadron in 1898, a few years after Kaiser Wilhelm II dismissed Otto von Bismarck as Chancellor. The aging Bismarck, realizing the ultimate outcome of such a procedure, had strongly opposed construction of a battle fleet to rival that of the British. However, with the rustication of the man who had really built the German Empire, Tirpitz, as navy minister, received almost unlimited funds to build a High Seas Fleet. After the repulse of his fleet's only serious foray, the grand admiral retired from active duty. He made one more public appearance; he was elected a member of the Reichstag from 1924 to 1928.

Destroying the enemy's merchant vessels has been a long honored facet of warfare from the beginning of recorded history. Americans partook gleefully in this process during the Revolutionary War but had an entirely different attitude "four score and seven years" later. The process was considerably reversed during the American Civil War when the English-outfitted, but Confederate-manned raiders, *Alabama*, *Florida*, and *Shenandoah*, and their auxiliaries, roamed the seas spreading more fear than destruction in Yankee civilian seafarers; in total, they destroyed less than five percent of the Union's merchant fleet. Of these ships, *Alabama* was finally destroyed off Cherbourg by USS *Kearsarge*, commanded by Captain Herbert Winslow, whose son and namesake was to command a battleship of the same name as a part of Teddy Roosevelt's "Great White Fleet." *Florida* was captured in the harbor of Bahia, Brazil, by the USS *Wachusett*. The assistant engineer of the *Wachusett* was George Wallace

Melville, later to become an Arctic hero, chief engineer for the entire American Navy, and the de facto designer of the "Great White Fleet." The *Shenandoah* compiled the best record of destruction, managing to sink 28 vessels of the Yankee whaling fleet in the North Pacific, *after* being told the war was over. She then turned south around the Horn and made it safely back to England where both ship and crew were interned.

At the start of World War I, the Germans had a number of warships on foreign station. It was expected they, too, would do their share of fighting. Their effectiveness was recounted with grudging admiration by the multitalented First Lord of the British Admiralty, Winston Churchill: "... nearly every one of these German cruisers took its prey before being caught, not only of merchant ships, but of ships of war. The *Scharnhorst* and *Gneisenau*[8] sank the *Monmouth* and *Good Hope*,[9] the *Königsberg* surprised and destroyed the *Pegasus*,[10] and the *Emden* sank the Russian cruiser *Zemchug* and the French destroyer *Mousquet*. Certainly they did their duty well."[11]

By the time of the Versailles Treaty in 1919, when the dust of the Great War's conflict finally settled, all but a handful of the equally well-constructed merchant ships of the Hamburg Südamerikanische, the Norddeutscher Lloyd and its then larger and older competitor, Hamburg-Amerika Packetfahrt, AG — most of which survived the conflict afloat — bore new names, sported new colors and responded to new masters. Several of these widely acclaimed German passenger vessels had also become involved in the war as auxiliary cruisers—*Hilfskreuzer*, in German — roaming the oceans, at first quite successfully, in search of enemy shipping.

The German Empire, through the actions of its precedent Kingdom of Prussia, had been signatory to the Geneva Convention on treatment of prisoners of war and to the several Hague Conventions on such matters as the flying of false colors. However, the German *Kriegsbrauch*[12] contained no mention of any such inhibitions and before hostilities began, both German and Allied military and naval commanders were comporting themselves accordingly.

As far back as April of 1914, Britain's First Lord of the Admiralty[13] was also sure that any forthcoming war would be fought in great measure for control of the sea, and that this contest would hold a very important place in determining the outcome of the greater conflict. "...Economic pressure will be put on Germany by the distant blockade of her shores which will cut off her trade, both export and import, as a whole.[14] If this is effectively done, it is of very little consequence to us whether individual German ships are captured as prizes, or whether they take refuge in neutral harbors until the end of the war." Actually, before the war was over, the British and their allies would be quite grateful that most of the German ships took such refuge rather than toughing it out in combat or trying to run for home.

As for the "distant blockade," it was enormously effective, as no less than the great Schlieffen had feared — hence the German need for a quick but dramatic push to eliminate France. The blockade brought the German production of munitions almost to a halt, until chemists could devise a means of abstracting nitrogen directly from the atmosphere. Statistics tell the story. In 1914, the Central Powers had a trade with America of $169 million; by 1916 that had dwindled to only one million. On the other hand, at the yet to be named "Arsenal of Democracy," the value of trade with the Allies had risen from $824 million to more than three billion dollars over the same period.

"...It is reasonable to suppose that German merchant ships, other than those armed and commissioned for warlike purposes, will run for neutral harbors as soon as war breaks out, and that very few will attempt under the German flag to return home running the gauntlet of the numerous British fleets operating in the North Sea."[15]

First Lord Churchill's thesis on this count was quite accurate, but his companion prediction of impending losses at their hands was considerably off the mark. Four of the large German merchantmen had been sold to foreign interests before the war began and only five of the justly respected, large, German merchant vessels were finally equipped for combat as auxiliary warships— and actually put to sea: *Cap Trafalgar, Kaiser Wilhelm der Grosse, Kronprinz Wilhelm, Prinz Eitel Friedrich* and *Berlin*. When these had all been hunted down and eliminated, several little-known German ships took over the game and played a very useful part in terrorizing the Allied merchant ships at sea.

It was planned that way! The Germans were realistic enough to know they could not manage a traditional "blockade" of England and France, but they did hope their auxiliary raiders— and later their submarines— would paralyze the enemies' overseas trade and force the British to assign so many of their warships to protecting merchant ships that the result would be an evening of the substantial disparity between the High Seas Fleet and the Home Fleet. The task of their auxiliaries was to harass and disrupt. The task of the numerous British auxiliaries, on the other hand, was purely defensive — to prevent the Germans from performing their assignment. A great deal of preparation went into the matter on both sides. In the end, the U-boats created the most havoc with Allied shipping, but it did not start out that way. A total of 75 British merchant ships (273,000 tons) was sunk through the end of January 1915, of which surface raiders accounted for 215,000 tons. However, the total British Empire shipping sunk during the entire war was 7,133,000 tons by submarine, against 442,000 by surface ships. The British also lost the use of 82 ships (182,000 tons) detained in Central Powers ports.

All governments were then and remain now in the habit of subsidizing their merchant fleets by one device or another and are thus legally enabled to direct the course of shipbuilding in the national interest — as well as in the interest of their private owners. Thus, in 1913, the German government issued a directive that required all future merchant shipping to be designed to the following minimal specifications:

• Speed of 18 knots.
• Fuel capacity to cruise 10,000 miles at 10 knots.
• Twin-screw propulsion.
• Enhanced subdivision, including a double hull along the waterline.
• Extra pumps and watertight doors.
• Two separate sets of protected emergency steam-operated steering gear.
• Boilers and other critical propulsion machinery protected behind coal bunkers.
• Decks strengthened for mounting of two 105mm guns forward and aft and four 150mm guns broadside.
• Increased coal ports in the sides and decks.
• Munitions storage facilities, capable of being flooded.
• Provisions for installation of high-powered searchlights and carriage of steam pinnaces.
• Taller masts for radio antennae and lookout positions.
• Carriage of radio (*funk*) equipment designed to operate on German Naval frequencies.

The British were not far behind. After two years on the job as First Lord of the Admiralty, early in 1914, Winston Churchill ordered that 39 merchant ships, mostly those on the more vulnerable Far Eastern runs, be equipped with stern guns, and by the end of the year 70 ships were so outfitted.

Soon after the hostilities of the Great War were concluded, First Lord Churchill — a prodigious keeper of memoranda — also wrote: "When war began[16] the Germans had the following cruisers on foreign station: *Scharnhorst, Gneisenau,*[17] *Emden, Nürnberg, Leipzig* (China); *Königsberg,*[18] (East Africa and Indian Ocean); *Dresden,*[19] *Karlsruhe* (West Indies). All these ships were fast and modern, and every one of them did us serious injury before they were destroyed. ... In addition, we expected that the Germans would try to send to sea upwards of forty, fast, armed merchantmen to prey on commerce."[20]

Unhappily for Germany, and due to poor foresight on the part of the German Generalstab, 18 of these 40 — all but two of the best — were "voluntarily" interned in originally neutral American ports, then seized before the war was over and used against the Fatherland. In a final, economic humiliation, another ten, having mostly been in home ports and thus escaping wartime service and damage, were turned over to the victorious Allies as part of the enormous war reparations imposed on Germany. They thereby made up for a small part of what the Kaiser's warships, auxiliary cruisers (*Hilfskreuzer*), mines and U-boats had sunk during the conflict.

Two of the 40 — *Kronprinz Wilhelm* and *Prinz Eitel Friedrich*— served both belligerents before the war was over. Three — *President Lincoln*, *Cincinnati*, and *Brasilia*— were torpedoed by U-boats, and *Kaiser Friedrich* was sunk by a U-boat–placed mine while on Allied wartime service. In a final irony, two of these ships survived long enough to be sunk by American submarines in the Second World War. One of these sinkings was a case of mistaken identity; the other came about after the vessel had been refitted as an auxiliary naval craft and used in early November 1941, to verify the moorage pattern and sea duty spells of American battleships before Admiral Yamamoto's fleet set out on its Kido Butai mission (code name for the Japanese sneak attack on Pearl Harbor).

Seven of the bigger German merchant ships had originally been made in the Belfast yards of Harland & Wolff; ten were launched from the Hamburg yards of Blohm & Voss; 14 slid down the ways from the Stettin yards of Vulcan; four came from those in the Danzig yards of Ferdinand Schichau (which were more famous for the construction of warships)[21]; and one each was built in the Weser yards of Bremen and Johannes Tecklenborg's yards at Geestemünde. Eighteen of these ships sailed under the company flag of the Norddeutscher Lloyd and most of the balance pertained to the slightly larger fleet of Herr Ballin's Hamburg-Amerika Line and its Elbe River–based associates.

Actually, despite First Lord Churchill's information, the Germans had not designated 40 of these merchant ships as wartime cruisers— it was only half that number. These included mostly NDL ships; HAPAG and Hamburg Südamerika had only two apiece; and the much smaller German East Afrika line, but one.

❖ ❖ ❖

For many generations the ports of North Germany, both on the North and Baltic Seas, were bound by the merchant's guild known to history as the Hanseatic League. While the league's Diet met for the final time in 1669, its seafaring legacy remained and is still remembered in the name of Germany's national air carrier. Thus, there were a number of shipbuilding firms lining the estuaries of the North and Baltic Seas. Other than those mentioned above and the Royal/Imperial warship facilities at Wilhelmshaven, Kiel and Gdynia, the biggest yards included — from west to east — two along the river Weser near Bremen; Deschimag and Vulcan; the Vulcan and Howaldswerke at Hamburg[22]; Germania, Deutschewerft, Krupp and Norddeutscher Schiff at Kiel; Neptunwerft at Rostock; and Danzigerwerft at Danzig. After the major Kriegsmarine construction effort began during the reign of Kaiser Wilhelm II, civilian ships were primarily constructed by Blohm & Voss and Vulcan, though the others built a few. The yards of Herr Schichau were preferred by the Imperial Navy, not only because of the elder Schichau's personal reputation for sound engineering, but because they were well up the Baltic Sea and thus the farthest away from England.

Regardless of where the ships were built, when the Great War was finally settled, the victorious Allies took over all the remaining NDL and HAPAG vessels but one. Germany was allowed to keep the large but deadbeat *Victoria Luise*; it was once the fastest ship afloat and a five-day wartime cruiser, but now its boilers and engines were deemed totally beyond repair. It was a sad ending for a merchant fleet that had, only five years earlier, been labeled by many, competitors and patrons alike, as the best in the world.

In June of 1914, when the world was at peace, there were 20,524,000 tons of oceangoing shipping registered to Great Britain and its overseas dominions. The Germans were in second place, considerably behind the British, with 5,135,000 tons, and the United States came in a close third at 4,287,000 (but only by including those ships used exclusively on the Great Lakes). Exactly five years later, when the war was over but not yet settled, the British Empire registered 18,208,000 tons — a net wartime loss of 2,316,000 tons, mostly sunk by U-boats. At that time the Germans still had possession of 3,247,000 tons, but the United States had picked up to 11,933,000 tons — a great deal of it at the expense of the Central Powers.[23] After the Versailles Treaty was implemented, Great Britain and her dominions weighed in at 20,143,000, not far from where the Empire started out the war. Germany was down to a measly 419,000 tons and the United States' total had risen to 14,525,000 tons. The other major shipping nations among the victorious Allies showed considerably smaller, but similar, statistics.

3

The Leadership

In the late spring of 1847 a group of Hamburg merchants seeking to open a transatlantic trade founded the Hamburg-Amerika Packetfahrt Aktien-Gesellschaft, soon to be known by its corporate initials only — HAPAG. The following year it began operations with three sailing vessels. Ten years later, a group of merchants in the other major Hanseatic city of Bremen founded the competing Nord Deutsche Lloyd and began transatlantic operations the following season with the first of a series of steamships bearing the hometown name. Starting in 1881 NDL began to construct increasingly fast — though not as fuel efficient — steamships, a practice not emulated by HAPAG until eight more years had passed. Thereafter the two lines brought ever greater comfort and quality into their operations such that, by the start of the Great War, they had begun to dominate the upper crust traffic between the United States and Europe. After twice having lost most of their fleets in two global conflicts, the two lines merged in September 1970.

Albert Ballin was born in Hamburg in 1857, the son of Jewish immigrants from Denmark. This was the year that James Buchanan took office as president of the United States, Giuseppe Garibaldi commenced his unification effort in Italy, Elisha Otis installed his first elevator, and Czar Alexander began the emancipation of Russian serfs. Ambitious and erudite, Ballin went to England as a teenager to learn the shipping business from the bottom up. He returned to Germany in 1883, aged 26, and then

Albert Ballin, Chairman of HAPAG and leader of the world's maritime industry. HAPAG/ Lloyd.

served three years as general passenger agent in Hamburg for the English Carr Line. His competitive selling ability was so great that he cut deeply into the business of the resident Hamburg-based lines, and in 1886, was lured away to head the passenger service of Germany's oldest transatlantic steamship company, the Hamburg-Amerika Packetfahrt. Rising to Director General of HAPAG after 1899, Ballin built that line into the world's largest shipping company, and with it built the port of Hamburg into Germany's second largest city. When he came to the line, it had 26 vessels aggregating 66,000 tons' capacity. Twenty-eight years later, when war broke out in 1914, HAPAG had (worldwide) 175 ships with an aggregate carrying capacity well in excess of a million tons and capable of transporting almost half a million passengers, including in its oceangoing fleet the two largest passenger ships in the world—*Imperator* and *Vaterland*. As his career progressed, it became clear to the world that Ballin was the prime figure of German shipping and principal spokesman for the industry worldwide.

In the year of Ballin's birth, North German Lloyd was founded by a group of Bremen-based businessmen and bankers under the leadership of Hermann Heinrich Meier (1809–1898), a sometime consul, who was variously known among his associates in Bremen as an "Unternehmer und Politiker" or a "Grosskaufmann"—i.e., an entrepreneur, politician, and wholesaler. Meier stayed at its corporate helm for the ensuing 31 years, retiring just two years after Ballin entered the employ of HAPAG. This rival line soon found its niche in building fast ships for the transatlantic run. These two major German shipping companies were often in severe economic competition but also almost always willing to make "adjustments" in rates and sailing capacity to reduce the excessive and ruinous aspects of that competition. Ballin presided at a rate- and capacity-setting meeting among European carriers held in London in 1908. Also included were the Canadian Pacific and various J. P. Morgan interests in what became known as the Atlantic Conference or "General Pool." A further sign of this friendliness was found in the basically common port facilities shared by the various German lines collectively, primarily HAPAG and Norddeutscher Lloyd at Hoboken, New Jersey, across the Hudson River from New York City.

Friendliness aside, there was never a case of failing to assist others in trouble at sea. When the British ship *Volturno* caught fire and was in extremis in October 1913, eight ships came to the rescue. They represented eight different shipping firms (including both the major German lines) and six separate nations. With the completion of the *George Washington* in 1908, Norddeutscher Lloyd rounded out the $50 million complete remaking of their fleet, which had begun in 1890. After the retirement of Meier, Norddeutscher Lloyd was led for the next two decades largely by Heinrich Wiegand, who was, in turn, succeeded in 1909 by Philipp Heineken, previously manager of NDL's freight operations.

Like those of other nations, the German ship owners received a variety of subtle subsidies from their government, in addition to their lucrative mail carriage contracts. But these also carried obligations to turn their ships over to the Kaiser's Kriegsmarine for wartime purposes when asked. Every captain of a major ship knew that in such an eventuality his duties to the Fatherland outweighed those to his employer. However, just before the Great War broke out, the German owners were on the verge of canceling their exclusive mail contract with the government, because their commercial services to Australia and the Far East were really prospering and the liabilities imposed by the subsidy seemed to far outweigh the benefits accrued.

Admired and respected even in Britain, Ballin was described by Viscount Richard Haldane, then Lord Chancellor of England, as "one of the most remarkable personalities of Germany." Despite his Jewish ancestry he had become a close friend and confidant of the Kaiser for many years prior to the disastrous war he had strongly advised against undertaking. Ballin was involved with several prewar conferences with the British on where the German naval construction program was forcing England, and was later quoted as saying: "Even a moderately skilled German diplomat

Albert Ballin sits surrounded by the top management of HAPAG, **21 July 1895, on board the *Augusta Victoria*.** HAPAG/Lloyd.

could easily have come to an understanding with England and France, which could have made peace certain and prevented Russia from beginning war."

Less than a week before the German armies were loosed against Belgium and France, Ballin attended an "unofficial" but very high-level meeting in London with Chancellor Haldane, Foreign Minister Sir Edward Grey[24] and Winston Churchill in an attempt to avert the impending conflict. The meeting ended with Churchill tearfully pleading with Ballin to restrain his Kaiser and keep Germany from going to war. Ballin returned to Hamburg on 28 July, where he was publicly quoted as saying that England wanted no part of a war with Germany. "The highest authorities in London are positively determined to take no steps based on participation in the war."

As that conflict progressed, with the global enterprise he had built being almost totally destroyed in the process, this one of Germany's foremost business leaders became increasingly critical of the manner in which the struggle was being conducted. Ballin was not alone in this process. No less than General Helmuth von Moltke (the younger) stated to the Kaiser on 14 September, after the French Army had held the line of the Marne River: "Your Majesty, we have lost the war!" He was replaced as chief of staff two months later by the more hawkish Erich von Falkenhayn, who was held accountable for the defeats on the Somme and at Verdun and was in turn replaced by the heroes of the Eastern Front, von Hindenburg and Ludendorff. There were also those who felt that Ballin's behind the scenes influence had caused the rustication of Grand Admiral Tirpitz in 1916.

Ballin, however, was a German, through and through. At the very start of hostilities he was party to a long-winded "Appeal to the Civilized World" the thrust of which was to place all blame for the war on the Czar of Russia. Also signing this document was a long list of world-renowned scholars and statesmen including general Prince Karl von Bülow, Field Marshal Colmar von der Goltz, Reichstag opposition leader Matthias Erzberger, scientist Wilhelm Roentgen, composer Engelbert Humperdinck and the world-renowned scholar, Count Ernst von Reventlow.

When the final "Ludendorff" offensive of June foundered and the war began turning unmistakably sour for the Central Powers late in 1918, because of the respect with which he was known to be held internationally and because of his longstanding American and British contacts, the now infirm Ballin was asked to help represent Germany at the upcoming armistice negotiations. Urged also by the Catholic party leaders, who had long sought a negotiated peace, he accepted the task with great reluctance. The aging magnate was never able to complete his final assignment for the Fatherland, however. On 9 November, the date on which Kaiser Wilhelm abdicated his throne and two days before the Great War was formally ended, HAPAG's ten-year-old offices on Hamburg's scenic Alsterdamm (now the Ballindamm) were ransacked by rampaging revolutionaries. Albert Ballin, the second most influential civilian member of the prewar German military-industrial-political complex,[25] withdrew to his home where he died of a self-inflicted overdose of medication. Thereupon, at the request of Marshal Hindenburg, Matthias Erzberger had to sign the humiliating armistice papers for Germany. The task of rebuilding the shattered HAPAG empire was left to Wilhelm Cuno.

Just a month after the war broke out, and when many large German ships were still in very good condition but afraid to venture out from the safety of American ports, a bill was introduced by Joshua Willis Alexander, Representative from the 3rd District of Missouri and Chairman of the House Committee on the Merchant Marine. Alexander, who had been

Chairman of the American delegation to the "Conference on Safety of Life at Sea," later served as Secretary of Commerce. His measure authorized the sum of $10 million for a government corporation to purchase or construct merchant ships. Everyone knew the sum would be used for the purchase of German liners, idle in American ports. The bill was passed and Secretary of State William Jennings Bryan transmitted the purchase offer to Germany, where it was rejected.

In mid–1917 Ballin had written to Clemens von Delbrück, the "taciturn and indolent" German Minister of the Interior and a long-time crony of the Chancellor's:

"When Your Excellency [finally] decided to permit the sale of our vessels in the United States it was too late to do so, because the U.S. Government had already seized them.[26] Previous to that, when we saw that war [with America] would be inevitable, and when we had received an exceedingly favorable purchasing offer from an American group, we had asked permission to sell part of our tonnage laid up in that country.

"Your Excellency, acting on behalf of the Chancellor,[27] declined to grant this permission. ... Our company, which was the biggest undertaking of its kind in the world, and which previous to the war possessed a fleet aggregating about 1,500,000 tons, has lost practically all its ships except a very few. The losses are not so much due to capture on the part of the enemy as to measures taken by our own Government. If our Government had acted with the same foresight as did the Austro-Hungarian Government with respect to its ships in United States and Chinese waters, the German vessels then in Italy, Portugal, Greece, the United States, Brazil and elsewhere, might have been either retained by us or disposed of at their full value.

"The Austrian ships,[28] with their dismantled engines were, at the instance of the Austrian Government, sold in such good time that the shipping companies concerned are not only in a position to-day to refrain from asking their Government to pass a Shipowners Compensation Bill, as we are bound to do, but they have even enriched the Austrian national wealth by such handsome additions that their capital strength has reached a sum never dreamt of before, and that they are now able to rebuild their fleet by drawing upon their own funds, and to make such further additions to their tonnage that in the future we shall not only be compelled to compete with the shipping companies of neutral and enemy countries— which have accumulated phenomenal profits— but with the Austrian mercantile marine as well.... [29]

"...Your Excellency, I am sure, is aware of the fact that the methods of the Admiralty Staff— ignoring, as it does, all other considerations except

Modern street signs near the offices of HAPAG/Lloyd. W. L. Putnam.

its own[30]— have caused one country after another to join the ranks of Germany's enemies. In view of the shortage of tonnage which Great Britain and other of our enemies systematically try to bring about — evidently with the intention of inconveniencing neutral countries as much as possible — these latter feel compelled, for the very reason of this lack of tonnage, to declare war upon us, because the politics of our country are guided by a body of men who, unfortunately, shut their eyes to the economic and political consequences of their decisions."

In this last phrase Ballin was referring mainly to the monumental blindness of the German military leadership which was so convinced that the long-projected Schlieffen Plan really would work to knock France out of the war in less than six weeks (as it did when properly executed 26 years later) that it: (a) had no real contingency for failure; and (b) failed almost completely to use the nation's merchant marine in the manner for which it had been subsidized. Because no warnings of the imminent hostilities (comparable to the Army's mobilization orders and those given the German railroads) had been given to the nation's shipping companies, they operated on a "business as usual" basis right up to the end.

Once the conflict began, of all the principal figures on both sides, only Britain's 64-year-old Secretary of State for War, Horatio Herbert

Lord Kitchener, the hero of Khartoum, repeatedly warned his colleagues in the cabinet that the contest would be long and exhausting of man-power and wealth for all parties. On the German side, the equally leg-endary von Moltke (the Elder), now long in his grave, had warned Kaiser Wilhelm II in 1890 that the resources of modern nations were so great that he believed the next war might last seven years, or even longer, before the sheer economics of the effort would force one of the contestants to capitulate.

Thus, of the five ships (85,631 gross registered tonnage) designated to be in the first rank of readiness as auxiliary cruisers, one was simply unfit, one stayed put in New York, one was so underarmed that it was sunk before it served any of its purpose and only two actually did some of what was expected of them. In the second line of auxiliaries there were four ships aggregating 57,287 GRT, of which only one put to sea effectively. Of the four ships (81,736 GRT) in the third line, none went to war for the Kaiser; and of seven in the fourth line, only two actually did wartime ser-vice. So inept was the planning for the Hilfskreuzer that one ship — never scheduled to go to war at all — was fitted out for combat as an incidental afterthought and struck the enemy its single most devastating blow. The Great War might well have gotten off to a better start and even had a much different outcome if the Kaiser's naval advisors — who had been so suc-cessful in getting his ear to build the High Seas Fleet — had thought, in a timely manner, to use even half the ships Churchill had expected to find against him in the way that would have matched their properly prepared capabilities.

The combined fleets of all civilian German flag craft included a great many mundane vessels, tankers, tramps and cargo ships, whose places in this narrative were not anticipated by Britain's erudite First Lord of the Admiralty. As the war progressed, however, some of them played very use-ful parts in the effort and are therefore discussed in Part Five (below).

Herr Ballin's and his lesser known associates' renowned fleets saw the final loss of their membership in a variety of sad endings. Six were sunk by submarines — three of them German, two American and one British; six others were almost totally consumed by fire. During their careers four of them suffered the great indignity of capsizing while tied at their piers; all but three of them finished their days of service in foreign hands and in the traditional manner — at the ships breakers.

❖ ❖ ❖

Any account of the demise of the impressive Hanseatic merchant marine as a result of the Great War requires a brief analysis of the one

1815

1914

1925

Growth of modern Germany: 1815, 1914, and 1925.

person who initiated that war and who could have stopped it at any time up to the penultimate hour of defeat. Kaiser Wilhelm II, headstrong grandson of "der Grosse," had little of his father's or his grandfather's loyalty to the stern though successful policies by which Otto von Bismarck had crafted a united Germany out of a welter of minor kingdoms, city states and semifeudal holdings.

Ostensibly a democratic monarchy — perhaps an oxymoronic term — Germany of 1914 was ruled by the Hohenzollern kings of Prussia who reveled in the title of "All Highest." It was true that an elected Reichstag appeared to have control of the imperial purse strings. But that body was almost invariably cowed by the residual prestige of the Hohenzollern dynasty into consistent agreement with whatever leadership came from above.

After the "fall" of Bismarck in 1890, Kaiser Wilhelm was served by a series of more compliant chancellors, none of whom had the courage to speak publicly of their private views on the folly of their Kaiser's naval policy: Leo von Caprivi, Chlodwig Hohgenlohe-Schillingsfürst, Bernhard von Bülow, and finally Theobald von Bethmann-Hollweg. All these political leaders — though perhaps knowing better in their hearts — abetted the vainglorious Kaiser in his consistent efforts to advance the prestige of Germany as an imperial power to rival the status of Great Britain.

No analysis of Kaiser Wilhelm II's personality, with its constant need to reinforce the trappings of competitive supremacy, could be complete without consideration of the birth defect that afflicted his left arm. This physical disability must surely have been influential in his never-ending search for means to substantiate his imperial glory and fitness to follow in the military footsteps of his Hohenzollern ancestors. In almost every photograph or painting of this ruler, his left arm is almost invisible — a right-side view, or the arm held behind his back is almost invariably all we see.[31] So anxious was this ruler to nevertheless demonstrate his worthiness to hold the imperial throne that he overdeveloped the strength of his good right arm. Occasionally it was noted that in pulling himself into the saddle of a horse — a place obligatory for any military chieftain to be — he would overshoot and a prior-placed aide would have to surreptitiously stabilize the imperial seat.

If there is one person who could rightly be singled out for blame for the holocaust of the Great War that engulfed the world and brought down several ancient thrones, it surely must be Friedrich Wilhelm Viktor Albert

Opposite: Kaiser Wilhelm II, as remembered in the lobby of Hamburg's Hotel Kempinski. W. L. Putnam.

Kaiser Wilhelm II, as pictured in one of his enemies' war posters. *Leslie's Photographic Review of the Great War.*

of Hohenzollern (1859–1941), the King of Prussia and Emperor of Germany for 30 years after June 1888. Integral to his upbringing away from the coldness and rejection of his mother (the eldest daughter of Britain's Queen Victoria) and surrounded by military figures, was the concept of his right and obligation to fulfill every aspect of imperial power and privilege. Upon assuming the throne this inbred attitude brought him into continuous conflict with almost all moderate political leaders of Germany — a condition aggravated by his uncheckable proclivity to make the grand gesture or belligerent announcement without full thought as to the fallout or consequences.

Torn, as head of state, between a boastful but essentially peaceful intent, in the crunch he invariably sided with the militaristic element in his nation's society. Even to the end of his rule — on 9 November 1918 — they prevailed; it was the aging Field Marshall Paul von Hindenburg who finally convinced him that he had to abdicate in order that something would be left of his nation. In the official abdication document, he said: "By the present document I renounce forever my rights to the crown of Prussia and rights to the German imperial crown. I release at the same time all the officials of the German Empire and Prussia and also all officers, non-commissioned officers and soldiers of the Prussian Navy and Army and of contingents from confederated States from the oath of fidelity they have taken to me, as their Emperor, King, and supreme chief. I expect from them until a new organization of the German Empire exists that they will aid those who effectively hold the power in Germany to protect the German people against the menacing dangers of anarchy,

Advertisement for North German Lloyd. *New York Times*, Wednesday, 29 July 1914.

famine, and foreign domination. Made and executed and signed by our own hand with the imperial seal."[32]

It was Kaiser Wilhelm's decision to build a navy to rival England's which brought on the alliance against him and it was his lack of concern for his nation's merchant fleet that gave his foes the means to deliver the troops which ultimately defeated him. But never, in his later memoirs and to the end of his life, did Kaiser Wilhelm acknowledge the total lack of logic by which he insisted that Russia was to blame for a war that started by his ordering a German invasion of Belgium and France. Nor did he ever appreciate the wisdom with which he had been served by Bismarck, who saw that Germany's power was best exercised on land, which would have complemented British control of the sea rather than compete with it.

The German leadership, of course, saw the fleet buildup differently. On page 192 of "My Memoirs," published in 1919, Grand Admiral Tirpitz wrote: "British statesmen naturally did not stress the fact in their conversations with Germans that it was mainly the presence of our nearly completed fleet in the North Sea that produced their respectful tone and had lessened the probability of a British attack. Of course they only spoke of their peaceful inclinations and not so much of the facts which strengthened those inclinations. ...Seventeen years of fleet-building had, it is true, improved the prospects of an acceptable peace with England."

Finally, the Kaiser never came to understand that it was the wanton cruelty and destructiveness of his own soldiers — as in the burning of Louvain — which made it easy for the whole civilized world to view him as a monster. Perhaps, as he lay dying and another egomaniac ruled Germany, the last Kaiser recalled his dismissed chancellor's rule never to antagonize England by competing for control of the sea and never to engage in a war against Russia.

While truth is always the first casualty in any conflict, with the passage of time history generally sorts things out properly. Thus it is very difficult when assessing overall military competence to overlook the record of the French. Despite the relative anarchy of having 42 war ministers in the 43 years prior to 1914, the French General Staff was able to procure a "leaked" preliminary version of the Schlieffen Plan as early as 1904. Even with this windfall of intelligence, however, they still proceeded to fight two wars with Germany over the next 40 years and were unprepared for the right-wing drive on both occasions.

For the purpose of this account, though, it is worthy of greater note

Opposite: Advertisement for Hamburg-American Line. *New York Times*, Wednesday, 29 July 1914.

that Kaiser Wilhelm II — or his hand-picked agents — ordered his High Seas Fleet into readiness a week before his armies invaded Belgium. He ordered the German railways to cancel civilian obligations and move his Wehrmacht reserves and regulars to their assigned positions for the Schlieffen Plan. But he never gave a word of warning to his merchant marine that war was in the winds — not one word right up to the actual moment he authorized the invasion of Belgium whose neutrality he was pledged to uphold.[33] This tremendous oversight had two important and largely overlooked results: (1) the loss of the entire Hanseatic commercial fleet; and (2) the delivery into the hands of America the means to transport massive reinforcements to the battlefields of Europe, without which the mutually ruinous war would surely have gone on much longer, and might even have ended quite differently.

What follows is the dolorous tale of the loss of the pride of Germany's merchant marine and the use of much of it against the Fatherland.

4

Inventory

In the text that follows, it is sometimes difficult to "tell the players without a program." This process was complicated because both major German lines used a number of the same names for their ships; it was made even more difficult because the German Navy used some of the same names for major warships as were applied to various important elements of the nation's merchant marine. For example, another *Königin Luise* was sunk on 6 August 1914, while laying mines, and there were two *Prinz Eitel Friedrichs* interned in American ports—one in New York and one in Norfolk. Then, during the surrender of the High Seas Fleet on 19 November 1918, warships bearing the following list of names were among those crossing the North Sea to their graves at Scapa Flow: *Grosser Kurfürst, Kronprinz Wilhelm, Friedrich der Grosse, König Albert, Moltke, Karlsruhe, Nürnberg, Emden,* and *Dresden,* all of which names had already been applied to ships that played a well-known part, as documented below, either for or against Germany, in the erstwhile war.

When the Great War broke out, there were three major German shipping lines working the Atlantic Ocean and some lesser players whose ships were not among Winston Churchill's "forty." We treat these ships collectively under several principal categories.

• Part Two—those that went to war for the Kaiser on the high seas, more or less as planned.

• Part Three — those which were commandeered (mostly in 1917 by the United States) and used against Germany.
• Part Four — those that stayed at home or otherwise played no significant part in the conflict and were mostly handed over at the end of the war.

Of them all, the second group (in Part Three) became by far the most significant, for American help in winning the Great War would have been very slow to arrive in Europe in 1917–18 if there had not been a score of excellent, unused and now enemy passenger transport ships fully available in American ports.[34] Of all these ships, though, those in the first category played the most romantic roles. A few of these German vessels fall into more than one category, as will become clear.

The nonnautical person often has difficulty with the different "tonnage" figures applied to ships. Displacement tonnage is generally applied to naval fighting vessels and refers solely to the weight of water that the ship actually displaces. Deadweight tonnage is a measure of the total weight of the ship, contents and fuel. Gross registered tonnage pertains to the volume and weight of useable (cargo capacity) space aboard a passenger or freight vessel and is used to calculate harbor entry fees. Determining the title of "largest ship in the world" is generally based on this last measurement but the criterion has always been constantly shifting. As marine architecture evolved, starting in the mid–19th century, few steamships held this title longer than one year regardless of the measurement criterion.

In fuel efficiency there are some other interesting comparisons. As most of us come to learn, it takes more energy to run than to walk; likewise it takes more energy to move a 50-kilogram rock than one of only five. The same considerations pertain to steamships and the much faster airplanes of later years. The 20,000-ton German liner *Kronprinzessin Cecilie* (a heroine of this narrative) burned one ton of coal per nautical mile, when moving at her "cruising" speed — some 30 million British Thermal Units, each one of which equals 252 calories. She burned even more when in a hurry. On a normal (3,000 mile) crossing of the Atlantic, that would amount to some 90 billion BTU. By comparison, the modern American aircraft carrier, *John F. Kennedy*, burns fuel at a rate of one gallon of oil for every 17 feet traveled, some 310 gallons (or 7.05 bbl) per mile. On a normal crossing of the Atlantic the carrier consumes some 22,000 barrels of oil, or approximately 128 billion BTU. The two ships would each carry some 3,000 passengers and other freight. On the other hand, a Boeing 767, commonly used in similar transatlantic service, burns some 18,000 pounds of jet fuel to make a similar crossing, carrying less than 200 people, but for an expenditure of 358.2 million BTU. The *Kronprizessin*'s BTU-passenger-crossing rate comes out to something like 30 million while to move a comparable number of bodies, in the same length of time, the 767 has a rate of nearly 2.7 billion.[35]

Another interesting comparison is shown in the relative speeds of such ocean crossings as they evolved over a century of steam-powered transportation. In July 1840, Nova Scotian Samuel Cunard's *Britannia* went from Liverpool to Halifax and then on to Boston in a total of 14 days and eight hours. By 1849, he was running nine such paddle-wheel-driven ships, had a contract to deliver the Royal mails to the United States and Canada and his *America* went from New York, via Halifax, to its docking in the Mersey in 11 and a half days. That same year his *Canada* had made the westbound run to Halifax in eight and a half days, and newer ships—not yet launched—of 1250 tons and 249 feet in length were expected to shave the "land to land" time down to one week.

The full "inventory" of such shipping in the hands of the two major German-owned lines that served the North Atlantic as of the outbreak of the Great War—Hamburg-Amerika Packetfahrt Aktien-Gesellschaft and Nord Deutscher Lloyd—is in the Appendix. Almost all of the vessels listed survived the war, and almost all of them were lost to Germany forever. However, a very few of them—as is indicated—later found their way home.

For ease of understanding the effectiveness of firepower in the descriptions of ships in the Great War, the following table shows the major differences in the progression of increased gun bore.

Bore		Weight of Projectile	
1"	25.4 mm	1 pound	0.45 kg
2"	50 mm	6 pounds	2.6 kg
3"	75 mm	12–15 pounds	5.3–6.6 kg
4"	105 mm	28–32 pounds	12.3–14 kg
5"	130 mm	50 pounds	22 kg
6"	155 mm	100 pounds	44 kg[36]
7.5"	190 mm	200 pounds	88 kg
9.2"	234 mm	380 pounds	167 kg
10"	254 mm	500 pounds	219 kg
12"	305 mm	850 pounds	373 kg
13.5"	343 mm	1250 pounds	548 kg
16"	380 mm	1920 pounds	842 kg

From this table it is clear that the weight (i.e., volume of explosive) of every projectile increased not only with the diameter of the gun bore, but also with the length of the shell that could be effectively used in a larger caliber gun. However, because of the difficulties in manhandling bigger guns, normal use of field pieces greater than 155 mm was out of the question except in the cases of the most enormous siege mortars. Bigger diameter guns were almost exclusively used aboard naval craft. At the very close of the Great War, some American battleships were equipped with 16-inch guns, but the largest ever used in combat in the war were the 15-inch guns aboard several British capital ships.

Early in the conflict on land, the Germans used some 350 mm pieces made by the Austrian armament works at Skoda, and some of Krupp manufacture with the enormous diameter of 420 mm. These were transported on tracks, pulled by teams of dozens of horses, served by crews of a hundred men and could only be moved at a rate of a dozen miles per day. It took hours simply to emplace them, but the shells these pieces fired were not as heavy as the 15-inch projectiles fired from several of the newest British battleships. Nevertheless, these land-bound colossi delivered an egg that was a meter in length, equipped with an armor-piercing nose and delayed-action fuses. They were enormously effective and pulverized the Belgian forts around Liège, Namur and Antwerp in short order. The "Big Bertha" shells that were used toward the close of the war to bombard Paris, were not as heavy — after all, they had to travel close to 75 miles to reach the target area. For the most part, German weaponry, in both this war and its sequel, was more effective unit for unit than that of her enemies, particularly that of the French. The "Boche" used field guns of 88 mm diameter, which became the most famous artillery piece of World War II and fired projectiles weighing 60 percent more than the French 75s — the best known piece of the earlier war, and that which the French Army continued to use a generation later.

PART TWO

The Ships That
Went Overseas to War

5

The Great Kaiser

Born in 1797, Kaiser Wilhelm der Grosse ascended the throne of Prussia in 1861. In that year — his 64th — and until his death early in 1888, the Kartätschenprinz[1] ruled the House of Hohenzollern and over an ever more firmly united Germany. Throughout most of his 27-year reign (though not in the four years of regency for his ailing father that preceded it) he was guided in almost all governmental decisions by the redoubtable Junker prince, Chancellor Otto von Bismarck — the man generally credited with the firm but wise policies that reunited the German peoples in the 19th century and that set a newly vigorous nation on the path toward global prominence in the 20th. Kaiser Wilhelm valued the stern-visaged Bismarck so highly that, despite their recurrent disagreements, he refused to be parted from his handpicked and most able servant. In 1877, the great Kaiser very publicly rejected the great Chancellor's attempt to retire. The "Social Security" system of the United States was patterned from that instituted by Chancellor Bismarck the very next year, when he was 63. One of its options is a retirement (with reduced benefit) at age 62.

Der Grosse's grandson, however, had no such loyalties and in 1890, barely a year after assuming the throne, dismissed the steady-handed but ageing statesman. The event was memorialized by Sir John Tenniel in one of the most famous political cartoons of all time which appeared in *Punch*, on 29 March 1890 and was entitled "Dropping the Pilot." The youthful Kaiser chose to call the matter a "resignation," but everyone knew that the immature and headstrong ruler — entranced by his studies of American Admiral Alfred Mahan's texts on sea power — had not only dropped the nation's pilot, but in so doing had also masterminded the loss of both keel and rudder of the growing German Empire. From this point forward, Kaiser Bill steered the German ship of state, taking advice only from those who pleased him in his ill-considered rivalry to be one up on his uncle Edward VII, and after 1910, on his cousin, George V of England.

The Iron Chancellor was to be honored by having his name applied to several merchant vessels, including the last of Herr Ballin's "Big Three," which finally put to sea in 1922 as the Cunard liner, *Majestic*. In addition, he was honored in the names of more than one warship, of which perhaps the most fitting and final namesake was the huge battleship of World War II which destroyed the much ballyhooed, 42,000-ton British battle cruiser, *Hood*, with one salvo in the frigid waters off Iceland in 1942. Within a week, though, that *Bismarck,* too, was on the bottom, but it took the combined efforts of five Royal Navy battleships and torpedo planes from two aircraft carriers to disable and then, circling around the powerless lion, pummel her mercilessly. The warship was unable to fight back but uninjured below the waterline when the captain ordered the 58,000-ton warship to be scuttled, with the loss of all but 115 men from her crew of 2,000.[2]

The great Kaiser's ship, however, was of dramatically lesser tonnage and belonged to the Norddeutscher Lloyd; she had come to a far less glamorous though somewhat similar ending 32 years earlier. Launched from Vulcan's yards at Stettin, in the presence of the grandson kaiser, one century almost to the day after her namesake's birth, the *Kaiser Wilhelm der Grosse* at the time of her completion displaced 24,300 tons and had a registered tonnage of 14,349. She carried four decks for her 1970 passengers, was 198 meters in length and 20 in width, with a draught of 8½ meters. With her triple expansion, 28,000-horsepower engines she was for two years the largest ship in the world and was soon to become known as the fastest. *Kaiser Wilhelm der Grosse*'s maiden voyage to New York began on 19 September 1899, and on her second such crossing, in November, she captured the coveted blue ribband from the aging Cunard liner, *Lucania*, which had held the record since 1893.[3] The newcomer's speed was a sustained 22.35 knots eastbound between New Jersey's Sandy Hook at the entrance to New York harbor and the rocky Needles off the Isle of Wight. She did not hold the title very long, however; it was taken away by one of her sisters within three years.

Less than a year after her maiden voyage, the *Kaiser* was tied at the Hoboken piers when a fire started in some damp bales of cotton and spread rapidly throughout the entire sprawling establishment and into several adjacent buildings. The fire was a big event, even causing consternation on the opposite side of the Hudson towards which some of the burning barges drifted. Reports of the event were on front pages of newspapers around the world the following day, and occupied the entire front page of the *New York Sunday Times*. Being berthed at the most distant point from the origin of the fire on the night of 30 June 1900, the *Kaiser* was the least damaged of the five German vessels in port at the time. Due to her celebrated status, the big ship had been opened for VIP sightseers and had little steam up. When danger threatened, the 150 special guests were quickly rushed ashore and two tugs pulled the liner away from the scene of disaster, but a lot of paint was blistered and she was sufficiently damaged to be out of action for several weeks. While undergoing repairs back in Bremerhaven, as if in partial recompense, the ship was then one of the first in the world to be equipped with radio apparatus.[4]

Kaiser Wilhelm der Grosse's well-advertised speed was considerably hampered on the night of 21 November 1906, when she was rammed in the port bow by the Royal Mail Line steamer *Orinoco* in the fog off the French port of Cherbourg. The *Kaiser*, moving at a swift 17 knots out of the harbor, was headed for New York and had just dropped the local pilot, while the British ship was inbound, coming across the Channel from Southampton. Eight passengers and five of the crew on the German liner were killed in the crush — an even larger number were injured — and the big ship was badly damaged, emerging from the impact with a hole some 35 feet wide by 15 feet high that put her in dry dock for months. Subsequent analysis indicated that the German ship's captain, Otto Cuppers, failed to steer past the *Orinoco* starboard to starboard, as the rules of the sea normally require. *Orinoco* lost much of her stem, including both anchors, and great panic ensued among her passengers, but there were no personal injuries from the impact.

An interesting sidelight of this collision was the "discovery" by British dock workers in Dover, where the ship put in for emergency first aid, that the forward deck of the German merchant carrier seemed to be especially reinforced, as if for the placement of gun mountings. Not much was made of this discovery at the time, and the German owners shrugged the matter off by observing only that their ships were always built to higher, and thus presumably safer, standards than those of other nations. This alleged discovery was not so much a reality as a reflection of Britain's concern about maintenance of its traditional maritime supremacy that was sweeping the country as the Kaiser's High Seas Fleet began to assume an ever more threatening reality. In actuality, the foredeck was not so reinforced for another seven years.

"Dropping the Pilot." *Punch*, 29 March 1890.

Kaiser Wilhelm der Grosse, built in 1897. Steam Ship Historical Society of America.

In 1913, responding to a perceived (but never to be realized) future need, the one-time speedster, now 16 years of age, was taken out of service for several months during which time she was refitted to a slightly lesser registered tonnage while her passenger quarters were compacted to third class and steerage traffic only reflecting the ongoing flood of emigrants from eastern Europe bound for the brave New World of America. Before the next year was out, though, she was taken over by the German Admiralty for the kind of wartime service that First Lord Churchill had feared might be in store for much of the German merchant marine. Commissioned as an auxiliary cruiser and commerce raider on 2 August, two days before the agonizingly drawn-out British ultimatum expired, she was well at sea when the maritime war broke out and was immediately loosed on the Allied commerce of the North Atlantic.

This time, when the *Kaiser* left port, she carried 5,000 tons of coal, enough to stay at sea for 11 days and go 5,000 miles at an economical speed of 12 knots. The ship was now armed with six 105 mm guns (400 rounds) — four of which were on that foredeck — and two 37 mm quick-firing pieces with 200 rounds under the command of 42-year-old Fregattenkapitän Max Reymann.[5] *Kaiser Wilhelm der Grosse* thus became the only German

Captain August Richter of *Kaiser Wilhelm der Grosse*. Deutsche Schiffarts Museum.

Radio operators' quarters on *Kaiser Wilhelm der Grosse*. HAPAG/Lloyd.

merchant ship to actually be fitted out for war according to the Admiralty's longstanding plan.

Fortunately for the British, that early in the Great War, maritime combat was still somewhat of a gentleman's activity, not the "sink first and ask questions later" exercise it was to become in the following year, the renewal of which a year later finally brought the United States into the conflict after January 1917. While the *Kaiser* did sink the first three relatively small enemy ships she encountered, they were all cargo carriers and she had plenty of room aboard for the captured crews. The *Tubal Cain* hardly counted, at a measly 225 tons; but the 11-year-old, New Zealand registered *Kaipara*, at 7,392, was more worthwhile. Making the destruction of 16 August more noteworthy still was the *Nyanga*, at 3,066 tons. This day, on the battlefields of northern France, 34 divisions of the German Army crashed onward, having finally overcome most of the unexpected but fierce resistance of the six-division Belgian army; the British Expeditionary Force was slowly moving up to a position of usefulness; and the French were beginning to face the reality that Colonel Grandmaison's "Plan 17" for an offensive stroke to paralyze the invaders, was simply never going to occur. However the 6,762-ton Union Castle liner, *Galician*, and the much larger *Arlanza* were different — they each carried a full load of civilian passengers

Steerage passengers coming up for air aboard *Kaiser Wilhelm der Grosse*. Steam Ship Historical Society of America.

and so were merely stopped for inspection and then allowed to proceed. After inspecting *Galician*, and removing two British army officers, the German commander flashed her a message: "On account of your women and children I will not sink the ship. You are released. Bon voyage."

The second of these ships became an intriguing prize. *Arlanza*, one of the finer vessels of the Royal Mail Lines, was equipped with both triple expansion reciprocating engines and a low pressure turbine to drive her three screws. Registered at more than 15,000 tons, she was bigger than the *Kaiser*, but not nearly as fast, for her engines could only generate 14,000 horsepower against the *Kaiser*'s still very impressive 31,000. Neither this discrepancy in speed, however, nor the gentlemanly release of the ship, deterred the British Admiralty from quickly commandeering *Arlanza* upon her safe return to her home port of Belfast. She was immediately armed and sent out to sea as an auxiliary with the Tenth Cruiser Squadron.

The *Kaiser*, though, was now beginning to encounter some of the same problems that were soon to be creating headaches for Captain Thierfelder aboard her companion vessel, the *Kronprinz Wilhelm* (more about which below) and Captain Wirth on *Cap Trafalgar*. Keeping all that horsepower available for high-speed operation meant the consumption of huge amounts of fuel, but her coal bunkers had only been designed for voyages of the 3,000-mile nature such as the Atlantic crossing. At normal cruising speed the big ships of this design consumed coal at a rate of approximately one ton per nautical mile — a figure which doubled to almost two tons when they were traveling at their maximum speed of 22½ knots.

A few days before the end of August, while the British were hastening some of their limited arms down the Atlantic to eliminate the annoying German presence in Africa,[6] the *Kaiser*, having been evicted only a few days earlier from the Spanish-controlled port of Las Palmas in the Canary Islands, was near the coast of then Spanish-owned West Africa in the narrow and shallow bay called Rio del Oro, off the still inconsequential port of Dakhla. By the most common understanding of neutrality then operative, a belligerent warship, except when in urgent need of repair, was allowed to stay in a neutral port for only 24 hours — long enough to take on water, fuel and victuals. Rio del Oro was then, and is now, pretty much off the beaten track.

The German admiralty had belatedly set out to organize fuel supplies for their warships at large on the oceans. Using some of their own unarmed freighters as well as those of friendly neutrals, the Kriesmarine did its best to make up for Germany's lack of overseas bases, of which the British had plenty. These ships, however, were ordered to various rendezvous points by radio and the British, aided by Marconi's expertise were able to keep track of these meeting points.[7] The Swedish freighter, *Magdeburg*, with a large cargo of dynamite bound for New York, had thus received orders from her owners to divert her course and meet the *Kaiser* to supply the raider with some of her coal, as had the German freighters, *Arukas* and *Bethania*.[8] While at anchor for this purpose, Captain Reymann had damped most of his boiler fires, and the *Kaiser* was immobile on the morning of 26 August 1914 when the 14-year-old British light cruiser, *Highflyer*, came churning in at top speed from the open ocean around the south end of the barren peninsula. Carrying two masts (the vestigial signs of Britain's earlier naval glory now essential for radio antennae) as well as three stacks, she did not have the speed of the German ship; but her steam was up, she was far better armed, and the latter was completely immobile and unable to get away.

Highflyer had already enjoyed one interesting and rewarding wartime episode. She had been party to the capture of the *Tubantia*, a German ship belonging to the East Afrika Line which was carrying a number of German army reservists and a substantial quantity of gold. Now a member of Cruiser Force "D," she was based in Gibraltar and assigned to the protection of British trade in the Central Atlantic. For this duty she carried 11 six-inch quick-firing guns, as against the six of only four-inch caliber on the *Kaiser*.

Upon sighting his long-sought quarry, whose location had been given away by indiscriminate use of her radio, 41-year-old Captain Henry Buller[9] signaled a demand that the German ship surrender, which Reymann promptly rejected. *Highflyer* then opened fire and for an hour and a half a ship-to-ship duel ensued. The British ship suffered only one death and five slightly wounded. Unfortunately for the *Kaiser*, her gunners were insufficiently trained and she ran out of ammunition before inflicting much damage on the considerably better-armed warship. Captain Reymann was forced to order the setting of explosive charges in the boiler rooms and others of the ship's 16 compartments. He then abandoned his almost undamaged vessel.

Captain Orgel of the *Magdeburg*, with his cargo of dynamite, who was lying to some distance away from the action awaiting his turn to offload fuel, wasted no time in getting out of the neighborhood after his ship was hit by a wild shot from the *Highflyer*. It was a very one-sided encounter that was reported in some detail by Captain Makepeace of the *Kaipara*. Moments after the last German crew member (along with 100 British captives) had taken to the lifeboats, the great ship that had once been the pride of the German merchant marine, was resting on her side in the mud of the shallow bay where she could be seen for decades. Her beam was two meters greater than the water depth and her starboard side showed for most of its length. The crew took to their boats, made it ashore and marched a dozen miles overland to a Spanish fort where they were interned. The Germans may have expected better, but all 24 officers and 503 of the crew soon went to England as prisoners.

Highflyer returned to less spectacular wartime duties, but her casualties were paradoxically higher. She was in Halifax harbor on 6 December 1917, when the French ammunition ship *Mont Blanc* caught fire after a collision. Buller was now assigned to shore duty as assistant to the Second Sea Lord, but his former command lost half a dozen men in a boat which had gone to the assistance of the French vessel, as well as having much of her superstructure severely damaged by the ensuing explosion of the *Mont Blanc*. *Highflyer* was able to be repaired and did more convoy duty, but was scrapped on 10 June 1921.

Later on the day following *Highflyer*'s successful encounter with a famous enemy vessel, First Lord Churchill took some pleasure in inform-ing the House of Commons that another tally could be entered on the scorecard of German ships sunk

It was the only good news of the week. Louvain, with its celebrated library, was a smoldering ruin. The British Expeditionary Force was in retreat, more from the funk into which its commander, Sir John French, had sunk than to the overpowering might of von Kluck's 1st Army. French Generalissimo "Papa" Joffre was in the process of removing half his army, corps and division commanders for their incompetence and cowardice. In addition, on the 29th, Parliament had to accept the dreadful news that the vaunted Russian "steamroller" had careened into an East Prussian swamp at the battle of Tannenberg where 55-year-old Alexandr Samsonov and his 2nd Army was effectively destroyed by Ludendorff's forces. The French government was making plans for its flight from Paris to Bordeaux where it had taken up temporary residence during the war of 1870–71 a genera-tion earlier, and was to do so again in 1940. This time the politicians were gone from the Quai d'Orsay on 3 September, but summoned up the courage to return to Paris just after Christmas.

6

Cap Trafalgar

The Hamburg–Süd Amerikanische Dampfschiffahrts-Gesellschaft was started in 1871 to serve the overseas trade between various ports of western Europe and those along the east coast of South America. In 1899, the line began to initiate a new series of "express" steamers, somewhat along the lines of those being built under the leadership of Albert Ballin for HAPAG — luxurious, but not overly speedy. This series bore names derived from the various prominent capes that could be seen from the ships making the long Atlantic passage to or from the Southern Hemisphere: Caps Frio (Brazil), Roca (Spain), Verde (Africa), Blanco (Africa), Ortegal (Spain), Vilano (Brazil), Arcona (Baltic Sea), and culminating in the larger "express" series of Finisterre (Spain), Trafalgar (Spain), Polonio (Uruguay) and Arcona (Germany) that were laid down starting in 1910. The subsequent career of the first vessel of this second series is described in the final chapter of this book — she might well have become one of the most infamous vessels of all time had she received adequate recognition.

The final ship of this series was to play a tragic and melancholy role in the sequel conflict a generation later. In early May of 1945, only hours before the German surrender went into effect, the aging luxury liner, *Cap Arcona*, was stationary in the Baltic Sea harbor of Lübeck, crowded with thousands of Jewish prisoners taken from Auschwitz and forced aboard. Spotted by English fighter planes, she was bombed, strafed and set on fire. Very few of the unfortunate captives escaped and the ship was a total loss.

The second ship of this more enhanced group of liners was named for the locale near Gibraltar which was the site of Horatio Nelson's famous victory in 1805 that decided the naval war against Napoleon. But the *Cap Trafalgar* slid under the waves in the summer of 1914 never having come near meeting the heroic stature of the epic events off that Spanish cape 109 years earlier. When war broke out in Europe, the Hamburg-Süd express passenger steamer *Cap Trafalgar* was a new ship, displacing 23,640 tons and fitted out from the Vulcan yards in Hamburg only the previous March. The 18,710 (GRT) liner was a triple-expansion, "Schnelldampfer" but, unlike the four-stacked royalty of the Norddeutscher Lloyd, definitely not a speedster. She had made her second voyage to South America and was tied up peacefully in Buenos Aires on 31 July 1914, when German armies completed their final preparations for the march into Belgium. Putting out unarmed into the basically British-controlled open sea was clearly an act of folly, but for two weeks nothing happened. On 14 August, however, the day that the forts around Liège succumbed to the 420 mm mortars of the German artillery and the Schlieffen Plan was set into full motion, tranquility ended for the 186 meter-long (610 feet) flagship of this smaller German line.[10]

Early that morning the Kaiser's naval attaché in Buenos Aires marched aboard to inform Captain Langerhannsz that, as was its right during time of war in regard to passenger vessels listed as first-line auxiliary cruisers, the Navy would take over his ship. All passengers (she had accommodations for 1587) plus female employees and male crew members beyond the age of military service, were required to disembark. Quite a few of the civilian crew were already in the naval reserve, so this made the transition easier. Besides its captain, *Cap Trafalgar* normally carried five other officers, two doctors, two radiomen, 112 in the engine room, 147 stewards and stewardesses and 37 in the kitchen staff. Langerhannsz, already well instructed in his new duties as were all such commanders of German vessels, then started to make the transition from a merchant passenger ship to a naval auxiliary. As soon as was possible his vessel would become a "Kriegsmarine Hilfskreuzer."

However, the first order of business, as always, was to take on sufficient fuel to enable the ship to do anything. The German skipper soon recognized that while the Argentinean port authorities seemed to have quantities of high quality coal on hand, no matter how exalted a price he was able to offer they remained reluctant to part with any. The Argentines had been easily persuaded to such an attitude because they imported all their coal from England and while the British suppliers had informed them that they would continue to ship coal to Buenos Aires during the war, the

Cap Arcona in her postwar salad days, off Rio de Janeiro in 1922. Steam Ship Historical Society of America.

South Americans were urged to be "very economical" with the fuel. Between the lines it became clear that the British would keep them adequately supplied as long as they were not so foolish as to use this fuel for purposes as unnecessary or frivolous as supplying enemy vessels.

Being further inspired to actions friendly to England, and despite the captain's assurances of the "cleanliness" of his vessel, Argentine officials searched the big German ship for guns and ammunition, but were unable to find a single item of contraband. Soon enough, this treatment told both the naval attaché and the Hamburg-Süd management that if the ship were to remain in Buenos Aires it would never be converted into the much wanted Hilfskreuzer. She was being watched night and day. On 18 August, while the civilian captain was still in charge, he raised steam and ordered his vessel north across the wide estuary of the Rio de la Plata to the hopefully more understanding folk at Montevideo in Uruguay.[11] By the evening of 23 August, *Cap Trafalgar*'s bunkers were filled to their 5,100-ton capacity, enough for almost three weeks at sea (if operated "economically," not at her top speed of 18 knots). The ship was now equipped for a range

***Cap Trafalgar*, starting on her maiden voyage from Hamburg. Hamburg-Süd.**

of 7,100 nautical miles at a speed of 15 knots and capable of a sea sojourn of 19 days.

Langerhannsz then steered his vessel from the safe harbor of Montevideo and headed out to sea making for the small mid–Atlantic volcanic island of Trinidad, a frequently deserted Brazilian outpost two days' steaming to the east. Here, *Cap Trafalgar* had been instructed to make a rendezvous with the Kriegsmarine gunboat, SMS *Eber* (boar), which was to transfer its armament and professional navy crew to the new Hilfskreuzer. En route, in an attempt to disguise the big liner, all available hands were set to work dismantling the ship's third smokestack. This, being a dummy erected only for ventilation, had no effect on her ability to raise steam for her maximum speed. A much more serious factor in that regard was the big ship's insatiable hunger for coal, a condition that afflicted every one of the German auxiliary raiders then at sea. Without the presence of well-equipped and well-defended bases, such as the British Navy had at strategic points around the globe,[12] the German ships were constantly strapped for fuel. In any case, her white, topped with bright red, Hamburg-Süd colors on the two remaining stacks were painted over to the black stripes above red that pertained to the Union Castle line.

On 28 August, General Joffre was finally able to convince Sir John French to join in an attack on the flank of von Kluck's army that became known as the Battle of the Marne. On that same date the diminutive (less than 67 meters, overall) but still two-stacked *Eber* ventured slowly into the harbor of Trinidad accompanied by tenders loaded with coal. Over the next three days, the professional naval crew of the small gunboat was effectively swapped with most of the remaining civilians aboard the large auxiliary cruiser, which was now taken over by Korvettenkapitän Julius Wirth, a 39-year-old career officer, formerly in command of the *Eber*. *Cap Trafalgar* now had 16 naval officers and a crew of 303 (of which 16 were to die in the ensuing action).

Trinidad (Trinity) is a much used name in areas of Spanish religious influence. Here it pertained to a volcanic island with crests reaching some 650 meters above the ocean about 800 kilometers east of Brazil. Measuring five kilometers by two, the best anchorage is on its southwest side. Of no economic value to anyone, it is definitely off the beaten track and was used as a shelter and rendezvous point by several German vessels during the war. SMS *Dresden* had been there only ten days earlier.

As *Eber* was both small and weakly armed, she did not have much to offer: two 105 mm (four-inch) cannons (with 482 rounds) mounted starboard forward and port aft. In addition she had six rapid-fire guns of only 37 mm (1½-inch) with some 9,000 rounds of ammunition. All remaining nonmilitary people were transferred from the liner to the coal tender *Santa Lucia* and *Cap Trafalgar* was now fully ready for the final act of her career. With his newly installed guns on the already strengthened decks, Captain Wirth formally commissioned the Kriegsmarine's latest auxiliary cruiser, Seine Majestäts Schiff *Cap Trafalgar*. *Eber*, also built by Vulcan, was the second German warship of this name. She had been commissioned on 15 September 1903, but was now officially "retired" from the Kriegsmarine. After outfitting the *Cap Trafalgar* she sailed for Brazil as an unarmed "merchant" ship to be interned at Bahia where she was finally burned and scuttled by her crew on 26 October 1917, the day that Brazil entered the European effort to subdue the Kaiser's ambitions.

However brilliant her name, the Hilfskreuzer's subsequent career was short and undistinguished. Wirth was ceaselessly troubled in his desire to inflict damage on the enemy by the need to feed his ship her daily minimum diet of several hundred tons of coal. Therefore, the Hilfskreuzer set a course to the north-northwest alone and at the relatively slow speed of 10 knots, following the unwanted Argentinean advice to be economical with their coal. Five days later, now well into the traditional route of ships between Europe and the major South American port of Buenos Aires (an area that was quite "profitable" for other Hilfskreuzers), they learned by radio that the previous plan to refuel them off the Brazilian Islas Rocas with coal from the *Crefeld* (a 20-year-old one-time NDL freighter of only 3,800 tons, now a naval auxiliary supply ship), would not come to pass. All of *Crefeld*'s spare coal had been commandeered by the regular naval cruiser SMS *Karlsruhe*, the last friendly fuel that vessel would ever take on.

No alternative source of coal being available, Captain Wirth turned back to Trinidad, where three additional "colliers," *Pontos, Eleanor Woermann* and the freshly chartered American ship, *Berwind*, which had also supplied the *Dresden*, were all resting at anchor. The Kriegsmarine, still unaware of the security problems stemming from indiscriminate use of the ether, had instructed Wirth by radio to find fuel wherever he could; so, on 13 September, the auxiliary cruiser, once again starved for coal, dropped anchor in the same little bay it had left only two weeks earlier. All that steaming around the South Atlantic and along the coast of Brazil and they had not sighted even one enemy ship! However, the ether was now humming with messages from and between British warships; the South Atlantic Ocean appeared to be crowded with them. The next few days were spent transferring more of the lighters' coal to the *Cap Trafalgar*'s bunkers.

By the morning of 14 September, this traditionally dirty task was largely completed and Wirth ordered his black gang to raise steam while he debated his next move. Suddenly, homing in on the German's radio, disaster appeared over the northwest horizon in the form of the equally new British auxiliary cruiser, the 19,524-ton, turbine-powered, recently renovated Cunard liner, *Carmania*. She, too, had been hurriedly converted from peacetime competition across the North Atlantic with the ships of NDL and Hamburg-Amerika to a war footing. On her last civilian voyage, she had left New York for Southampton on 28 July.[13] As well as being slightly larger, the British vessel was considerably faster and a far more advantageously equipped adversary — she sported twelve rifles of 12.7 (five-inch) caliber. Unsure of the strength of this looming opponent, but determined to do his duty, Wirth was not about to turn tail; in any case his steam was not up sufficiently to even to try to escape. SMS *Cap Trafalgar* detached herself from the smaller unarmed craft, weighed anchor, and moved gingerly out to more open waters in order to gain maneuvering space.

The rapidly approaching British ship was first to open fire. The much lighter armed German shot back. Both scored hits. Before long, however, *Carmania*'s heavier armament was able to show its value; each of her shells weighed a good 60 percent more than one from *Cap Trafalgar*, and she had

Cunard liner *Carmania*, built in 1905, later the nemesis of *Cap Trafalgar*. Steam Ship Historical Society of America.

six times as many guns. Though the Germans scored one devastating hit on the Cunarder's bridge, killing several officers, the British holed their enemy's hull repeatedly and soon *Cap Trafalgar* became unmaneuverable, listing so heavily—despite her 12 watertight compartments—that her lifeboats, those that had not already been destroyed by gunfire, could not be lowered. Sadly, but in keeping with the Kaiser's standing orders, Captain Wirth ordered the sea cocks opened and explosives detonated in the engine room.

The English ship was set on fire and severely damaged, and the officers and crew suffered nine fatalities. Interestingly, they were so badly mauled that they were sure the Germans had possessed a much heavier armament than was the case. Nevertheless, at 11:10, barely an hour after her adversary had come over the horizon, *Cap Trafalgar* sank, bows first.[14] Captain Wirth had been seriously wounded during the action and was among the 16 persons who drowned during the sinking, but most of the survivors were rescued from the water by the quick action of the unarmed coal tender, *Eleanor Woermann*, and put ashore at Buenos Aires. *Carmania*, aware that her late adversary (using *Berwind*'s facilities) had radioed about her engagement and that major German naval forces were somewhere in South American waters, departed the scene as quickly as possible after dispatching her foe. In those days before SATCOMs and other types of "eye-in-the-sky" devices, it was hard to be sure exactly where these other vessels might be. In any case, Admiral Graf Spee's Far Eastern Squadron was known to be at large, and soon inflicted a crushing defeat on three British cruisers off the south Chilean port of Coronel. At the moment of *Cap Trafalgar*'s need, Captain Thierfelder on the newly commissioned SMS *Kronprinz Wilhelm*, was only an hour's steaming away, but thought better of joining the fray when he learned of *Carmania*'s victory. The latter ship, still seaworthy, but not really up to any further combat, made her way unmolested to Gibraltar for repairs.

The Argentinean authorities on land were, of course, somewhat put out that all this belligerent action had taken place despite their diligent but safely neutral search for arms on the German ship; they promptly interned all the surviving naval personnel for the duration of the war — four long years. Because both before and during the short battle the German officers had not identified their ship and due to the pains taken to disguise her, the victorious British were not sure what enemy ship they had sunk. Furthermore, because of the unexpectedly substantial damage inflicted by the German gunners, the British were certain they had been dealing with a very heavily armed craft. Only when the survivors reached Buenos Aires did the name of the sunken ship come out. Then, inspired by further British guile, the Uruguayans formally accused Captain Langerhannsz, who had stayed with his ship in a subordinate capacity to Wirth, of having given false information to the port authorities at Montevideo. He had allegedly perjured himself when he asked permission to keep his unarmed ship in their port. The Argentineans therefore extradited him back across the wide estuary to Uruguay where he was put on trial.

After his arraignment Langerhannsz's lawyer presented his client's full report to the court, which then sent it on to Noel Grant, the Royal Navy's captain of the *Carmania,* for his comments. Embarrassed at the discovery that he had suffered so much damage from such a vastly outgunned foe, the Englishman never replied and Langerhannsz's testimony went unrebutted; he was thus acquitted and released. Despite the highly touted traditions of the Royal Navy, German naval gunnery was consistently better throughout the Great War than that of the British. At Jutland, for instance, the vastly outnumbered Germans inflicted twice as much damage on Jellicoe and Beatty's fleets as they suffered themselves. During the entire war, the British lost 16 of their capital ships to the German two, and 13 heavy cruisers to six. Only in submarines was the German loss rate more than the British — 99 to 54.

❖ ❖ ❖

Back in Wilhelmshaven, having lost one Hilfskreuzer commandeered from Hamburg-Süd, the German Admiralty now decided to go for another. *Cap Polonio*, a slightly larger sister ship, was just nearing completion at Blohm & Voss. In the Fatherland it was still felt that the war would be a short one, at the latest over by Christmas, so Grand Admiral Tirpitz believed it wise to continue sending swift but lightly armored surface raiders to sea despite having already lost NDL's *Kaiser Wilhelm der Grosse* to HMS *Highflyer*, and now the *Cap Trafalgar*. Tirpitz's decision was of questionable merit on another count, for the big, and admittedly fast, German passenger ships were enormously coal-consuming (and coal was still the fuel of choice for most steamships). The British Navy, however, was fast being converted to the use of oil for fuel, a process begun in 1912 when the first contracts were signed with the Anglo-Persian and Royal Burmah oil companies. For the British anyway, oil was cheaper to procure; for all users it was vastly easier to handle, less labor-intensive and enabled steam to be raised more quickly.

Though *Cap Polonio* was listed in the second line as a "stand-by" auxiliary cruiser, the managers of Hamburg-Süd were understandably unenthusiastic about seeing another of their expensive ships lost, so they took their own sweet time in preparing their flagship for her new status. Nevertheless, by 8 February of the new year the alterations were complete and the ship was sent out into the relatively safe waters of the Baltic for her sea trials under her new and very temporary wartime name of *Vineta*. (See Part Five for more on ships of this name.) Despite everyone's best efforts the boilers were unable to produce sufficient steam to move her faster than a maximum of 19 knots and then for only a short time. It was assumed that low-grade German coal was the reason for this shortfall, but the fact was nevertheless obvious; even with better fuel, her triple-expansion reciprocating engines could not hope to move her fast enough to outrun almost anything that the British might put to sea. Faced with that sad reality, on 14 February 1915, *Cap Polonio* was laid up in her home yards and thus became part of the war reparations in 1919, after which she ended up briefly in the hands of the very line whose ship had sunk the *Cap Trafalgar*. Bought back in 1921, the 20,000-ton ship continued her services for Hamburg-Süd to South American ports until 1936.

7

Kronprinz Wilhelm

Another on the British First Lord's list of "forty ships" was the passenger vessel *Kronprinz Wilhelm*. Launched in 1901, she was five years older and somewhat smaller than the very similar *Kronprinzessin Cecilie* (more about which below). Both were built on the same lines with two pairs of funnels dominating their distinctive silhouettes. Also owned and operated by the North German Lloyd, *Kronprinz Wilhelm* was a slightly slimmer ship, 663 feet in length and just one tenth of that in width. Drawing almost 30 feet when fully laden, she displaced 24,900 tons of ocean water and had a registered capacity of 14,908 tons. But, pursuant to Herr Wiegand's acceptance of Herr Ballin's dictum (enhancing passenger comfort at the expense of an extra knot), she was never one of the serious contenders for the North Atlantic speed record. The *Kronprinz* was a sturdy ship, typical of those built by Vulcan at Stettin on the Baltic Sea, and for 13 years carried passengers and light freight between North America (mostly New York, but occasionally Baltimore or Boston) and the North Sea ports of Europe (mostly Bremerhaven, but with occasional stops at Antwerp, Rotterdam and Plymouth).

Vulcan was a highly regarded shipbuilding firm; it was one preferred by the German Admiralty, an honor it shared with the Schichau yards farther east in Danzig. Both of these facilities were on the Baltic Sea, safe from naval assault by what was becoming the most feared of the Fatherland's potential enemies.[15] It was along these protected shores that the great bulk of the Kaiser's High Seas Fleet was also built — something that gave rise to the need for a wide and deep passageway. The Kaiser Wilhelm II, a.k.a. Kiel, Canal was ultimately cut across the Duchy of Holstein to enable these warships to reach the more open waters of the North Sea and to avoid the tedious and possibly hazardous transit through the sandy shoals and channels among the Danish-owned islands scattered in the Kattegat and Skagerrak.

The need for the canal through the low-lying moraine and glacial outwash soils at the base of the Danish peninsula, in turn made possession of Schleswig-Holstein an important political consideration for the expanding Prussian state and thus led to more than one international crisis in the mid–19th century. The famous waterway was built between 1887 and 1895. Its length of almost 186 kilometers makes it the longest waterway built by man. Known as the NordOstsee Kanal in present-day Germany, it now handles more than 100,000 ships each year. As the size of dreadnoughts and then superdreadnoughts, grew in the early years of the 20th century, the canal was widened and deepened to handle ships of ten-meter draft in the seven years just before the outbreak of the Great War. By the end of the century its dimensions were no less than 100 meters in width and 12 meters in depth, making it traversable by ships exceeding 1,000 feet in length and up to 130 feet wide.

In appearance, the *Kronprinz* was typical of the North German Lloyd speedsters; four pale gold-colored stacks arranged in two pairs was the unique nautical trademark of her class. As in the case of numerous such vessels, the German Admiralty had a hand in her design, then assisted in her construction, and thus also had a handle on her activities in case of war. Among the qualities that marked her design, therefore, was an unusually high degree of compartmentalization in her lower decks — a condition insisted upon by Grand Admiral Alfred von Tirpitz's draughtsmen. This element in her construction made life aboard the ship slightly more inconvenient for the crew and civilian steerage passengers, but also made the vessel much less vulnerable to catastrophic flooding if wounded below the waterline. Like the person for whom she was named, she would be ready for an active role in war, should the need arise.

Many German warships were also built by the Vulcan shipbuilding firm of Stettin. During the frenzied naval buildup prior to the outbreak of World War I, these yards were fully occupied, as were the comparable British shipyards at Belfast run by Harland & Wolff, and those along the Clyde below Glasgow, as well as others along the Tyne, the Mersey, the Thames and numerous other estuaries around Great Britain. Sometimes, in those hectic years, before the waves had subsided from the launch of a

First-class passengers on the promenade deck of *Kronprinz Wilhelm*. Steam Ship Historical Society of America.

merchant ship, workmen would already be filling the vacated way with the keel of a warship, and vice versa. While the equally highly compartmentalized nature of German warships also made them more difficult to sink, it made life notoriously uncomfortable and inconvenient for the personnel onboard.

Kaiser Wilhelm II, and his son, were so imbued with the traditions of their Teutonic Knights heritage that they, and others of the German royalty, still took a personally active role in the conduct of war. Rupprecht, the last Grand Duke of Bavaria, led the German 6th Army in the Great War; Albrecht, the Crown Prince of Württemburg, led the 4th; and the Imperial Crown Prince headed the 5th. In peacetime war games, however, the Kaiser had the custom of pulling rank and always having the divisions under his command declared the winners, regardless of how badly they were outmaneuvered in the field. Finally, his generals' very justified complaints forced him to "get real."

At the start of the Great War, the 32-year-old Crown Prince William was next in line to the throne held by his father, Kaiser Wilhelm II. True to his militaristic heritage he held command of the German 5th Army, which was stationed in Alsace along the upper Rhine. It was this army

group that later participated in the enormously wasteful assault on the French fortress complex at Verdun where more than one million men died in the process of attaining no appreciable result. It was here that the later tragic Marshall Pétain commanded the French forces and made his famous declaration of defiance: *"Ils ne passeront pas!"*— "They shall not pass!"

With inherited royal arrogance the Crown Prince would insist on having a greater part in the opening offensive on the Western Front than that envisioned in the famous 1905 plan of Graf Alfred von Schlieffen for a strong right wing to bypass the fortified areas and swiftly eliminate France. The consequent reassignment of two "right wing" divisions to his command, plus the unexpectedly determined Belgian resistance and German reaction to the surprisingly swift mobilization of the Russian 1st and 2nd Armies, turned out to be just enough to enable French General Joseph-Simon Gallieni[16] to assemble sufficient reserves from Paris to finally hold the line. Some members of this force had just arrived from Africa and were rushed 50 miles north into combat — by taxi! They commandeered all 600 cabs in the French capital for two round trips— and helped win the first and crucial Battle of the Marne.

In the early summer of 1907, the *Kronprinz* had her most dangerous confrontation, exceeding anything she later encountered in wartime. Very shortly after midnight on Monday, 8 July 1907, a sudden sharp decline in air temperature told Captain August Richter of the presence of ice. But the weather remained generally clear, though the night was dark with the moon barely a thin sliver that would not make its appearance until just before dawn. A strike on the part of her regular crew of boiler room stokers now turned out to have a fortunate by-product. The green replacements could shovel coal to the boilers at a rate barely sufficient to keep the ship's speed at 16 knots. When the westbound vessel was off the Grand Banks and only a hundred feet from what had at first seemed to be a mere fog bank, they recognized the true nature of what they were gazing at — it was a massive but now blessedly sun-softened iceberg. By putting the helm hard aport and reversing his quadruple-expansion engines, Richter was able to avert a head-on collision. Nonetheless, the big ship did strike the berg a glancing blow which dumped tons of ice onto her starboard well deck, dented her bow, and scraped away all the paint — as well as the lifeboats— on the starboard beam.

A quick examination showed that the ship had received no damage below the waterline, though just prior to the impact her officers on the

Opposite: ***Kronprinz Wilhelm*, approaching the NDL pier in Hoboken after her bruising encounter with an iceberg. Steam Ship Historical Society of America.**

bridge had had the foresight to throw the switches so that all 20 doors to her 17 watertight compartments were electrically closed before the moment of impact. The *Kronprinz* was soon back up to speed and docked at Hoboken three days later, where she disembarked a distinguished list of passengers headed by the longtime German ambassador to the United States, Baron Hermann Speck von Sternberg.[17]

Seven years later, on 1 August, when the Kaiser's Army started pouring across Germany's western border, *Kronprinz Wilhelm* was again at her pier in Hoboken, New Jersey. She had arrived from Bremerhaven ten days before and disembarked all her passengers prior to refueling and revictualing for the return voyage. It was an open secret among the captains of all German merchant ships that the Fatherland's high commanders had been itching for a chance to eliminate the century-old British domination of European politics, and — unlike their more democratic, complacent and trusting opponents — had made extensive plans for use of *all* their potential resources well in advance of the actual outbreak of hostilities.

On 5 August, the British grapneled to the surface and severed the German transatlantic cables thus making communication momentarily more difficult. One day before this action, early on the morning of 4 August, and exactly on schedule, the *Kronprinz*, having canceled all future passenger bookings, departed quietly from her pier leaving word only that Captain Grahn was returning her to home at Bremerhaven. Coal, however, had been loaded into every available cranny (including the previously ornate grand saloon) and longshoremen at Hoboken had commented openly on the unusual amount of fuel that had been taken on. They even told reporters that the ship's coal bunkers were crammed so full the hatch covers could not be fastened.

This purported destination was immediately found questionable when the distinctive ship was sighted some distance outside New York harbor by the incoming steamer *Seguranca*. The Ward liner's captain told the press that the big German ship was headed south, thus giving credence to the rumors along the waterfront that the NDL ship's extra coal supply was to be used to replenish the fuel needs of several German cruisers stated by U.S. Navy officials to be operating in North American waters—*Dresden, Karlsruhe, Nürnberg, Strassburg* and *Leipzig*.

Upon being questioned, the New York spokesman for the Norddeutscher Lloyd denied only that she was armed, explaining, "All we know about the *Kronprinz* is that we received orders to have her returned to Bremen as quickly as possible. The *Kaiser Wilhelm der Grosse* [subject of Chapter 5] is in Bremen and we are forwarding an extra crank shaft to her. It was placed on the forward deck with its wooden casing to protect it from the weather, and this is evidently the cause of a report that the *Kronprinz* was going out armed.

"The liner ordinarily carries about 4,000 tons of coal, and we loaded her with 6,000 tons because she may have to make a dash for a neutral port. She burns 700 tons of coal daily and, therefore, is likely to have use for the 6,000 tons. We don't believe she headed south as has been reported. The *Kronprinz* will take a northerly course and reach a German port as soon as possible. It would not be practicable for her to coal German cruisers, and there is no reason why those cruisers should not enter an American port to coal."

However, despite this extravagant and inconsistent statement of gross misinformation, in the warm waters of the Gulf Stream, midway between Grand Cays of the Bahama Islands and Florida's Cape Canaveral, but out of sight of each, waited Seine Majestäts Schiff, the light cruiser *Karlsruhe*. Built at the Germania yards of Kiel at a cost of more than eight million marks, she was launched on 11 November 1912, and commissioned for overseas service under the command of Captain Köhler. She carried twelve 105 mm (four-inch) guns and a variety of torpedoes and mines, plus considerable lesser armaments and a crew of 373 officers and men. In addition, like most other naval vessels, she carried spare armaments for equipping potential auxiliaries, such as the *Kronprinz*.

Before the end of daylight on 6 August, the cruiser had transferred to the liner two 88 mm (3½-inch) guns, which were mounted on the starboard foredeck, with close to 300 rounds of ammunition, as well as numerous rifles and a machine gun. In addition to this materiel, the *Kronprinz* received a new commanding officer and 15 enlisted men trained to handle the weapons. Her smoking room was now fitted out as a hospital and the civilian speedster became the third, and close to the last, of Churchill's "forty fast, armed merchantmen"—an auxiliary cruiser, or Hilfskreuzer, of the Imperial German Navy under the command of Kapitänleutnant Paul Wolfgang Thierfelder,[18] previously navigation officer of the *Karlsruhe*.

A widely circulated but apocryphal and undocumented story has it that immediately upon departing from Hoboken, it was found that the *Kronprinz* suffered from an infestation of large and rabid rats. No verifiable evidence has ever come to light for this rumor, but it generated numerous tales of an embattled crew more occupied with their internal enemies than with those they had set out to destroy. The 27-knot warship was to play its own significant part in the destruction of French and British commerce, and now the *Kronprinz* was on its way.

Her precise whereabouts unknown for several subsequent months, as the Royal Navy searched vainly for her, *Karlsruhe* accosted and sank 15 ships, concluding on 27 October 1914, with the British passenger ship, *Vandyke*, bound for New York from Buenos Aires. Then the warship developed internal problems, apparently from interaction between an oil storage area and her aging munitions. The exact cause was never determined, but the cruiser's entire forward section blew apart on the evening of 4 November (less than three months after her meeting with the liner) in the open ocean north of Surinam and east of Trinidad, with the loss of Captain Köhler and 259 men from her complement. Since the survivors were taken aboard an accompanying supply vessel this event was not confirmed for several months until wreckage washed up on the beach at the British-owned island of St. Vincent in the Windward Group, 500 miles from the disaster site.

The big passenger ship's abrupt departure from Hoboken and New York harbor was an event the British were anxious to prevent recurring. There were quite a few more German express liners tied up at Hoboken, several of which had the necessary speed and had been earmarked for wartime service. In a memo of 26 October 1914 regarding the quickly instituted British cruiser patrol a few miles off Sandy Hook, First Lord Churchill wrote: "I have felt very uncomfortable about this for some time. Although it is strictly legal, it must be very galling to the Americans[19] to see their capital port picketed in this way.... [T]he closest watch should be kept on shore upon the Hamburg-American liners, and our cruisers should be given the earliest warning if they are seen to be getting up steam.... The prevention of these Hamburg-America liners leaving armed and fueled is practically the whole duty of our vessels off New York, and as long as they are in a position to discharge this they need not be too obtrusive in their other duties."[20]

While the *Kronprinz* was going about its business in the mid–Atlantic on 26 August 1914 the ship *Madgeburg*— very similar in both age and design to *Karlsruhe*— became lost in the fog off the coast of modern Estonia. After stranding on a sandbar she was scuttled and abandoned by her crew, then cannibalized by the Russians who also salvaged the German naval code books that had been tossed overboard. In due course, this stupendous find was given to the British admiralty, thereby greatly aiding in their future war effort. In the meantime, the Germans were not naive or arrogant enough to think that the Royal Navy was in complete ignorance of their basic plan for disruption of British commerce. They knew that superior ships would be on the lookout for just such a rendezvous as the *Kronprinz* and *Karlsruhe* were making, and the more redoubtable HMS *Suffolk* as well as the light cruisers *Berwick* and *Bristol*,[21] were known to be in the vicinity of the Bahamas.

Thus, the midocean arming of the *Kronprinz* was broken off after only one day and before she could receive further weaponry. After spending several more days cruising, holidaylike, in the warmth of the Gulf Stream, hoping to run across British merchantmen en route from their Caribbean "sugar" islands toward the homeland, Thierfelder gave up this task and steadied on an easterly course for the Azores with a view toward helping the *Kaiser Wilhelm II* in the disruption of British attempts to bring additional manpower from their overseas dominions of India and Australia to enhance the strength of the expeditionary force in France.

On 17 August, as the French armies were being driven back at all points of contact and the German right wing under generals von Kluck and Bülow was regrouping from its belated reduction of the Belgian frontier forts, *Kronprinz* met with the German freighter, *Walhalla*. Again by prearrangement, this was in longitude 25°W just off San Miguel, the largest island of the Azores. For most of the next week the *Kronprinz* received coal and other supplies from the *Walhalla* as the two ships again glided leisurely in warm waters, this time toward the Canary Islands. So far little success had come her way and now the *Kronprinz* learned with dismay from the German agent at Las Palmas that all sources of coal and supply in the Azores and Canary Islands had just been closed to German vessels — the strong and traditional friendship of the British with the Portuguese government was making itself felt.[22]

Captain Thierfelder then determined that his basic purpose would be equally well served by disrupting the important British commerce in foodstuffs from South America as by trying to intercept the transport of supplies being sent to aid the Indian Army forces being sent to seize what is now the nation of Tanzania, then known as German East Africa. Furthermore, given the important positions held in Argentina, Brazil and Chile by persons of German ancestry, the neutral ports of those countries might well turn out to be more hospitable and generous with respect to his neverending need for fuel. He set a course west-southwest across the equatorial doldrums of the South Atlantic Ocean for that vicinity. Along the way, the heretofore civilian crew perfected their training as naval personnel and completed the emplacement of their recently acquired armament. In preparation for capturing enemy merchantmen, a prize crew was organized and its members trained in the techniques of boarding a hostile vessel and manning it, as well as the ammunition-saving alternative — placement of explosive charges below the waterline with which to quickly sink one.

At this time, the Great War was barely a month old and going poorly for the Allies of the Triple Entente on both land and sea. The new German battle cruiser, *Göben*, fresh from a courtesy and repair visit to the Austrian naval base at Pola, had left the still friendly waters of Italy soon after the outbreak of hostilities and, accompanied by the light cruiser, *Breslau*, eluded a much superior British dragnet of battle cruisers to reach safety within the Sea of Marmara. Her arrival there and the political haymaking that ensued, was added to the Turkish resentment at the abrupt British expropriation of the battleship later named *Agincourt*,[23] which had been in an English dry dock being rebuilt to the order of the Sultan's Navy. This combination of events soon became decisive in bringing Turkey into the war on the side of the Central Powers. *Göben*, later surrendered intact but for the moment renamed *Jawas* with its German crew still aboard and in charge, went off into the Black Sea on 28 October to shell the Russian ports of Odessa and Sevastopol. German diplomats had been angling for weeks, trying to get the Sultan's forces into the conflict and engage their traditional Russian enemies on another front. This foray so outraged the Czar that he made the decision for the Turks.

In the decades leading up to the Great War, British shipyards were the world's busiest. Ships, both merchant and naval, for all nations were built on British ways. When war broke out at the end of July 1914, in various stages of completion around the British Isles were two battleships for Turkey, three flotilla leaders and one battleship for Chile, four destroyers for Greece, one cruiser for the Netherlands, and three monitors and one battleship for Brazil. In dread fear of losing their two-to-one margin over the High Seas Fleet, the entire lot was expropriated. In this process the Turkish *Osnan I* became HMS *Agincourt* and *Reshadieh* became HMS *Erin*. The latter ship was so near completion that a Turkish crew was waiting off Armstrong's yard in the harbor on the Tyne, when British marines marched aboard to claim her for the Royal Navy.

On the critical battlegrounds of Europe, the minuscule British army of only five divisions (but with reinforcements slowly coming in from various overseas dominions) was endeavoring to hold its assigned place in Flanders while the massive German right wing crashed across southern Belgium and into the industrial region of northeast France. Marshall Gallieni had been successful in commandeering the taxis of Paris, but at this moment his success on the battlefield was still dubious. The contest along the Marne was to be the critical battle of the war, though its outcome would not be known for another week; but "just in case" the French seat of government had already been evacuated to Bordeaux. On the eastern front, 67-year-old Paul von Hindenburg, called from retirement to head the Kaiser's much smaller forces arrayed against the potentially huge masses of Russian manpower, had been assigned Erich Ludendorff as his chief of staff. This team was on the verge of stunning everyone with a quick series of major victories.

On 3 September 1914, the *Kronprinz* slanted across the Equator to meet with one of the *Karlsruhe's* tenders, the steamer *Asuncion*, off the Atoll Rocas north of the Brazilian port of Natal. The very next day, soon after sunset, the 2,846-ton British merchantman, *Indian Prince*, bound from Bahia to New York with a cargo of coffee and cocoa, had the misfortune to cross paths with the now fully prepared German auxiliary cruiser. The *Prince* stopped on being hailed, foregoing the necessity of using any of the *Kronprinz's* limited supply of ammunition. The boarding party took control without a hitch but heavy seas prevented immediate transfer of much-needed coal from the bunkers of the *Prince* to those of the *Kronprinz*. By the morning of 9 September, however, the process was complete, the *Prince's* passengers and crew were safely aboard the *Kronprinz*, and three explosive charges were detonated to complete the sinking of the four-year-old British steamer.

A profitless four weeks ensued for the *Kronprinz*. This was while the French Army was receiving major reinforcements from her older classes of reservists and desperately stabilizing the defense line that was now holding along the Marne, pretty close to where it was to stay for most of the next four blood-soaked years. In the meantime, fuel for the big vessel's hungry boilers was of most immediate concern. This problem was eased only somewhat by sporadic visits of small and unarmed German-controlled vessels sent out from various South American ports with hastily filled bags of coal. The issue of major fuel replenishment was one which never left Captain Thierfelder's mind.

On 7 October, in latitude 20°S off the port of Rio de Janeiro, the *Kronprinz* hailed a more substantial and even newer British steamer, the 8,529-ton *La Correntina*, bound from Buenos Aires to Southampton with 121 persons and 2,800 tons of frozen beef. Though armed (per Churchill's order) with a pair of stern-mounted guns (120 mm or 4.7-inch) larger than those of her captor, the British steamer had no ammunition for them or crew trained to use these more powerful weapons. Despite the strong appearance of splinter shields and heavier mountings, the "little messenger" had no claws. Unfortunately for the Germans, who were quick to remount them aboard the *Kronprinz*, these newly acquired guns, while impressive, remained fundamentally useless; they could fire only homemade blanks. A far more useful capture was that of the *Sierra Cordoba*, with its 700 tons of coal, on the 23rd.

At this stage of the Great War none of the belligerent powers had fully grasped the virtues of radio silence and, while continuing to offload passengers and supplies from *La Correntina*, the German's radioman learned that a sister ship, *La Rosarina*, would be coming along soon. Unfortunately she did not follow the same course and thus escaped capture. Not much happened until the end of the month when the German raider accosted the 2,183-ton French bark *Union* with a crew of 24; *Union*'s cargo of 3,100 tons of coal was carefully removed before she was sent under the waves. On 21 November, the *Kronprinz* dispatched another and almost identical Frenchman, the 2,063-ton *Anne de Britagne*. On 4 December, the Germans were lucky and came across two Allied steamers, *Bellevue* and *Mont Agel*, totaling 8,617 tons. The former had a delightful 4,000 tons of high quality Welsh coal aboard, but the latter, a French ship, was in ballast. Just after Christmas another Britisher, the 3,486-ton *Hemisphere*, provided a further welcome present of 5,500 tons of coal. All of them were relieved of this essential item before being sent to the bottom.

The New Year of 1915 saw a continued run of success. On 10 January, the *Kronprinz* put an end to the *Potaro* at 4,419 tons, with another cargo of meat. On the 14th, the Germans thought themselves really lucky and dispatched the 7,634-ton *Highland Brae* after helping themselves to much of her cargo of clothing. However, on that same day Thierfelder made the mistake of trying to sink the 251-ton schooner *Wilfred M.*, bound from St. John's to Bahia, with a cargo of salted fish, potatoes and lumber. Low on ammunition, after taking off the Newfoundlander's edibles, the Germans rammed the schooner in order to preserve their dwindling supply of explosives, but the schooner's cargo of lumber was sufficiently durable to dent in some of the steel plates in the *Kronprinz*'s bow and also kept *Wilfred*'s disabled cadaver above water.

By now the raider had acquired a total of 493 extra passengers, all of whom had to be quickly locked up below whenever another ship came in sight. The business of feeding them had also become tedious, and the persistent leakage around the recently damaged bow became a growing concern. But the Hilfskreuzer mission for the Fatherland had to go on. The 2,280-ton Norwegian bark *Semantha* with a crew of 23 and a cargo of foodstuffs for Great Britain was sent to the bottom on 5 February, and on 22 February, the 4,583-ton British steamer *Chasehill*, with 4,000 tons of coal, was stopped and relieved of its cargo. The next day she captured the smallish (6,600-ton) French passenger liner, *Guadeloupe*, with a manifest of 293 persons, a crowd that would more than fill up her prison quarters. *Chasehill* was laden with the sunken French liner's unhappy passengers and packed off to Pernambuco.

Toward the end of March, the *Kronprinz* ran across two more British steamers, the 3,207-ton *Tamar*, with a welcome cargo of 68,000 sacks of coffee (much of which was offloaded) and the 3,824-ton *Coleby*. Both ships were sunk and the number of prisoners grew by 61. Food supplies were now getting seriously low and the diet imposed by a lengthy voyage without many fresh edibles was beginning to take effect; the first signs of beriberi and scurvy began to appear among the crew and captives.

On 27 January 1915, the First Lord of the (British) Admiralty composed a memorandum to his First Sea Lord: "...All German cruisers and gunboats abroad have been sunk, blocked in, or interned, with the exception of the *Karlsruhe* and *Dresden*, which are in hiding.[24] There are great doubts as to the efficiency of the *Karlsruhe* of whom nothing has been heard for nearly three months. There are believed to be 2 German armed merchantmen at large (the *Kronprinz Wilhelm* and *Prinz Eitel Friedrich*). All the rest of the 42 prepared for arming and which it had been intended to let loose on the trade routes have been blockaded, interned [the greatest number in American ports], sunk or captured."[25]

On the evening of 28 March, steaming northward to a further rendezvous point on the equator with a supply ship, *Macedonia*, sent out to revictual the raider, the *Kronprinz* sighted in the distance two British warships in company with an unknown steamer. Captain Thierfelder then spent the next several days cruising the vicinity in search of his support vessel, not knowing that what he had seen in the dusk of the 28th was its capture by British cruisers. *Macedonia*, never expected to be any kind of warship, nevertheless became a problem for the British. She had been interned at Las Palmas on 13 November, but had managed to slip out in mid–March to attempt this rendezvous. The ship was subsequently used as a supply vessel for Admiral Sturdee's force that had eliminated Graf Spee's squadron off the Falkland Islands.

Finally, in early April, with his coal supply running very low and a sick list becoming alarmingly high, Thierfelder, whose crew had now been at sea for 250 days, had little alternative but to make for the nearest neutral port capable of handling such a large ship. By 3:00 A.M. on Sunday, 11 April 1915, the *Kronprinz Wilhelm*, with all lights out, had successfully eluded the British cruisers patrolling the American East Coast, picked up a local pilot off Cape Henry, Virginia, and proceeded to a safe and neutral anchorage at Newport News. The *Prinz Eitel Friedrich* (about which see the following chapter), after her similar adventures, had been formally interned two days earlier. Captain Thierfelder's ship had been at sea for more than 37 weeks, steamed close to 38,000 miles and destroyed 15 vessels[26] representing more than 60,000 tons of Allied shipping. She arrived in port with only 25 tons of coal, ten tons of potable water and 86 men disabled by scurvy and beriberi. With her formal internment two weeks later, the first wave of German surface raiding was over and this element in the Kaiser's war plan was not to be resumed until the following November, when *Meteor* was sent out to sea. Nevertheless, the wartime career of the *Kronprinz* was only half completed.

❖ ❖ ❖

Later moved to Philadelphia, the *Kronprinz* floated interned and idle for the next two years but was formally seized by the United States on 17 April, 11 days after the country declared war on Germany. On 9 June, refitted with new weaponry after her long idleness, the distinctive four-stacker was renamed *Von Steuben*, appropriately enough, and placed under the command of U.S. Navy Lieutenant Charles Bullock, for further service as an American auxiliary cruiser.

The historical Friedrich Wilhelm Rudolf Gerhard Augustin von Steuben was 46 years of age when recruited by Silas Deane to the cause of American independence. He had been a staff officer in the Prussian army in the Seven Years' War and was highly recommended by LaFayette. He arrived at Portsmouth, New Hampshire, in the autumn of 1777, and Congress created him a major general and ordered him to Valley Forge where the effectiveness of his drill instruction earned him a place in all subsequent American history books. Less well known was his active participation in the campaigns leading up to the British catastrophe at Yorktown and his subsequent work in planning the further defense of the nascent American Union. Honorably discharged from the military in 1784, Steuben stayed on in America, was elected an American citizen by act of the legislatures of both New York and Pennsylvania, became a founder of the Society of the Cincinnati, president of the German Society, and a regent of the University of New York. The Congress voted him a pension of $2,500 per year in 1790 and he died four years later.

Before long it dawned on the ship's new masters, despite the ongoing U-boat menace which reached its crescendo in April 1917, that Allied control of seaborne traffic was sufficiently solid that a role of commerce raiding was no longer fruitful. There were simply no more enemy merchantmen or surface warships on the high seas; that aspect of the Allied strategy which Britain's First Lord had propounded had really been completed two years earlier. Barely three months later, the big liner was again engaged in her original function, once more as a passenger vessel on the North Atlantic run.

In convoy on 9 November 1917, during her very first voyage as an American troopship, and with a manifest of more than 1,200 fighting men,

Von Steuben collided with one of her former teammates *Kaiser Wilhelm II*, now renamed USS *Agamemnon*. The collision was caused by faulty execution of a collective zigzag maneuver within the large convoy. *Agamemnon* suffered only minor damage, but *Von Steuben* had opened her bow to the sea; while her damage control personnel made emergency repairs, the ship was able to maintain only 12 knots for the balance of her voyage into Brest. Repaired once more and returning to North America, the 16-year-old German-built ship was approaching the important British base of Halifax on the morning of 6 December, just as the French munitions ship, *Mont Blanc*, caught fire and blew up in a catastrophic explosion that killed 1,600 people, totally demolished the harbor's waterfront, and damaged most of Nova Scotia's capital city. *Von Steuben*'s crew was able to land and provide help in the initial rescue efforts before proceeding to Boston for more first aid to her injured bow.

Throughout most of 1918, after a trip to Balboa, in Panama, for full dry docking and completion of repairs to her bow, *Von Steuben* ferried American fighting men to the Western Front in France. On one of these voyages, three of her crew were killed in the premature explosion of a five-inch shell being fired at a supposed German U-boat periscope. On another such trip, she was about to pick up survivors of the torpedoed British merchantman, *Dwinsk*, when it was realized that these men were safe enough in their lifeboats, but were very probably acting as unwitting decoys for the *U-151* which was suspected of remaining in the area. *Dwinsk*'s crew was finally rescued on 21 June, by the USS *Siboney*, a newly launched 11,000-ton ship whose handling had been responsible for the collision (see Chapter 13) only eight weeks earlier between *Aeolus* and *Huron*.[27]

On another such voyage, *Von Steuben* was the only ship in the vicinity when the transport, *Henderson*, a relatively new American-built ship, loaded with some 2,000 men, caught fire in her forward hold. After two of the escorting destroyers, USS *Mayrant* and USS *Paul Jones*, ferried the human cargo across the waves, the former German liner ended up crammed with twice her rated capacity. Nevertheless, she completed the eastbound trip to Brest on 9 July while *Henderson*'s crew stayed aboard their vessel and finally managed to put out the fire. On further trips, *Von Steuben* survived hurricanes and influenza outbreaks, and was used to bring American troops back home throughout most of 1919.

The big ship's final years as a civilian were hardly an appropriate encore to her exciting wartime career. Laid up in Virginia's James River, with a lot of other surplus tonnage, she was chartered to take a world tour as a showcase for American manufacturers—and to be renamed *United*

States. When that plan fell apart from lack of interest, in 1924 the *Kronprinz* was sent to her grave in Baltimore. The man for whom she was originally named lived on in his Dutch exile. He returned to his homeland in the 1920s and stayed there through another World War. He died in 1951, 27 years after his namesake ocean liner was broken up.

8

Prinz Eitel Friedrich

Johann Kalb (1721–1780), though born in Bavaria during the reign of Elector Maximilian II, served with distinction in the French Army, rising to the rank of brigadier general. In 1768 he was sent to visit the American colonies on a secret mission for the French government, still smarting from their recent loss of Canada, to determine the extent of potential anti-British sentiment among King George III's increasingly restless overseas subjects. Eight years later he was recruited to the cause of American independence by Silas Deane and then given the rank of major general by Congress on 15 September 1777. One of George Washington's ablest supporters at Valley Forge during the discouraging winter that followed, he is known in American history books as "Baron de Kalb"[28] and gave his life for American freedom at the Battle of Camden, South Carolina, in the fall of 1780.

The German-built ship that ultimately bore de Kalb's name was ordered in 1900 by Norddeutscher Lloyd and constructed in the Vulcan yards of Stettin. When launched on 18 June 1901, the hull was christened after a prince of Prussia, an uncle of William the Great. Displacing more than 16,000 tons (GRT 8,797), *Prinz Eitel Friedrich* was one of the larger ships of her day — 506 feet in length, with a beam of 55 feet and a draught of 26 feet. She was about three quarters of the dimensions of the soon to appear express steamers, and with considerably smaller engines— only 7,000 horsepower. Interestingly, though, despite her plodding speed and only average accommodations, in their authoritative post war *Source Records of the Great War*, the British editors described the *Prinz* as being "swift and sumptuous." She sailed the Europe to Far East run without incident, at her unspectacular but profitable 15 knots, for a dozen relatively uneventful years until World War I broke out, at which time she was just departing Shanghai.

Knowing by radio of the 31 July order to all German civilian ships, Captain Carl Mundt immediately steamed his ship north at full speed to the German treaty city and naval base of Tsingtao. This excellent port on the south side of the Shantung peninsula in northeast China had been seized by Germany in 1897, soon after a similar British exercise at Hong Kong, and legalized (along with similar takeovers in Tientsin and Hankow) and solidified by a 99-year lease extracted from the weak imperial authorities of Peking in a protocol of 7 September, 1901. Over the next dozen years the city was rebuilt with Teutonic order and thoroughness to a fine modern standard and became Germany's main Far Eastern base.[29]

In this takeover of Chinese territory the Germans were latecomers (as they were in Africa, too). The process had begun in 1834 when the British began to crowd the imperial authorities on trade matters, finally receiving extraterritorial privileges at five ports. Six years later, Caleb Cushing negotiated a similar treaty for the Americans. Then everyone else started getting into the act — the French in 1844, then the Belgians and the Swedes. The Portuguese, though early on the Far East trading scene, had not taken part in the acquisition of extraterritorial rights— they were content with their position on Macao. It was during the Opium War of 1839 and the subsequent Treaty of 1860 that the Russians managed to acquire Vladivostok and other once Chinese territory east of the Ussuri River.

In Tsingtao lay the SMS *Emden*, a five-year-old light cruiser (and sister ship of the *Dresden*), many of whose crew were soon destined for a spectacular wartime "cruise." The *Emden*'s captain, Karl von Müller, was the senior commanding officer in the port. Though aware that his base and probably his ships, would very likely soon be overwhelmed by various enemies, he was obligated to do everything he could do in the face of such inevitability and rapidly set about making life as difficult for them as possible. Heavy guns were taken from the aged and ailing gunboats *Kormoran* and *Luchs*, and used to arm another of First Lord Churchill's "forty," the biggest merchantman in Tsingtao's harbor.

As the crisis deepened in Europe during the final days of July 1914, Japan announced that she would stand firmly by her British allies. Within a matter of weeks, Japanese forces had surrounded Tsingtao. The city and base were occupied on 29 September the day after all the vessels remaining in the harbor had been burned and sunk. When the Chinese also formally entered the war on 14 August 1917, many observers felt this was simply a device to prevent Japan from occupying even more of the Chinese mainland.

While the *Prinz* was being outfitted, *Emden* looked outside the harbor and apprehended the passing freighter, *Rjäsan*, of the Russian Volunteer Fleet. This ship had been built by Schichau at Elbing in 1909 and was not any sort of speedster; with only one screw, she could barely make 13 knots. But she had four holds in her eight-compartmented hull, could carry 2,500 tons of coal and had a 40-day endurance span at sea. Once escorted into harbor by *Emden*, this ship received all the residual armament from *Kormoran* and other aging gunboats of the Kriegsmarine that were now becoming recognized more as liabilities than assets. Rechristened as another *Kormoran*, after the ship from which she had been armed and which was to be scuttled only six weeks later, the once Russian mail steamer now sported eight five-inch (127 mm) guns and was manned by a force of 335 men. She could have had a bright future in the service of her new owners, but ended up milling unprofitably around the western Pacific Ocean for the next several months and was finally interned at Guam in mid–December, where she stayed idle until April of 1917.

The task of converting North German Lloyd's *Prinz Eitel Friedrich* into another Hilfskreuzer was completed in record time. Now manned by a total crew of more than 400 men, she put out to sea ready to do battle for the Fatherland on the evening of 7 August 1914. On this date in St. Petersburg, the 48-year-old Grand Duke Nicholas was desperately trying to organize the Russian Army to battle against the weakly garrisoned German forces in East Prussia. Ambassador Maurice Paléologue of France had become increasingly insistent, then frantic, in urging action of any sort that would serve to draw troops from the battlegrounds of Belgium and France and relieve the pressure that was forcing his nation's troops steadily backward. In the end, more than 30 trainloads of German soldiers were withdrawn from the western front and shifted eastward to Hindenburg and Ludendorff.

Since British merchantmen, as almost everywhere, dominated the Far Eastern cargo trade, there were ample opportunities at hand for inflicting injury on the commerce of the Fatherland's prime maritime enemy. During the first several days at sea, the former merchantman — now commanded by 40-year-old Kapitänleutnant Max Thierichens,[30] formerly skipper of the gunboat SMS *Luchs* (lynx) — kept company with *Emden*. *Luchs* was a slightly older sister ship of SMS *Eber*, which had furnished the armament for *Cap Trafalgar*. Then, having decided to separate in the hope of being able to cover a wider expanse of "profitable" ocean, the much speedier warship headed off southwestward to sink two enemy warships, the Russian light cruiser *Zemchug* and the French destroyer *Mousquet* on 28 October 1914, when Captain von Müller caught them napping at dawn in the harbor of Penang on the west coast of Malaysia. The *Emden* went on to sink a further 20 enemy merchantmen, aggregating 80,000 tons, in the East Indies and adjacent Indian Ocean.

At dawn on 9 November, First Officer Hellmuth von Mücke headed a landing crew on Direction Island to dismantle and destroy its annoying British radio relay station. This is now a part of the Cocos Group some 1800 km northwest of Australia's North West Cape. The radio operators, however, sent out word that a strange warship had entered their harbor before the invaders managed to disable the transmitter. Hearing this potentially distressful call, the HMAS *Sydney*, already on the lookout for *Emden*, and one of the newer, faster, and better armed cruisers of the Royal Australian Navy, put on all possible speed to reach the area before the smaller and slower German cruiser could once again get away with a quick hit and run.

Knowing of the island's "APB" and seeing the smoke of impending disaster looming on the horizon, Captain von Müller abandoned his landing party in order to attempt to save the ship. It was to no avail. By noon that day, after a two-hour pummeling by the *Sydney*'s heavier guns from a range beyond that of the *Emden*'s, she was a burning wreck, beached on North Keeling (Cocos) Island and out of the war.

The landing party, meantime, was not out of the war. There was a tired schooner named for the favorite wife of the Prophet Mohammed, at anchor in the small harbor of Direction Island. Within hours, the *Emden*'s first officer had commandeered supplies from the stunned British garrison and was well out to sea before the enemy could repair the damage and get their transmitter back on the air to tell the world what had happened. Making a painful and tedious way to Sumatra in the leaky *Ayesha*, the German crew finally boarded the German-owned freighter, *Choising*,[31] and set out westward across the Indian Ocean — now a basically British lake, criss-crossed by dozens of unfriendly warships— in hopes of reaching succor in a Turkish-held region near the Red Sea.

The friendly freighter successfully evaded all enemy craft, and the 50-man party left it near the straits of Bab el Mandeb on 8 January 1915. They took small boats and various camel caravans northward along the east side of the Red Sea until they finally reached the end of the railway line to Constantinople at the modern town of Ma'an in southern Jordan, the temporary terminus of the much touted "Berlin to Baghdad" railway. With a special train now at their disposal, and having outrun Major Thomas Lawrence's irregulars, Leutnant Hellmuth von Mücke's men were soon back in the hands of their own forces—and back in the war—while all the *Emden*'s other survivors were in prison camp.[32]

Prinz Eitel, meanwhile, was now quite heavily armed. She sported four 105 mm guns (900 rounds), six of 88 mm and four of 37 mm (with 9,000 rounds). She had 10,000 tons of coal which gave her a 30-day span at sea and a range of more than 10,000 miles at her optimum cruising speed of 14 knots. Captain Thierichens turned her eastward across the Pacific. He learned intermittently by radio of the successes and then the terminal fates of other German warships as the much larger British Navy, operating from well-equipped bases around the world, relentlessly scoured the seas and one by one hunted them down. The crew was cheered by learning the outcome of the battle off Coronel, Chile, on 1 November 1914, where Admiral Maximilian Graf von Spee's squadron of five cruisers largely destroyed an inferior British force of only three. All hands, 1,600 men, were lost when the British light cruisers, *Good Hope* and *Monmouth*, were sunk. Six weeks later, on 9 December, they learned with sadness of the subsequent battle off the Falkland Islands the day before, when Admiral Sir Doveton Sturdee's much superior force of battle cruisers and other heavy craft put an end to the German heavy cruisers *Scharnhorst* and *Gneisenau*, the lighter ships *Leipzig* and *Nürnberg*, and all of Admiral von Spee's activities. In that area of the ocean only *Dresden* and *Prinz Eitel* were still at large.

For the next six months the *Prinz* and her distant parent, the *Dresden*, were both hunters and hunted, one cruising in the Indian and South Pacific Oceans, the other working across the South Pacific and then into the southern Atlantic Ocean, in search of enemy merchantmen they could catch up with and destroy. The adventures of SMS *Dresden* are not part of our story, but she outlived the *Eitel*'s cruising career by four days, until cornered, then scuttled, off the coast of Chile. Meanwhile, many of *Eitel*'s captures were almost routine—deceive by flying false colors, hail, stop, inspect, offload some coal and finally sink. But three of them were more noteworthy.

On 11 March 1915, the Norwegian steamer *Nordic* reached Panama and disembarked 37 seamen. They were all but eight men from the crews of the British bark, *Kildalton*, and the French bark, *Jean*, which had been landed—"marooned" in their words—on Easter Island since 11 December, when Captain Thierichens put both groups ashore and then sank their ships. Giving question to the matter of their marooning, the captain of the French boat and seven of his crew refused to be "rescued" by the *Nordic* because, for reasons never disclosed, they wanted to go to Chile, rather than Panama. *Jean* was also one of the few ships encountered by any of the German raiders that put up some sort of real fight before being taken.

On 20 February, now well into the Equatorial doldrums of the Atlantic, she accosted the small, 3,630-ton British steamer *Willerby*. Captain Wedgewood ignored the order to stop and kept on his course. But when it became obvious that his craft was about to be rammed by the much larger German ship, he hove to. By now the two vessels were almost in contact as at the crossing of a "T." Wedgewood, knowing that his lightly laden ship was doomed in any case, but not knowing that his captor was loaded with unwilling passengers taken from various liners and cargo ships that had been dispatched to the bottom, saw his chance to strike a blow for his side. It was an understandable standard practice on the German raiders to herd all prisoners below decks at the first sign of any potential new capture. It was felt that, if given any chance, they would make some sort of signal about the true nature of the approaching Hilfskreuzer. As the two vessels drifted slowly apart, Willerby suddenly ordered his engines full astern and attempted to ram backwards into the *Eitel*. Unfortunately for the effort, the British ship could not get up sufficient speed to make the contact and the ships passed some 15 feet apart. Thierichens was not amused. *Willerby* was then boarded, her crew was removed, and she was promptly sunk. It was *Prinz Eitel*'s final blow for the Fatherland.

Prinz Eitel's most controversial and costly capture was that of the 2,998-ton American sailing vessel *William P. Frye*, one of four "shipentines" owned by the Sewall Company, a local partnership of Maine citizens with 128 shares. The ship was accosted and sunk in the South Atlantic, soon after the *Prinz* had rounded Cape Horn. The 28th day of January 1915 was to become a date the Kaiser's exchequer would not recall with pleasure. Named upon her launching at Bath in 1901 for the senior senator from the state of Maine who had been a longtime supporter of American maritime construction subsidies, the *Frye* was the second largest square-rigger in the world (her rival being a sister-ship that had a somewhat larger deck house) and as such she had been a source of much pride to her namesake politician. Though Senator Frye had been in his grave for three years at the time of the sinking, he remained fondly remembered in Maine, a condition that exacerbated the expressions of outrage at the ship's sinking. The shipentine's value, according to one of her owners, was $175,000, and her cargo at the time the *Eitel* accosted her was $300,000 worth of wheat, loaded at Seattle and bound for Queenstown. Thierichens, who had originally ordered *Frye* to simply jettison the cargo and then go about her business, became incensed when the 31-man crew did not move to this distasteful

William P. Frye just before going under the waves. *Leslie's Photographic Review of the Great War.*

task with sufficient alacrity. At that point he lost patience and sank the ship.

The question of what was contraband and what could be allowed to move without hindrance, was a matter that excited much emotion during the war, mostly on the part of neutrals. Fairly soon, it became obvious that the British were not about to let *anything* move in the direction of Germany. That was First Lord Churchill's concept of a "distant blockade." Therefore, it was not without reason that the Germans took the next logical step of looking upon any ship at sea as being potentially in aid of their enemies, and therefore deserving of being sunk.

When *Prinz Eitel* finally ran dangerously low on coal, became overloaded with 342 unwilling passengers, and developed too much scale in her boilers for efficient functioning, she ran north until abreast of the Virginia capes and then turned sharply west to seek the entrance to Newport News, where she arrived on 10 March 1915. Almost immediately a smallscale but rapidly widening diplomatic flap erupted over the *Frye* incident. Graf Johann-Heinrich von Bernstorff, scion of a family famous in German diplomatic service and successor to the late Speck von Sternberg as ambas-

Captain Thierichens and a Captive

FRYE AN ALL-AMERICAN SHIP

Was Owned by 38 Individuals, Six of Whom Are Women.

WASHINGTON, March 11.—Destruction of the ship William P. Frye by the German commerce destroyer Prinz Eitel Friedrich struck from marine lists the pride of the American sailing fleet in point of size and equipment and one of the largest square-rigged craft in the world.

Her loss falls not upon a corporation, but upon individual members or connections of the Sewall family, famous among New England shipbuilders and owners since the days when American clipper ships carried the commerce of the world in all the seven seas and fought the losing battle against steam craft that ended American maritime prestige.

The Frye was built in Bath, Me., and was registered in 1901, with thirty-eight individuals, six of whom are women, appearing as joint owners. That ownership has never changed and those who hold allotments of the 128 shares into which the venture was divided are scattered from the Atlantic to the Pacific Coast. The ship was named after the late Senator Frye of Maine and to the day of his death was a source of pride to the Senator. It is recorded that he declared himself more honored in having his name upon the stern of an American-built, owned, and operated sailing vessel than if the fleetest of Atlantic steam liners had borne it.

The Frye was a sister ship of the Star of Lapland, also built at Bath, and because of a minor difference in the size of a deckhouse of the latter, was seven tons smaller in measurement, the Lapland leading American sailing ships with 3,381 gross tons, against 3,374 recorded for the Frye. Of the 128 ownership shares in the Frye, only half a dozen persons hold more than one or two shares apiece.

Commander of the Prinz Eitel and Mrs. Kiehne, wife of the Captain of the American ship Frye.

today and inquired whether there would be any objection to the Prinz Eitel Friedrich's being placed in dry dock and repaired at the works of that company. He spoke of the fact that the dreadnought Pennsylvania, which is being built by the company, was about to be launched there from a slip that would be almost immediately adjoining the dock where the German auxiliary would be repaired and asked whether the Navy Department would object on that account. Mr. Daniels said the department had no such objection.

The question for the State Department to determine is how long the German cruiser may, under international law, and without violating American neutrality, remain in an American port for repairs. When this decision has been reached, should the German Captain elect to remain longer than the period allotted, he would be compulsorily interned. The rules of international law do not allow a vessel to make repairs to an indefinite extent. The only repairs allowed in the case of the Eitel Friedrich would be those absolutely necessary to enable the vessel to proceed to the nearest German port. It would not be permissible for the vessel to increase her armament or military strength.

WIRELESS SAVED THE EITEL.

ONE EITEL PRIZE ALMOST SANK HER

Continued from Page 1.

bottom, and he was eager in his descriptions of the different ways in which the doomed hulks sought their last resting places.

"The finest sight," he said, "was the sinking of the French steamer Floride, because her cargo of wine and spirits took fire and burned away into the night. The next best, and in some ways the most beautiful of the wreckings, was the sinking of the bark Jacobson. She was square-rigged, like all barks, on her first two masts, and schooner-rigged aft, and she went down with very sail set, everything braced.

"From the German point of view the sinking of the Floride was a fizzle. They set off a bomb lashed against her bow, but while it tore a hole in the side of the ship the hole was above the water line. Then they set off another bomb. This time she started to settle slowly. It was late in the afternoon and we cruised away to the east, leaving the

guarded separately, but the others wherever they went were watched by armed marines. Indeed, the crew was armed today when visitors approached the ship, every man having his bayonet in his belt.

Many women were on board the Prinz Eitel by the time the Willerby was captured, and their discomfort was the cause of some complaint.

"My heart bleeds for these women," said Commander Thierichens, according to Capt. Wedgewood of the Willerby.

"Then why don't you put them on my ship, without a cargo, and let them go to port in her?" Capt. Wedgewood replied.

"But, instead," he says, "the German sent us to the bottom."

"The care with which the Germans guarded their shiftul of prisoners worked some discomforts on the prisoners," added Capt. Wedgewood. "They were locked up whenever anything was suspected, and of course their prison was below decks.

"Just before we passed the Capes they told us not to be afraid if a British cruiser should appear and open fire. They said they'd reply to the fire as long as the top of the Eitel's mast remained above water, and told us to stay down in the hold and not to worry. That was rather cheering for us, wasn't it?"

The members of the crew are de-

Picture of Captain Thierichens and his "captive," Mrs. Kiehne. *New York Times* of Friday, 12 March 1915.

sador to the United States, was quick to assess the volatile nature of the issue and its likely impact on American opinion. He stated his government's concern and promised to aid in the fullest possible inquiry.

However, the German position had an element of justification: the ship had been carrying foodstuffs to Germany's enemy, clearly an act of assistance to their war effort. But should she have been sunk? The Declaration of London (in regard to the movement of contraband during time of war) had not been accepted by the United States and so was not binding relative to American-owned vessels. In the end, and after a lot of posturing, recourse was had to some hundred-year-old agreements between the United States and the Kingdom of Prussia — the German government paid more than $200,000 to the *Frye*'s owners and officially apologized. Inciting American wrath was never on the Kaiser's agenda. That matter was closed.

In the meantime, NDL's *Prinz Eitel Friedrich*[33] was still in Newport News "undergoing repairs" when the time limit for such expired. It was common knowledge that a British cruiser patrol was on close station just outside the three-mile limit, waiting for the raider to try getting back to sea. Within a month, discretion overcame valor, and the ship was legally interned. Her unwilling passengers had already been freed, and the crew was sent to internment camps. Thierichens was subsequently awarded the Iron Cross, First Class. The ship was tied up to await her next assignment. She had enjoyed a good career as a commerce raider, 11 ships sunk in all: five British, four French, one Russian and, of course, the *Frye*.

By the 24th of October, however, the Secretary of the British Admiralty was able to report that "...German overseas trade has practically ceased to exist. Nearly all their fast ships which could have been used as auxiliary cruisers were promptly penned into neutral harbors or have taken refuge in their own. Among the comparatively few German ships which have put to sea, 133 have been captured, or nearly four times the number of those lost by the very large British mercantile marine."[34]

Soon moved to Philadelphia, the *Eitel* was formally seized in the name of the United States, along with dozens of other German and the small handful of remaining Austrian ships, on 6 April 1917. Reconditioned and refitted as a troop transport, she was rechristened after the German-American patriot and placed in commission on 12 May, under the command of Commander W. R. Gherardi. One month later, she took the very first troops of the American Expeditionary Force to France. Over the next 18 months she made ten more round trips, carrying a total of 11,334 soldiers to fight against the Fatherland. At the end of the war, she brought an even larger number home from Europe in another eight voyages.

On 22 September 1919, *De Kalb* was decommissioned by the Navy. She was returned to the United States Shipping Board for disposal, and briefly renamed *Mt. Clay*. However, as soon as normal relations were restored, she was soon sold back to her original owners, the North German Lloyd, who refitted her to 14,180 tons and used the now 16-knot craft peacefully for another several years (until 1927), once again on the Far Eastern run.

9

Batavia and *Berlin*

Batavia's part in the active war against England and France was very limited. The 15-year-old HAPAG liner had been outward bound to America when the Great War broke out. Built by Blohm & Voss with an original registered tonnage of 10,178, she was typical of the five "B" class liners that had been constructed during the years 1897–99 (see Chapter 15). Her engines could generate only 4,100 horsepower, sufficient to move her along at a sedate 12½ knots. But she was economical to operate, and radio-equipped, as were all ships with capacity for more than 50 passengers that called at American ports after the enactment of the Mann-Elkins Act of 1910.

Told, by radio message from the Kriegsmarine on 31 July of the imminent outbreak of war, she altered her course by some 100 degrees and set out on a return to Hamburg by circling north of Scotland, rather than by the shorter and quicker but now far more risky passage via the English Channel. The British had not yet managed to set up the intensive cruiser patrol across the top of the North Sea that became the most effective hallmark of their naval patrol system a few months later. Thus unhindered, *Batavia* regained her home port unmolested.

Hampered by her limited speed, this ship could never rate with many of the other much faster vessels owned by HAPAG and NDL that had been designated by the Kriegsmarine for commerce-raiding purposes. Nevertheless, she was at hand and could be converted without much effort into

Batavia, built in 1899, entering pier at Hoboken. **Steam Ship Historical Society of America.**

a troop transport for use in the Baltic Sea. This marine option for supplying the Eastern Front was necessary to take pressure off the German railroads in supplying manpower and munitions in the war against Russia. As such, *Batavia*'s years of war service were uneventful and unharmful to her. In 1919 she was still afloat and in good enough repair to be wanted by France as part of the wartime reparations exacted by the victors. By 1924, however, with the postwar economic slump, she was deemed no longer competitive and was scrapped.

❖ ❖ ❖

NDL's *Berlin*, on the other hand, was a far more likely candidate for wartime duty, though she was never listed among those ships set for that purpose. Nine years younger than *Batavia*, *Berlin* had been built at the Weser yards and was in the same 17,000-ton class with *Cap Trafalgar*, *Cincinnati*, *Cleveland* and *Prinz Friedrich Wilhelm*. Her registered tonnage was an impressive 17,323 and her 16,000 horsepower engines could drive her at a quite respectable 19 knots. Her owners had assigned *Berlin* to the

HMS *Audacious* going down by the stern off Lough Swilly. *Leslie's Photographic Review of the Great War.*

Naples–Genoa–New York service, as part of their complicated contract with the federally subsidized Lloyd Sabaudo Line. On the critical date of 1 August 1914, though, she was out of service at home in Bremerhaven undergoing routine maintenance.

This was a well compartmented ship with 11 watertight subdivisions and four passenger decks. Her bunkers could hold 4,000 tons of coal, sufficient to last her quadruple-expansion engines for 16 days at sea, if held down to a sedate 10 knots. On 18 September 1914, she was officially commissioned as a Hilfskreuzer-minelayer and put out to sea four weeks later under the command of Kapitänleutnant Hans Pfundheller.[35] By this date, the British had set several minefields in the narrowest part of the English Channel and were controlling the gaps with intensive destroyer patrols. This passage was thoroughly out of bounds to German ships of all types. Later in the war, however, a number of U-boats attempted this route — a few of them successfully, others less so.

Berlin's glory days of war were short but sweet. HMS *Audacious* had been commissioned late in 1913, as one of the Royal Navy's newest battleships. She displaced 23,000 tons, carried ten 13.5-inch guns in her principal armament and was one of His Britannic Majesty's most prized possessions. *Audacious* was the final member of the *King George V* class. She also carried 16 four-inch guns, had several torpedo tubes, and was capable of 22 knots. On the evening of 26 October 1914, she was just outside the British naval base at Lough Swilly in Donegal, in the waters between Ireland and Scotland, not far from the Malin Head Marconi station. Here, she ran afoul of a mine that had been set by the *Berlin* only a few days earlier.

It took hours for the well-compartmented battleship to finally go under, in the course of which the distressing sight was witnessed by people on several passing vessels, including the famous Cunard Liner, *Olympic*, which was inbound to Liverpool from New York. Though many of His Majesty's seamen were saved, the sinking of such a new battleship had the potential to be a staggering blow to British morale, which was already reeling under the successes of German arms almost everywhere else in the world. With their great dependence on an overseas supply of food and other raw materials, the British were constantly fearful throughout the war years of an escape to the open ocean of the High Seas Fleet. For their peace of mind, they felt the necessity of maintaining a two-to-one ratio of capital ships over the Germans, even prior to hostilities, hence the abrupt expropriation of the Turkish battleships and the dire feelings of insecurity at the loss of *Audacious*.

When Prince Louis of Battenberg, one of his staff assistants, informed the First Lord of the Admiralty about the sinking, Churchill asked that the matter be kept quiet for as long as possible. The British press was aware of the event, however; there had been too many eyewitnesses. Nevertheless the general public, and more importantly, the enemy, were kept in the dark for another five weeks. Long before then, *Berlin* had run so low on fuel that she had to make for the neutral port of Trondheim where she was interned for the balance of the hostilities. However, her actions had brought about far and away the largest single catastrophe to strike the Royal Navy in 20 years and was considerably more devastating to official thinking than anything later accomplished by the much feared High Seas Fleet whose existence had brought England into a French alliance and now the war.

Having laid the "egg" that struck one great blow for the Fatherland, Captain Pfundheller soon began to feel the same difficulty that was plaguing all the other Hilfskreuzer at large — no fuel! Indeed, of the 248 days which *Prinz Eitel* had spent at sea, 70 (more than a quarter) were occupied with the tedium and dirtiness of refueling from their captures. No matter where one of them turned, there was not a single port, friendly or neutral, into which a German ship could put without, at the very best, news of her presence getting out so that one or more warships of the much larger Royal Navy would take up their deadly watch just offshore.

In later life, *Berlin* was surrendered to the British government and used for postwar troop transport duties under contract with the P&O Line. Late in 1920 she was sold to the White Star Line and refitted as the *Arabic*; she served the transatlantic trade for the next five years. In 1926 the now 18-year-old ship was chartered to the Belgian Red Star line and four years later returned to White Star, and was always on the same transatlantic service between various European ports and New York. By early 1931, she was becoming passé; she soon became a victim of the Great Depression and was sent to the breaker yards at Genoa.

PART THREE

The Troopships
of America

10

The Crown Princess

Cecilie was the daughter-in-law of the last German Emperor, Kaiser Wilhelm II, and wife of Friedrich Wilhelm Viktor Albert, the Crown Prince of Germany. She had been born the Princess of Mecklenburg. In keeping with the autocratic nature of the nation, the Crown Princess's name was given to two ships, one each of North German Lloyd and HAPAG. That pertaining to the Hamburg-based line was only half the tonnage of the ship that is the principal topic of this chapter, but it was to play an interesting, if minor, part in the Great War. This was a dowdy vessel, capable of only 14.5 knots. Built as hull #108 by Germaniawerke in Kiel, she had a maximum passenger capacity of 1284 and was used mostly on the Hamburg-Tampico run. The nine-year-old ship, with a registered tonnage of 8,689, had been trapped by the sudden outbreak of war in the small Cornish port of Falmouth, near the southwesterly tip end of England. Destined for use thereafter in a unique manner by her new masters, she was outfitted with considerable false work, and made to resemble one of the newer British battleships—at least in silhouette. Thereafter she was put on parade, so to speak, as HMS *Princess*. Always kept sufficiently distant from detailed scrutiny, she served her purpose quite well—to convince the casual observer that there was a powerful presence in the neighborhood. To some who saw her, she might have been the late and sorely lamented *Audacious*.

A far different ship was that owned by the Norddeutscher Lloyd. Designed to serve on the busy and lucrative North Atlantic passenger run to New York, Crown Princess Cecilie's other namesake vessel was built in 1906 by the famous Vulcan firm of Stettin, where the vessel had at first been known more simply as "Hull #267" until it was launched and christened on 1 December. A few weeks later a distressing event occurred as the ship was being completed and elements of her superstructure being added. On 20 July 1907, water entered the hull through an open coal port and before anyone could correct the situation she had filled enough to settle into the mud a few feet below her keel at her pier. Pumped dry and completely fitted out by mid–August, the *Kronprinzessin Cecilie*'s maiden voyage from Bremerhaven to New York, though delayed by several weeks, was completed at an average speed of 23 knots.[1] Seven hundred and seven feet from stem to taffrail and a trim 72 feet in beam, she was rated at 19,360 tons by the British measurement system of gross capacity. Fully laden, she required a channel depth of 32 feet and a crew of more than 600 men to run her smoothly. At this moment Admiral George Melville, recently in charge of motive power design for American naval vessels, was bemoaning the fact that most of his nation's naval bases could handle ships of no more than 28 feet draft and his colleagues in the fleet were constantly demanding larger and more heavily armored battleships.

A sister ship of that named for her father-in-law, *Kaiser Wilhelm II*, her cabins could carry 742 passengers amidships in the first class staterooms, three hundred twenty-six in the bow and stern quarters entitled second class, and 740 persons in the below-waterline barracks of steerage. Despite these and other impressive statistics, the *Kronprinzessin* was never meant to be a contender for the blue ribband speed record across the ocean. By the time of her design, Herr Ballin had pushed the German shipping industry into concentrating more on passenger amenities and luxury than on the ever more costly and less fruitful pursuit of more speed. Thus the *Kronprinzessin* was known as a comfortable ship, and though setting a few transatlantic speed records[2] for German-registered vessels, was always outdone, both in speed and size, though only slightly, by the newer major ships of Samuel Cunard's line, *Mauretania* and *Lusitania*. One of Herr Ballin's most successful innovations in providing passenger amenities had been to hire the famous Swiss hotelier, Cesar Ritz, to oversee the design and operations of the dining facilities. Ballin also made equally good use of his consultant's already well-known name.

Nevertheless, NDL's crown princess sailed from Bremen in distinguished company. Her Norddeutscher companions bearing the German flag included three Kaisers and her crown prince sibling. From the port of Hamburg the friendly competitor line managed by Ballin had also ordered one ship of the same design and from the same Vulcan yards which had

LATEST RACERS FOR

THE ATLANTIC SPEEDWAY.

THE NEW NORTH GERMAN LLOYD
STEAMSHIP KRONPRINZESSIN CECILIE.

Highest Types of Ocean Navigation Attained in Rival Steamers Coming from Germany and England.

For Size, Speed, and Equipment the Lusitania and Kronprinzessin Cecilie Never Before Equalled.

tania and Mauritania may be said t'
in a class by themselves. With
cated horse power which
work out at 80,000, with
45,000 tons, and a
mately, of 25½
comparison
steamer'
cent.
the he
tor. T
88 feet,
provide
capacity
steamships.   are
wider and lo   coupled
with the ab   ation, will do
much to here   omfort of transatlantic travel."

Luxury of German Steamer.

But while now admitting that the Kronprinzessin will be no match for the Lusitania when it comes to fast going, the
German company maintains that its newest
creation, which was named for the Crown
Princess Cecilie, is inferior to none in
superb equipment. In this vessel, they
assert, has been installed the very latest
in the way of luxury and comfort.

The first cabin rooms are situated upon
the upper and lower promenade decks, the
upper and the main deck, and, besides the
regular staterooms, the steamer contains
two imperial suites, consisting of a parlor,
dining room, bedroom, and bathroom;
eight other suites, consisting of parlor,
bedroom, and bathroom, and twelve cabins
de luxe, consisting of large bedroom and
adjoining bathroom. All the regular

Story on *Kronprinzessin Cecilie* with comparison to Cunard's *Lusitania*. *New York Times* of Sunday, 11 August 1907.

built all but one of the others. The *Kronprinzessin* was also the last major passenger ship to be equipped with reciprocating steam engines and hers were the largest ever installed. With quadruple expansion and the final cylinder reaching a diameter of more than seven feet, they developed 45,000 horsepower. Her North German owners described the luxury liner, with reference to her motive power and with typical Teutonic word-smithery, as "Doppelschrauben Schnellpostdampfer"— more literally translated as "twin propellored, fast mail steamer." Her massive pistons pumped faithfully up and down without fail throughout her career, but from her day onward, German-built steam turbines, licensed by their inventor, British engineer Sir Algernon Parsons, became the motive power of preference for all large German ships, both civilian and naval.

The ceiling of her first class dining room towered four decks upward to a skylight between the second and third funnels. Norddeutsche Lloyd's promotional brochures noted that the first-class men's smoking room was done in "the modern Roman style, decorated in white, with leather tapes-try. ... The pictures show scenes from the home of the Crown Princess— Mecklenburg." In addition to the luxurious interior, which was fulsomely described in her promotional literature, the ship was built to the highest standards of safety with "a double bottom, which is divided into twenty-six watertight compartments extending over the entire length of the vessel. Seventeen watertight transverse bulkheads, of which six extend to the upper deck and one to the main deck, and a bulkhead between the starboard and port engine rooms, divide the hull into twenty watertight compartments, of which two could be filled without affecting the flotation of the vessel. Water entering the hull can be expelled by four centrifugal pumps, four engine pumps, four steam pumps and five duplex pumps, which are able to dispose of 5,000 tons of water in one hour." Before her seagoing career was ended, the "boast" contained in these last two sentences was to be tested and found to be completely accurate.

Thereafter, for seven more or less uneventful years, while other German vessels had perilous encounters with icebergs and other ships, the *Kronprinzessin* competed profitably on the North Atlantic run carrying upper-crust passengers between her home port of Bremerhaven — with alternating stops at Plymouth and Cherbourg — and the major ports of the northeastern United States, generally New York, but occasionally Boston, Baltimore and even New Orleans.

After May 1913 her captain was Karl August Polack, well known to the American travelers, who had been employed for some years on the much smaller and older *Spree*. His habit of passing out expensive Cuban cigars to any male passenger he met surely contributed to the goodwill that his owners had achieved with the better-off American passengers. The ship was equally popular for her engines and drive system which were very well balanced and she had little of the perpetual vibration that disturbed the patrons of HAPAG's faster but also slightly older *Deutschland*, or NDL's much later *Europa*. The *Kronprinzessin* was a happy and well-operated ship.

Her final westward voyage for the Norddeutscher Lloyd began in mid–July 1914 from Bremerhaven; she was bound for the German lines' piers at Hoboken. These facilities lay just across the Hudson River from midtown Manhattan Island, whose then less impressive skyline was readily visible from the massive 30-year-old array of piers, warehouses and other accommodations. The German lines' major docking facilities in the New World had been completely rebuilt since the disastrous fire of June 1900 and were kept up to date; they were always regarded as among the finest in the world.

Despite the reports of imminent war from several places in Europe, soon after midnight on 28 July, Captain Polack eased his big ship out of her slip into New York harbor exactly on schedule for the return voyage to Europe. The comfortable *Kronprinzessin* carried a typically distinguished list of passengers—capitalists, politicians, sportsmen—a roster that was published in full in the *New York Times* nine days later. Under a different captain, the *Kronprinzessin* had carried Prince Heinrich, the Kaiser's brother, to the United States on a goodwill tour in 1907. The behavior of competing radio interests with respect to this voyage was cited by President Theodore Roosevelt as requiring an act of Congress to compel more cooperation among such users in "the public interest." Though many of the midsummer travelers of 1914 sensed that war was brewing among the imperial powers of the world, their crossing was smooth and uneventful until three days later, on the evening of 31 July (midnight German time) when the radioman received a midocean wireless from Bremen. The ship was now some 1,000 miles west, two days steaming, of Plymouth, the first scheduled port of call in Europe.

More than coincidentally, this was the same day that another German liner, HAPAG's much touted *Imperator*, by a few feet and a few tons the largest ship in the world, had been abruptly ordered to stay in her home port. The wireless message to the *Kronprinzessin* was part of a notice sent out from Wilhelmshaven to all German merchant ships around the world. It was also most unusual, so the radioman rushed it to his duty officer and then his skipper, who read it slowly: "Erhard hatte einen Blasenkatarrh Anfall; Siegfried."[3] Polack recognized this message as instructions to open immediately a sealed envelope he had been given on assuming command of the ship a year earlier.

Captain Karl August Polack on the bridge of his ship, *Kronprinzessin Cecilie.*
Deutsche Schiffarts Museum.

The midocean day had been clear and now an almost full moon was shining brightly on the waves to the ship's starboard; some of the first-class passengers who were gregariously consuming their postprandial drinks in the massive lounge amidships commented on the beauty of the scene. Without any ostensible reason and in a fairly calm sea a few of them noticed that the ship began to heel slightly toward the starboard as she commenced a gradual curve in course while maintaining her normal cruising speed. Before long, almost all the passengers in the lounge noticed that the same moon seemed to have reversed its position. While continuing to shine brightly, it was now high above the port beam. Where were they going? At this point the burly Captain Polack, accompanied by First Mate Carl Gastmeyer, called the male first- and second-class passengers into the ornate smoking room to explain what, indeed, was happening. Aboard the *Kronprinzessin* were 1,892 passengers: 354 Americans, 667 Germans, 406 Austrians, 151 Russians and several citizens of other, smaller European nations, including some, as noted by Justice William LeBaron Putnam in a subsequent dissent (see Chapter 11 below), "of nationalities that would have been hostile, if war had broken out, to any port she might touch, including her port of final destination."

Polack was easily approachable, a well-known and popular figure among the better-off American transatlantic passengers. He had commanded the *Kaiser Wilhelm der Grosse* in 1910 as part of the German lines' routine policy of shifting their experienced captains between their major vessels.[4] With the aid of his sealed instructions, he had deciphered the mysterious wireless message and then reacted promptly to the long-awaited secret orders. The gist of them was that he should run for cover in a neutral port, preferably New York; war was breaking out and it was felt that the oceans near Great Britain and France would soon be unsafe for German ships.

He explained to his passengers the thrust of his orders—after all, many of them were innocent and friendly American neutrals, loyal customers who were well deserving of his continuing good will and confidence. In those years, the German element within the American body politic was second in size and prosperity only to those of British descent. Many Americans, of all ancestries, recalled with warm gratitude the arbitration of the current Kaiser's grandfather in 1872, which settled the "Pig War" over jurisdiction of islands in Puget Sound very much to American liking. Besides, there was nothing any of them could do to change things while aboard his ship. He told them the truth, their voyage was being aborted as it was expected that British warships would be quick to blockade all ports friendly to German interests and seize any of their ships found on the high seas. They were on a new course, 180° different from that of an hour earlier and were headed back toward New York. Once inside the neutral territorial waters of the United States (then established by international agreement at three miles) the *Kronprinzessin* would be safe from the omnipresent Royal Navy, which unfortunately had a well-populated base at Halifax.

The grouse hunters, eagerly set to debark at Plymouth and head for a Scottish vacation, were dismayed; the politicians, including two members of the United States House of Representatives[5] bound for the International Peace Conference in Stockholm, were shocked. What could any of them do? "Buy the ship," someone suggested, and continue their journey under the American flag. While there was some question as to whether such action was possible under American shipping laws, in any case Polack's owners had not authorized such an act, though clearly Chairman Ballin soon wished they had. Much to his regret, as the captain unhappily explained to his patrons in the lounge, no matter how attractive the offer, he was required to refuse. Orders were orders and his were now explicit; despite the very attractive blandishments of the several American tycoons[6] traveling with him he had to follow his owner's instructions.

By dawn of 1 August, fortunately another clear day, the ship's crew was busily repainting the ship's four funnels. With luck — and poor visibility — they could touch up the *Kronprinzessin* and get her to resemble the White Star's almost equally sized liner, *Olympic*, a sister ship of the tragic *Titanic*. The appropriate red and black band was hastily painted around the four massive gold-colored funnels and the ship raced westward at her maximum speed consistent with fuel economy. At this moment the *Kronprinzessin* had insufficient coal to maintain her maximum speed for the time necessary to reach a neutral port. Fuel efficiency was much greater at a lower speed, and any reserve would have to be saved in case she had to run from an enemy warship. Polack's attempt at disguising his ship was the best he could do on such short notice and it would work only if the daytime lookouts on any hostile vessel were inattentive, hampered by fog, or half blind. The German four-stackers carried their massive funnels in two pairs, to allow space for the elaborate first-class dining room directly amidships where wave motion was the least. The White Star Line's four-stackers carried theirs equally spaced. The difference in silhouette appearance was considerable and easily recognizable, regardless of color.

The captain's concern was enhanced by the fact that the well-known German ship had been spotted earlier on the previous day by the French liner, *Savoie*, which had done him the disservice of then reporting her own position by wireless. Immediately upon altering course, he ordered all the ship's running lights extinguished and portholes covered with canvas during the dark. The numerous patches of fog encountered on the ocean were a mixed blessing — when thus surrounded the ship could not be seen by the various British and French warships suspected of prowling the North Atlantic sea lanes. On the other hand, neither could the *Kronprinzessin*'s lookouts see what might be immediately ahead. No matter! Polack's orders to the engine room were absolute: "Keep up all possible speed commensurate with economy of operation." He needed to husband his dwindling supply of coal in case he had to outrun one of the numerous British cruisers rightly feared to be at large.

Now that concern took on greater urgency. As the news from Europe became ever more ominous the radioman began receiving increasingly strong signals from the British cruiser, *Essex*, another of the *Monmouth* class and as fast as the *Kronprinzessin*, which was known to carry a dozen six-inch guns and appeared to be heading for a station off New York harbor. That refuge would now be dangerous and an alternative had to be determined. Boston was also a routine stop for NDL ships, but it was also a major port of call and without doubt the British would be quick to install warships on lookout there, too. Portsmouth's harbor was two hours nearer and it also had the depth to handle the *Kronprinzessin*, but that was a naval facility and she might not be welcome. Portland, Maine, even nearer, could also fit her in, but it, too, was a popular port and much frequented, particularly by ships plying to British ports in Canada.

Adding supplementary anxiety to Captain Polack's predicament was the most valuable element in his ship's cargo — stated in press accounts to be as much as $25 million in barrels of gold coins and $3.6 million in silver bars, mostly from New York's Guaranty Trust Company and National City Bank in remittances due several European firms.[7] This item of cargo was no secret; the *Kronprinzessin* had taken a similar shipment to Europe in 1910. Its capture by a British ship would be a double disaster for the North German Lloyd; the cargo was worth far more than the ship and the line had contracted for its safe handling and delivery.

There was much anxiety in European financial circles as a general European war seemed ever closer. On 27 July, Lloyds was asking for premiums of 40 percent on coverages against the outbreak of war. Bankers everywhere were experiencing runs on their reserves, and gold shipments — mostly from American sources — were increasingly frequent. *Carmania*'s final voyage from New York on 28 July carried a shipment of bullion almost equal to that on the *Kronprinzessin*. Before the war was two weeks old, the German raiders had achieved one objective: a major panic among British shipowners. The government was forced to subsidize maritime insurance rates to a maximum of 6 percent of value. However, matters were soon seen more realistically, and and a few weeks later Lloyd's was quoting rates of only 5 percent. The anticipated damage to British shipping from those "forty" Hilfskreuzer had simply failed to materialize. Sinkings there were, but nothing on the scale that had been feared. The 40 turned out to be only four.

The captain was very aware that it would now be against his owners' specific instructions and exceedingly perilous to attempt a return to Bremerhaven, but he was also aware that it might be good for him to have the imminent enemy think that was his intent. While steaming westward, he broke radio silence to contact the Marconi station at Malin Head, on the extreme northern tip of Ireland. Ordinarily such an eastbound ship's first wireless communication with Europe would have been to the Fastnet Station, at the other extreme of the country; thus Polack gave an indication that he would be taking a northerly course around the British Isles, rather than the normal but shorter route through the English Channel. This ploy was an excellent ruse and a very successful red herring; word of the unusual radio contact was immediately printed in newspapers both in London and New York. Following up on that piece of deception, general agent Heinz von Helmuth, North German Lloyd's main man in America, said, in a magnificent gem of understatement, that though the *Kronprinzessin* was scheduled to stop at Plymouth and Cherbourg, "the situation may have changed in international relations since she left this country." He added, in a remark similar to that which he had used to mislead everyone concerning the actions of the *Kronprinz Wilhelm* that very same day, that the *Kronprinzessin* had "only 300 tons of express freight aboard."

Among Captain Polack's passengers was one Clinton Ledyard Blair, a 47-year-old Princeton graduate and partner in the upscale New York investment banking house of Blair & Company. His office was in the heart of American finance at 24 Wall Street and he was among those heading for Scotland who had attempted to buy the *Kronprinzessin* in order to continue the trip; indeed, his dealmaking ability was a critical element in arranging the proposed purchase. Blair's home was in Peapack, New Jersey, whence he maintained membership in the famous New York Yacht Club, then the perennial holders of the America's Cup.[8] For the moment, however, it was more significant that Blair also maintained a summer domicile at Maine's tony Bar Harbor; he sailed his 1,000-ton yacht, *Diana*, in the nearby waters regularly. Bar Harbor was deep enough for the

Opposite: Kronprinzessin Cecilie, built in 1906, at anchor in Frenchman's Bay. Steam Ship Historical Society of America.

Kronprinzessin and several hours steaming closer than even Portland. "Could Mr. Blair find the entrance to Frenchman Bay and guide the massive liner to a safe anchorage?" "Why certainly!" He had sailed in and out of Bar Harbor dozens of times for many years. He could get them safely past the rocks off Schoodic Point and the Porcupines to a fine anchorage well within the three-mile safety zone. Less than 36 hours later Blair had completed his impromptu piloting job so well that on the morning of 4 August, while German troops continued their assault on southern Belgium and the British finally had to accept the obvious (that their withdrawal ultimatum to imperial Germany had been ignored), the residents of Bar Harbor awoke to find a most unusual sight in their harbor. Interspersed with the usual summertime flotilla of steam yachts and small craft was a huge ship that some of the summer folk were sure was the *Olympic*. It certainly very much resembled the *Titanic*, mental images of which were vividly recalled by quite a few of the Bar Harbor vacationers, several of whom had lost relatives only 28 months earlier when the great ship went down. The *Olympic* was to earn her own share of opprobrium some 20 years later when she made her landfall at the Nantucket Lightship, directly abeam. The lightship, the easternmost navigational beacon of New York harbor, was cut completely in half. On this day, however, *Olympic* was securely tied to her pier in Manhattan. In due course this ship also did its share in the war effort; on 12 May 1918, she rammed and sank the eight-month-old *U-103* in the English Channel.

The navigation laws of the United States prohibit any foreign-flag carrier from discharging passengers or freight at an unauthorized destination within the United States. While now safe from the enemy in a neutral port, Captain Polack soon found himself with a horde of restless passengers aboard, many of whom were anxious to find an alternative means of reaching their intended destinations. But there was a fine of $1,000 for each and every violation of the passenger landing prohibition. The master already had enough troubles and thus refused to let his passengers debark until he had obtained a special clearance from American customs authorities. It was several hours before Secretary of Commerce William McAdoo wired his consent for a waiver and the passengers could go ashore and set about their hastily revised business and travel plans.

Failure to deliver the gold and silver as contracted carried its own separate set of penalties and a belligerent nation's ship in faraway Bar Harbor was felt to be not nearly as safe as their vaults in Manhattan. Thus, the bankers in New York were quick to charter a special armored train to return their specie. While the environs of the ship were guarded by the U.S. Revenue cutter, *Androscoggin*, on 8 August an armed squad of United

Anxious passengers await debarkation from *Kronprinzessin Cecilie* at Bar Harbor. Steam Ship Historical Society of America.

States Marines supervised the transfer of the bullion from the ship into her boats and thence across Frenchman Bay to the Maine Central Railroad terminal at the Mount Desert Ferry dock. Then, "securely locked in four steel express cars and accompanied by an armed guard of forty express messengers and detectives," the special train preceded the regular New York Express and arrived safely to return their gold to the bankers early the next day. None of this, however, precluded the bankers from kicking a man while he was already down and subsequently suing North German Lloyd in the Admiralty Court of Boston for $1,040,467 in damages (including the cost of the marines and the train) because of the line's failure to deliver in accordance with their shipping contract.

Following the removal of the gold and the debarkation of her passengers, the *Kronprinzessin* was moved to the upper harbor, above Bar Island, where the new destroyer, USS *Warrington*, could take up a custodial position nearby. So the remainder of the summer passed by, while everyone wondered what would become of the big ship, and her band went ashore almost every afternoon to entertain the assembled, vacationing summer folk. Germany was no enemy of America at this time, indeed American sentiment regarding the European conflict, except in certain quarters of the Northeast, was quite neutral. Americans of German descent held many positions of prominence and respect in all walks of the nation's life.

"The crew of the *Kronprinzessin* had a lovely summer and autumn. The passengers had left the ship. The gold was back in New York. The ship became the sensation of the summer season. They [the Boston & Maine Railroad] put on special trains for tourists to visit the ship. The German crew was received as welcome guests of Bar Harbor and treated as such."[9] It was also the high point of her career.

While the band played on, and much to the distress of the local chamber of commerce, fears were publicly expressed that ice might damage the great ship if she stayed for the winter at Bar Harbor. But, on the other hand, if she were to brave the open ocean and make for a more southerly port, she would risk capture by the omnipresent British cruiser patrol. With the precious metals safely returned to New York, that element of potential loss was removed, but the ship itself was still worth close to $5 million, a fair sized fortune in those days of a nickel subway ride and a one cent daily newspaper. Could she stay within the three-mile limit all the way to Boston, where North German Lloyd had docking facilities?

In addition, more lawsuits now began to pile up. The bankers had been at the head of the line, claiming damages continuing at $1,500 per day because of the failure of Norddeutscher Lloyd to make delivery as contracted. Then followed some of the passengers, who should really have been grateful to NDL and Captain Polack but instead claimed various monetary injuries because they had not arrived in Europe when promised. These included the far-fetched contention of one Maurice Hanssens, who asserted that, somehow, his nonarrival at Plymouth had caused $200,000 in damages to his property in Brussels at the hands of the invading German army. Nevertheless, the combination of all these claims presented a sufficiently strong case that United States Marshal, Eugene Harmon, was instructed to seize the ship as collateral for all the potential damages.

Later in the fall the *Kronprinzessin*, now a ward of the United States courts, was towed to Boston, complete with a destroyer escort to prevent British interference, and formally interned in President Roads, off East Boston's Shirley Point, near Deer Island. Here, at least, she had company: the German freighters *Willehad*, *Köln* and *Ockenfels* and the big new liners, *Amerika* (advertised to sail for Europe at 9 A.M. on 1 August) and now *Cincinnati*, all of them holed up indefinitely because of the British control of the seas. To all German sympathizers, headed by the Kaiser but including many Americans, the war was only going to be a short affair, perhaps six weeks, but surely over by Christmas. There was no sense of

USS *Mount Vernon,* the former *Kronprinzessin Cecilie.* U.S. Navy photo.

overwhelming urgency about the unremunerative inactivity of these costly assets. Yet! In due course, all the litigation was consolidated before Federal District Court Judge, Clarence Hale, sitting in the Admiralty Court at Boston, who heard all the arguments and rendered his decision on 1 February 1916. It was during this trial that the text of the message from "Siegfried" came out, along with its hidden meaning.

❖ ❖ ❖

The United States entered the European conflict on 6 April 1917,[10] after Germany's unwise resumption of unrestricted submarine warfare in the German-declared "war zone" off the coasts of England and France which had generated great American public outrage. The sinking of the *Lusitania* in 1915 was the spark that ultimately brought the United States into the conflict two years later. Despite published advertisements warning people that the ship was carrying arms to the enemy and was entering a war zone, British propagandists managed to obscure the truth about a major element of the ship's cargo for half a century. The *Kronprinzessin*'s days as a German ship, however, were already over. Two months earlier, on 3 February, U.S. marshals had been ordered to proceed to her Deer Island anchorage and claim the liner as a delinquent for various harbor and towing fees. Within ten weeks she was to be rechristened as *Mount Vernon*. Because of her ancestry, and in the fervor of wartime anti–German enthusiasm, many of the enlisted men aboard the vessel coined yet another name for the ship—*Mount Vermin*. By now many of her original crew had spent time in Boston area colleges, obtained civilian employment in American stores and industries and begun to scatter across the continent on their way to becoming naturalized citizens. Only a minimal skeleton crew remained for internment and they were packed off to a YMCA-operated camp at Hot Springs, North Carolina.

For example, long before Germany became an enemy, several of the *Kronprinzessin*'s famed culinary staff migrated as far as western Massachusetts and found their way into the employ of Robert Jahrling, a longtime functionary of the local turnverein and proprietor of downtown Springfield's Highland Hotel. In due course, their exceptional talents and hearty food made this eatery one of the best known in New England. "Graduates" of the Highland Hotel became sought-after employees and eventually proprietors of a number of well-regarded restaurants across the region. The hotel itself, however, fell victim to urban renewal in 1964.

By the end of October 1917, her machinery repaired and her quarters refitted for troops, the ship once named for the crown princess of Germany made the first of her nine voyages to carry personnel and war materiel swiftly across the ocean and bring the growing weight of American manpower and industry into the effort to thwart the ambitions of the lady's father-in-law, Kaiser Wilhelm II.

Turnabout has always been thought of as fair play. On 5 September, 1918, while some 200 miles off Brest, on the return voyage to New York, the German *U-82*, one of the faster such ships with a speed of more than nine knots submerged, scored a direct hit in *Mount Vernon*'s starboard boiler room. Although 36 men were killed outright and another 13 wounded, the highly compartmentalized nature of the ship — a quality insisted upon by her German designers and noted in her sales brochures — enabled the port boilers and engine of the vessel to return her to Brest for emergency first aid before she headed west again to Boston for more permanent repairs.

Back in full operation several months later, she sailed again for Europe, this time largely empty, to begin the process of returning American servicemen. During her wartime service, the *Mount Vernon* had carried a number of distinguished governmental passengers: the Secretary of

War, the Army's Chief of Staff, the Chief of Naval Operations, and at the end of the war, President Wilson's special advisor and representative at the first phases of the peace negotiations, Colonel Edward Mandell House.

After her wartime duty was completed, which included one trip to Vladivostok to help repatriate the Czech Legion, the *Kronprinzessin* a.k.a. *Mount Vernon* was assigned to the custody of the United States Shipping Board. There was no possibility of a return to her prewar German proprietors; the enormous reparations demanded of that nation precluded such an act. She was laid up in 1920. A plan was then advanced — sensible given the efficient hull speed of the liner — to replace her massive steam-driven engines with diesel motors, but no action was ever taken. By mid–1924, the once great ship was firmly berthed in Virginia's James River estuary, along with a number of other surplus and momentarily uneconomical or inefficient vessels.

Another generation and another war later, the seeds of hatred left over from the humiliating terms imposed on Germany in 1919 at Versailles finally burst into bloom under Hitler's warped leadership of a rearmed nation. The *Kronprinzessin* was still laid up, rusting in quiet while lashed to similarly ageing piling in the James, cheek by jowl with one of her sisters and other relatives. While shipping was again in great demand by the British, who were once more witnessing the woeful pruning of their merchant marine by U-boats, age had taken the beauty off even a crown princess. Offered, as is, to the Allies early in 1940, she was spurned and soon thereafter towed away to Baltimore for interment. It took place on 13 September 1940. The scrappers paid $178,300 for the cadaver of the once famous lady.

11

The Litigation

The decision of United States District Court Judge Clarence Hale[11] was handed down on 1 February 1916. In the light of the times and three generations later, his recitation of the events in the quick rush from peace to war in the summer of 1914 makes interesting reading.

"In this case, No 1069, the Guaranty Trust Company of New York seeks to recover damages for breach of contract, by the steamship, in failing to carry a consignment of gold from the port of New York to the port of Plymouth, England. The libel alleges that on July 27, 1914, the steamship was lying in the port of New York, bound for Bremerhaven, Germany, by way of Plymouth, England; that on that date the libelant [the bank] delivered to the steamship in good order and condition 93 kegs of gold bullion, of the agreed and declared value of $4,942,936.64, to be carried to Plymouth, England; thence to be forwarded to London, there to be delivered in like good order and condition to the order of the libelant, in consideration of $9,268, prepaid freight; that the steamship delivered to the libelant a bill of lading therefore; that, in violation of her contract, the steamship, when about 900 miles from Plymouth, abandoned her voyage and put back to Bar Harbor, Me., where, on or about August 8, 1914, the libelant accepted redelivery of the 93 kegs of gold from the steamship, under an agreement that such redelivery should not constitute a waiver of libelants' claim for breach of contract. By reason of such failure of the steamship to deliver the gold at Plymouth, the libelant says it has suffered damage exceeding the sum of $1,104,467.43...."

"The answer admits the receipt of the 93 kegs of gold bullion, and alleges that the carriage of the same was undertaken by the claimant [steamship] subject to the conditions and exceptions contained in the bill of lading, which is made a part of the answer, subject also to the possibility of the ship being prevented from concluding her voyage and being forced to put back into a port of refuge, in case of outbreak, or threatened outbreak, of the European war. It admits that the steamship turned back on her course, and says that at the time of turning back she was about 1,070 miles from Plymouth. It alleges that the decision of the master to return to a port in the United States was based on credible information received by him from the North German Lloyd office at Bremen by wireless message that war had broken out, involving Germany and Russia, France and England, and that this message, considered in conjunction with the information with respect to the European crisis received by him prior to sailing, furnished reasonable ground for him to apprehend that the steamship and cargo would be captured if she continued on her voyage, and required him, in the exercise of sound judgement and discretion, to put back to a port of refuge; that, though war had not actually broken out at the time of the receipt of this wireless message, still the master, in anticipation of an outbreak of hostilities, and the consequent danger of arrest of the members of his crew, the arrest or probable detention and discomfort of his passengers, and the capture of his ship and cargo, was fully justified in adopting the course which he did adopt...."

[Here followed a recitation of several other legal defenses that North German Lloyd's attorneys[12] advanced to indicate the company's good faith and lack of liability to pay such exorbitant damages as the Guaranty Bank was demanding.]

"Certain historical facts are agreed upon, as part of the proofs. Those stipulated as having happened before the ship sailed from New York are as follows: On June 23, 1914, Archduke Francis Ferdinand, of Austria, and his wife, the Duchess of Hohenberg, were assassinated at Sarajevo, the capital of Bosnia. On July 23rd Austria sent an ultimatum to Servia,[13] the terms of which appear in the German White Paper and the British White Paper. On July 27th Russia urged that Austria abandon the time limit of her ultimatum —'in order to prevent consequences equally incalculable and fatal to all the Powers which might result from the course of action followed by the Austro-Hungarian government.'"

Until the advent of undeclared wars in recent generations, White Papers were traditionally documents issued by governments to explain (or excuse) subsequent positions or behavior. In this instance, though Judge Hale did not dwell on it, the heterogeneous Austrian Empire, in a slap at

Slavic interests, had swallowed up Bosnia and Herzegovina only five years earlier. The ten-point ultimatum reflected Austria's frustration with ongoing Serbian insults and anti–Dual Monarchy propaganda. It called for apologies for the shooting; the execution of Gavrilo Princip, the perpetrator of the murder; dismissal of numerous hostile officials; a jointly administered program of public education on topics favorable to Austria-Hungary; and "collaboration in enforcement of the suppression of the subversive movement directed against the territorial integrity of the Monarchy."

Judge Hale continued. "The Russian government [through Foreign Minister Sergei Sazanov] informed the other Powers that, if the Austro-Hungarian government should make war on Servia, Russia could not allow the conflict to be settled between those two countries alone. The French ambassador at St. Petersburg [55-year-old Maurice Paléologue] gave the English ambassador at St. Petersburg [Sir George Buchanan] to understand — 'that France would fulfill all the obligations entailed by her alliance with Russia, if necessity arose, besides supporting Russia strongly in all diplomatic negotiations.'

"The German government emphasized to other Powers its opinion that there is only question of a matter to be settled exclusively between Austria-Hungary and Servia, and that other Powers ought to reserve it to those two, because interference of another Power, owing to different treaty obligations, would be followed by incalculable consequences. On July 25th Austria declined the Russian request for extension of time limit to Servia. Servia replied to the Austrian ultimatum at 6 p.m. [accepting all but the most humiliating of its demands in language described by no less than the Kaiser as dissipating "every reason for war"]. The terms of the reply are shown in German and British White Papers. Austria advised Servia and the other Powers that she considered Servia's reply unsatisfactory.

"The Austrian minister [Baron von Gisel de Gieslingen] left Belgrade at 6:30 p.m. The Servian government moved from Belgrade to Nish[14] the same evening. Germany confined her Alsace-Lorraine garrisons to barracks, and placed the frontier works of Alsace-Lorraine in a complete state of defense. The populace of Berlin made demonstrations in favor of war[15]; Servia ordered mobilization; Russia began to take military precautions; martial law was proclaimed in Austria. On July 26th Austria severed diplomatic relations with Servia, and sent passports to the Servian minister. Austrian mobilization against Servia was decreed. Austria advised Russia that she sought no territory of Servia, and did not intend to impair the sovereignty of that country, but that, aside from that, she was prepared to go to the 'furthest extremes' to obtain satisfaction of her demands.

"The Austrian ambassador at Washington [Dr. Constantin Dumba] instructed consuls in the United States to tell reservists to prepare to return home for service. The Servian army began mobilization. There was panic in Belgrade as the people filed from the city. American tourists left Carlsbad and other resorts.[16] Belgium increased her army to enforce her neutrality.[17] The German fleet was concentrated in the home waters. Germany indicated to her railroads the measures preparatory for concentration. Germany urged the other Powers not to interfere with Austro-Hungarian plans to discipline Servia. The German ambassador at St. Petersburg [Count Friedrich von Portalès] was directed to make the following declaration to the Russian government: 'Preparatory military measures by Russia will force us to counter measures which must consist in mobilizing the army. But mobilization means war. As we know the obligations of France toward Russia, this mobilization would be directed against both Russia and France. We cannot assume that Russia desires to unchain such a European war. Since Austria-Hungary will not touch the existence of the Servian kingdom, we are of the opinion that Russia can afford to assume an attitude of waiting. We can all the more support the desire of Russia to protect the integrity of Servia, as Austria-Hungary does not intend to question the latter. It will be easy in the further development of the affair to find a basis for an understanding.'

"The Russian Secretary of War [66-year-old Vladimir Alexandrovich Sukhomlinov[18]] gave the German military attache [Captain von Eggeling] his word of honor that no order to mobilize had been issued, merely preparations were being made, but not a horse mustered, nor reserves called in. If Austria-Hungary crossed the Servian frontier, such military districts as are directed toward Austria, namely Kiev, Odessa, Moscow, Kazan, would be mobilized; under no circumstances those on the German frontier, namely, St. Petersburg, Vilna, Warsaw. He added that peace with Germany was desired very much. The military attache told the Secretary that Germany appreciated Russia's friendly intentions, but considered mobilization, even against Austria, as very menacing. [It was this limited mobilization — of Russia to defend the rights of Serbia — that was seized upon by Germany and strangled and twisted into a pretext for invasion of Belgium en route to France. When asked for the right of passage for their troops, Luxembourg had agreed, but Belgium's King Albert had said: "NON!"]

"Sir Edward Grey proposed to the Powers a conference in London between himself and the ambassadors of Germany, France and Italy for the purpose of discovering an issue that would prevent complications. If agreed to, the representatives of these Powers were to request authorities at

Belgrade, Vienna, and St. Petersburg to suspend active military operations pending results of a conference. Russia asked Austria to take back her ultimatum, and modify its form, and, if this were done, offered to guarantee the result.

"Russia informed Italy that the Austrian-Servian conflict could not be localized. Austria notified the Powers that the refusal of Servia to accept the Austrian demands in full, without reservations, would compel Austria to force Servia by the most drastic measures to a complete submission. Russia announced [in shades that would be repeated twice more in the 20th century] that she could not be asked to allow Servia to be crushed. The German fleet in Norway put to sea, and Austria ordered partial military and naval mobilization. On July 27th, Germany completed requisitions, and placed her covering troops in position in Alsace-Lorraine. Russia notified Austria that, if war broke out between Austria and Servia, Russia would not give way. The Vienna and Budapest bourses closed. A skirmish occurred on the Danube between Austrian and Servian forces. England stated to Germany [through British Ambassador Sir Edward Goschen and German Foreign Minister Gottlieb von Jagow] that, if Austria, notwithstanding the terms of the Servian reply, should invade Servia, she would prove she wished to crush a small state. This would raise a European question, and a war would ensue in which all the Powers would take part. France, Italy and Russia agreed to Sir Edward Grey's proposal of the 26th for a conference of ambassadors in London.

"State of war declared in the Russian province of Kovno [modern Lithuania]. Belgian army was mobilized. Shots were fired by a Cossack patrol on a German patrol at the Russian frontier. [Actually, the Germans had occupied three towns in Russian Poland — Bedzin, Kalisz and Czestochowa.] The Fourteenth corps of the French army discontinued maneuvers, and returned to its garrison.[19] Information to this effect was received in Berlin. Germany refused Sir Edward Grey's proposal for a conference of ambassadors at London. [The German ambassador, Prince Karl Max Lichnowsky, and the Austrian ambassador, Count Albert von Mensdorff, had been instructed from home to avoid any such conference.] The czar informed the crown prince of Servia,[20] if all efforts for peace failed, Russia would not disinterest herself in the fate of Servia. Russia proposed to Austria that desired modifications in the latter's demands on Servia be the subject of direct conversations between St. Petersburg and Vienna.

"The proofs [offered by NDL's attorneys] show that a newspaper called the *Ocean Gazette* was printed on the steamship, and that on July 29th a copy of the paper contained a wireless dispatch from London announcing that: 'A formal declaration of war was made by Austria on Servia to-day and active hostilities between the two countries have already begun.[21] Two Servian steamers were to-day attacked on the Danube, the Servian colors hauled down, and the Austrian colors hoisted…. Orders for the German fleet to concentrate in home waters have been issued, and the British first and second battle squadrons are in readiness for service. [At this juncture, the Kaiser broke off his vacation cruise in Norwegian waters.]

"'A dispatch from Berlin says a Russian force has occupied positions near the frontier of Russian Poland and that a squadron of German cavalry has also advanced to the frontier. Emperor Franz Josef has granted complete amnesty to all Austro-Hungarian subjects who have deserted from the army or who emigrated to other lands to avoid military duty.'"[22]

The declarations of war formed a lengthy daisy chain that continued throughout the next four years, culminating on 19 July 1918, when the inconsequential war-making ability of Honduras joined the conflict against Germany. It all began on 28 July 1914 with the Austrian declaration against Serbia. During the balance of 1914, this was followed as in the table below:

1 August	Germany against Russia
3 August	Germany against France
4 August	Germany against Belgium
4 August	England against Germany
5 August	Montenegro against Austria
6 August	Austria against Russia
6 August	Serbia against Germany
8 August	Montenegro against Germany
12 August	France against Austria
12 August	England against Austria
23 August	Japan against Germany
28 August	Austria against Belgium
2 November	Russia against Turkey
2 November	Serbia against Turkey
5 November	England against Turkey
5 November	France against Turkey

Seven more declarations of war against the Central Powers were made in 1915; six in 1916; 15 in 1917; and five in 1918, concluding with that of Honduras. By then belligerency was truly a worldwide condition and it was a great deal easier to list those nations which had not been drawn in — Andorra, Argentina, Chile, Colombia, Denmark, Ethiopia, Liechtenstein, Monaco, Netherlands, Norway, Paraguay, Persia, Spain, Sweden, Switzerland, and Venezuela. Being at war with Germany was all the rage.

Karl August Polack with his wife in retirement after the war. Deutsche Schiffarts Museum.

Judge Hale continued. "The text of Austria's declaration of war was also printed. On July 31st, the *Ocean Gazette* published another wireless dispatch from London: 'Germany sent an ultimatum to Russia, demanding an explanation for the latter's mobilization. The answer is to be given within the next 24 hours. Fighting between Austrian and Servian forces is reported to-day at several points and the invading forces are meeting with stout resistance. Dispatches received at the Servian legation in London say that the Austrians were repulsed while trying to cross the Danube 20 miles east of Belgrade and at Losnitz, west of Belgrade. The southern column of Austrians in Bosnia is reported to be watching the Montenegrin troops. In a severe battle at Fotcha, in Bosnia, the Austrians defeated the Servians with several hundred killed on each side. The gravity of the international situation is recognized in all European capitals. Russia proceeded with her mobilization of a large number of troops,[23] while the French defensive forces took extensive precautions.

"'Business was practically suspended on the London Stock Exchange to-day, pending the serious war situation. Dealers refused to make prices. The consols[24] reached a record low price of 69½, the lowest in a century. Seven failures were reported to-day. St. Petersburg, Vienna, Budapest, and Brussels Exchanges also remained closed, two failures were announced on Glasgow Exchanges. The *Shinbum* [*sic*], a semiofficial newspaper of Japan, declares to-day that, if England is attacked, Japan will give assistance to the British arms.

"'Washington. Administration officials are awaiting additional developments in European politics. If other nations than Austria and Servia are drawn into the conflict, probably a proclamation of neutrality covering the entire situation will be determined upon by the State Department.'

"Captain Polack, the master of the steamship, testified that he had followed the sea since 1875; he had been in the North German Lloyd service since 1886; he had been a master since 1900, and in command of this steamship since May 1913. When he was given command of the ship, he was given a sealed package, and was instructed to open the package at any time in the future in case he received a message, signed 'Siegfried' and relating to some disease. On July 31st, at 10 o'clock in the evening, ship's time (11:45 Greenwich time), a wireless message was brought to him on the bridge by the chief officer. The message was in German, and it related that somebody had fallen sick; it was signed 'Siegfried.' Upon opening the sealed package, he found a code which enabled him to translate the wireless message as follows: 'War has broken out with England, France, and Russia. Return to New York.'"

While all these events were occurring in Europe, a small-scale war erupted in the American press between Serbian Consul-General, Michael Idvorsky Pupin, a 56-year-old sometime professor at Columbia, from his offices in New York, and Austrian Ambassador Constantin Theodor Dumba, vacationing along with numerous other foreign diplomats at the scenic upper-crust town of Manchester-by-the-Sea in Massachusetts.[25] They each sought to persuade American public opinion as to the merit of their respective nations' positions. Among other interesting events, the swift rush of actions caught Baron Wilhelm Schön, the German Ambassador to France, on holiday in Bavaria; he hustled back to Paris. Serbian Commander-in-Chief, General Radomir Putnik, on vacation among the mountains of Styria, was detained by Austrian police as he attempted to return home, but was released on the personal order of Emperor Franz Josef. Russian bonds deservedly sank to an all-time low and even shares of the highly prosperous Canadian Pacific Railway tumbled, as German investors sought to unload foreign holdings.

The balance of Judge Hale's 40-page finding dealt largely with legal issues, including a lengthy analysis of the plaintiff's contention that war did not, in fact, break out in a manner that would have resulted in preventing the normal completion of the steamship's voyage. Upholding Polack's judgment, given his finite supply of fuel, Hale ended his decision solidly in favor of the *Kronprinzessin* and North German Lloyd, dismissing the Guaranty Trust's claim and even going so far as to assign all the costs of the litigation to the parties which had brought the suit. Hale's decision noted that completion of the voyage would have been very risky and that a turnabout decision had to be made in a timely manner that would still allow the ship to reach some port safely. Had Polack delayed 24 hours in obeying the instructions from "Siegfried" he would have been beyond the "point of no return" and committed to entering waters and ports that everyone could see were becoming increasingly risky if not downright hostile. A similar, but only slightly smaller, claim by the National City Bank, which had been consolidated into the same suit, was likewise dismissed, as were the claims of two passengers, Charles W. Rantoul, Jr., and Maurice Hanssens, that they had been damaged by the failure of the steamship to make port in Plymouth as scheduled.

That, however, was not the end of it.

Judge Hale's decision, dismissing the entire business, was handed down on 1 February 1916. The following November, an appeal was taken up to the First U.S. Circuit Court of Appeals—Justices Bingham, Dodge and Putnam. This was a distinguished panel. George Hutchins Bingham (1864–1965) of Littleton, NH, had served on the Supreme Court of New Hampshire for 11 years prior to his appointment by President Wilson to the 1st Circuit Court in 1913. Frederic Dodge (1847–1927) of Cambridge, MA, had been a judge for the Federal District of Massachusetts from 1905 and was elevated to the Circuit Court in 1912, where he served until his retirement in 1918. William LeBaron Putnam (1835–1918) of Bath, ME, was older and more experienced in maritime law than his associates and had been on the 1st Circuit bench since 1892. His reputation had been established by his very successful representation of American fishing interests in negotiations with Great Britain in 1887.

The appeals hearing was held on 17 November 1916, and the Appeals Court's decision was handed down two months later, on 23 January 1917. In a split decision, Putnam in the minority, the justices reversed the lower court's finding in part and upheld it in part. The two passengers, Rantoul and Hanssens, were still found undamaged, though the two banks were deemed eligible to collect. Even this was not the end of it, however.

Appeal of this defeat was taken by the North German Lloyd (despite the newly declared state of war between Germany and the United States) up to the Supreme Court of the United States. The matter was argued on 16 and 17 April 1917, and firmly decided in favor of the newfound enemy's steamship and her owners, who by now had already lost their ship. The famous Chief Justice Oliver Wendell Holmes, Jr., at this point in his life the senior member of England's prestigious Alpine Club, wrote a very firm upholding of the good judgment, properly exercised, by Captain Polack. America's top jurist summed up his conclusion with the typically sound pronouncement that: "Business contracts must be construed with business sense, as they naturally would be understood by intelligent men of affairs."[26]

12

Kaiser Wilhelm II

Never comparable as a statesman to his grandfather, "der Grosse," Kaiser Wilhelm II led the German state into its ill-fated naval armament race that climaxed in the Great War of 1914–18. In 1881, while the great kaiser still ruled, his grandson, also a grandson of Britain's Queen Victoria, had married Augusta Victoria (see Chapter 17 for more on her namesake vessel) heiress of the northern duchy of Schleswig-Holstein, a territory long coveted by Prussian rulers. His ailing father, Friedrich III, next in the line of succession, had held the crown for a bare three months in the spring of 1888 when he died of throat cancer on 16 June.

The youthful Kaiser's wife bore him a large family. After the Crown Prince, who was to follow his father into exile, they were christened Eitel Friedrich, Adalbert, Augustus Wilhelm, Oscar, Joachim, and finally the only girl, Victoria Louise. Ships, both mercantile and for war, were named for all of these children of which only Eitel Friedrich's played any meaningful role in the Great War. Kaiser Wilhelm II lived a long life, from 1859 to 1941, survived his "beloved" first wife by 30 years, and was well into a second marriage. The last 23 years of his life were in exile (barely tolerated by his host nation) at Doorn, southeast of Utrecht in the Netherlands, where he had taken up residence after his unwisely ambitious and militaristic policies resulted in the destruction of his own rule, the loss of his people's prime manhood, and the humiliation of his nation.

The ship that was given his name was launched for NDL from the

Vulcan yards at Stettin during earlier and better days. She was completed on 30 March 1903, and three years later broke her sister ship, *Deutschland*'s, transatlantic speed record by maintaining 23.58 knots between Sandy Hook and the Eddystone Light. Four years later, in 1907, this record was lost to the four-screwed, 31,550-ton *Lusitania*, the latest to hold the title of "largest ship in the world." That Cunarder in turn lost both titles the following year to her newly launched sister ship, the 32,000-ton *Mauretania*, whose average speed of 26.06 knots for the full voyage was unchallengeable for the next 20 years.[27]

The 45,000 horsepower of her engines enabled this *Kaiser* to outstrip most of her competitors in the transatlantic trade. Many of these "races" were chronicled, with barely suppressed glee by the winners, in newspapers on both sides of the ocean. One such "race" in late December 1906, was excitedly enhanced by use of the ship's "wireless telegraph," which the German lines had installed in 1900 and which became a mandatory item of equipment for all passenger vessels calling in American ports after enactment of the Mann-Elkins Act in 1910. Instead of using this newly found communications device for its primary purpose — safety — the two ships cordially taunted each other in Morse code across the ether, with Captain Poirot of the considerably lesser powered and losing French liner, *La Provence*, finally explaining in a subsequent press statement: "The great trouble with the French people is that they do not know how to brag. What we did, however, is shown by the result. We reached the [Sandy] Hook just a minute behind the *Kaiser Wilhelm II*."

Just a few weeks before the outbreak of war, the *Kaiser* got into her own conflict — with the British freighter, *Inchmore*, off the Needles, near the westerly end of the English Channel. Although soon repaired at Bremerhaven, she was out of commission for several weeks and was put back into service just in time to be approaching New York on 3 August 1914, when the agonizingly reached British ultimatum to the Kaiser and his armies expired at midnight to engulf the whole world in the Great War. The big ship continued full ahead on course toward safety in New York, but after that deadline the danger of capture was suddenly increased — the frighteningly numerous British cruisers were sure to be already at sea and on the lookout. Nevertheless, Captain Dahl managed to get his command safely by the Nantucket lightship and then raced across the open waters south of Rhode Island to where he could sidle along the south coast of Long Island — carefully within the American three-mile limit — for the final hours of her passage. In this exercise he duplicated the almost simultaneous performance of Captain Witt in command of HAPAG's slightly smaller liner, *President Lincoln*.

Arriving at her Hoboken pier on 6 August (while the band from her sister ship, *Kronprinzessin Cecilie* was beginning its regular afternoon concerts for the entertainment of summer folk at Bar Harbor) the *Kaiser* spent the next 31 months in immobility. Upon reaching her berth, the passengers learned that NDL's *Brandenburg* and HAPAG's *Prinz Oskar* had also just docked, unmolested, in Philadelphia, where they, too, were to rest and rust in idleness until needed by the United States for its belated entry into the war against Germany.[28]

Twenty-seven German-owned vessels in New York harbor were seized as prizes of the newly declared war, on 6 April 1917. After her long idleness *Kaiser Wilhelm II* was found to have suffered so greatly from neglect, compounded since the end of January by such deliberate "tampering with the machinery," that she was unfit for duty until repairs were completed by employees of the Brooklyn Navy Yard late the following August. Then, on 1 September, the big ship was renamed *Agamemnon* by order of Secretary of the Navy Josephus Daniels, to honor the leader of the Greek forces in the lengthy Trojan War. Tried out for seaworthiness and the reliability of her repairs, the onetime pride of the German merchant marine began life as an American troop transport at the end of October.

Midway on her first such voyage, the *Von Steuben* (a.k.a. *Kronprinz Wilhelm*) *Agamemnon*'s one-year-older sister ship, made a turn within the convoy which put her on a collision course with the younger vessel. As soon as the error was recognized, the former Hilfskreuzer made a correction, but it was too late to prevent the consequences. The older ship's bow smashed a hole in the younger one's forward well deck and then crunched beam to beam, destroying several lifeboats. One of the soldiers aboard *Agamemnon* fell off during the impact, but landed uninjured on the other ship's deck. The actual damage to the two ships' hulls were slight, so both of them resumed the voyage, but subsequent repairs delayed her second round trip until mid–January 1918.

On *Agamemnon*'s sixth such passage, early on the morning of 6 September in a westbound convoy barely a day out of Brest, her lookout spotted a periscope only 100 yards off the port bow. Sounding her siren and simultaneously firing one of her six-inch guns at the periscope to warn the other ships, she turned up to flank speed so as to leave the area. It was too late. A torpedo from *U-82* hit the former *Kronprinzessin Cecilie*, now working for the United States as *Mount Vernon*, directly amidships. After ascertaining that the younger ship was not mortally wounded and, thanks to the high degree of compartmentalization insisted upon by her designers, still able to move under her own power, *Agamemnon* cleared out of the danger area and left the offending U-boat to the escorting destroyers, while *Mount Vernon* limped back to port for emergency repairs. Three months later, *Agamemnon* was engaged in bringing doughboys home from Europe, a task accomplished without hazard and free of the tedium of convoying. This more pleasant duty was completed by midyear 1920, and the ship was then laid up in an inlet off Chesapeake Bay south of Baltimore.

During the war years a great many ships had been sunk, but a great many had also been built. Another large number had simply been frozen in place for the duration, particularly in German or other Central Powers–controlled ports. Soon after the coming of peace, all these vessels were released to civilian pursuits and they could all move at their most efficient speeds— no longer hampered by the convoy system which required all to move at the top sustainable speed of the slowest. With a postwar decline in demand there was suddenly a glut of shipping and though the big ship's name was again changed in 1927, to *Monticello*, no one really wanted her. Tied up to her relatives, she grew weedy and rusty for the next 20 years in the Patuxent River. Still sound, however, when the sequel war broke out, she was offered to the British early in 1940. Her machinery was too tired, though; she had become obsolete. She never went to sea again and, like the *Kronprinzessin*, was broken up in September 1940.

13

The *Barbarossa* Class

Eleven large ships, of 11,000 tons GRT, pertaining to HAPAG and NDL were known collectively within the seagoing community as the *Barbarossa* class. By the start of the Great War in 1914 these ships were the largely unsung but worldwide workhorses of the German merchant marine. They came in two series: four ships of the group launched in 1896, and a second group of basically similar design that started to come off the ways three years later. Of the total class, six of them were built in the Vulcan yards, three by Blohm & Voss, and two by Schichau. When war broke out, the first four members of the class had been in service for 18 years.

All ships of this class were originally intended to have names beginning with the same letter, but things went astray in several cases. The original order placed by Norddeutscher Lloyd included *Friedrich der Grosse*, *Barbarossa*, *Königin Luise*, and *Bremen*.[29] The youngest of the group were HAPAG's pair of generals, *Blücher* and *Moltke*, both launched in 1901. While all 11 were built to the same general dimensions and specifications, they were not all on the same transatlantic run from North German to North American ports. However, by unhappy coincidence, five of these 10,500-ton craft were berthed — in reality trapped — in New York harbor when the opening guns of the European war sounded on 1 August 1914.

To drive their twin propellers, all of the *Barbarossa* class were endowed with quadruple expansion, reciprocating steam engines, generating 7,900 horsepower in the 1896 group and up to 9,900 horsepower in the last of the seven younger ships. All members of the *Barbarossa* class had an identical silhouette, sported two stacks, and made up to 16 knots with working crews ranging up to 252 men. Averaging slightly more than 550 feet in length, they were all equipped to carry some 2,350 passengers, though the actual number varied slightly between ships and the classes of passenger. Aboard each of them, however, close to three quarters of all capacity was devoted to steerage travelers, quite commonly emigrants from the ghettos of East Europe intent on starting a new life in the New World.

An oft-told story has it that one such immigrant to the United States found himself in the bowels of a *Barbarossa*-class ship, crammed into the steerage with hundreds of his Yiddish compatriots from eastern Germany (an area later defined as Poland). Interminable discussion had centered on a choice of "good Anglo" names that they might assume, in order to enter the New World with a new identity, and each head of a family selected an appropriate handle. Upon arrival at the immigration wicket on Ellis Island, the unfortunate man was unable to recall the name he had selected and struck his forehead in dismay: "Heimos! Vergessen." —("Omigod! I've forgotten.") The immigration clerk thereupon wrote down Shamus Ferguson.

BARBAROSSA

Named for Friedrich, the aggressive and red-bearded ruler of the Holy Roman Empire between the years 1152 and 1190, the name ship of this class was commanded by August Riditer when she made her maiden voyage in January 1897, halfway around the world from Bremerhaven to Australia. Thereafter, North German Lloyd used her alternately on that run and on transatlantic duty between Bremen and New York.

Since Kaiser Wilhelm II's satraps and advisors had neglected to direct all civilian German shipping homeward in a timely manner, relative to the notices given his railroads and armed forces, Captain Gottfried Meyer found his ship, *Barbarossa*, securely tied up at her Hoboken pier on 1 August 1914, when the Kaiser's million-man army began its assault across southern Belgium and into France.

The aging ship had plenty of company. Also trapped in New York were many other Central Powers ships, some larger and newer, and four of her sisters: *Friedrich der Grosse*, *Grosse Kurfürst*, *Prinzess Irene*, and *Hamburg*. *König Albert* and *Moltke* were tied up in Genoa, another initially neutral port, where they stayed until taken over by the Italian government.

NDL's *Barbarossa*, built in 1896. Steam Ship Historical Society of America.

Blücher was in Pernambuco, where she stayed until the Brazilian government decided to enter the war. On the Far Eastern run, *Prinzess Alice* was caught in Manila and stuck there. She was taken over as a transport in the war effort against Germany, and two years later was given to the Japanese as part of their reparations from the defeated Central Powers.

Of all in this class, only *Königin Luise* and *Bremen* were safely at home in Bremerhaven, where they sat out the war. Herr Ballin later complained that a total of 64 HAPAG ships—close to 1.5 million tons' capacity—had thus been caught flatfooted in various United States ports and were interned, lost forever to HAPAG and to the Fatherland. He did not offer the comparable arithmetic for the competing Lloyd line; his own corporate disaster was sufficient. The ultimate result of the Kaiser's Oberkommando's failure to alert German merchant ships to the long-planned outbreak of war was that very few of them actually did what Britain's First Lord of the Admiralty had feared. Only one was actually equipped as planned in a timely manner, and only four others of the "forty" merchant ships actually performed a serious wartime function. Most of them ended up in the possession of Germany's ultimately most important enemy, where they played a monumental role against the Fatherland before the war ended. Indeed, the very logical argument has been posited that it was the merchant

Königin Luise, **built in 1896. Steam Ship Historical Society of America.**

and passenger ships of Germany that made the Allied victory possible in 1918.

Most of *Barbarossa*'s sisters languished at their piers in Hoboken for 31 bleak, forlorn, and increasingly friendless months while most of their crews dispersed into the American hinterland and their machinery gradually deteriorated. Quite a large number of the German crew members were eminently employable, many being skilled machinists or trained in other useful occupations, and American manufacturers needed exactly such workers for their huge new business of making war materiel for the Allies. Germany was regarded in those days as the world's leading source of skilled machinists and many of those who got stuck in America landed well-paying jobs. During these war years, the United States of America also went from being the world's largest debtor nation to being the world's largest creditor. It was a remarkable fiscal turnaround and one for which American political and financial leaders had no experience or preparation.

However, during this lengthy period of some 30 months, it became ever more clear that the German strategy of unrestricted submarine warfare—complained about by Ballin and enhanced for its propaganda value by continuous British guile—was driving the United States into the Allied camp. Those few caretakers left on board the liners were still loyal to their native land and saw that their ships might soon be commandeered by an increasingly hostile America. Critical elements of the propulsion machinery in many of the interned German liners were quietly dropped overboard, sold as scrap or otherwise damaged beyond repair. Some years earlier disgruntled French workers had used their wooden shoes for similar purposes and thereby created a new word for the process— sabotage (from *sabot*, clog).

On 6 April 1917, *Barbarossa* was suddenly, but not unexpectedly, ordered back to work. That afternoon a team of United States marshals marched through the cavernous warehouse piers of the North German Lloyd and Hamburg-America lines in Hoboken to formally seize everything within sight in the name of the newly belligerent United States of America. A few ships of the smaller German lines were also caught in this dragnet, but their part in the conflict was minimal.

It took four months for machinists of the Brooklyn Navy Yard to repair the damage to her machinery caused by three years of neglect and a few more recent weeks of deliberate mischief. Before the year was ended, she was christened *Mercury* by order of Navy Secretary Josephus Daniels and placed into service as a troop transport. Under her new name, she made seven round trips between New York and Brest, carrying a total of more than 18,000 men (approximately two divisions' worth) of the American Expeditionary Force to the battlegrounds of northeastern France. When the Great War was concluded, she made eight more trips to reverse the flow of fighting men until her decommissioning in mid–September of 1919.

Ten months of further idleness occurred before *Barbarossa/Mercury*, still maintaining her wartime name, was chartered by the United States Shipping Board to a postwar upstart "Baltic Steamship Corporation of America." But postwar times were economically tough and politically uncertain for the nations lining the inland sea of northern Europe; the new owners filed for bankruptcy before *Mercury* could even leave port. A year later she was mothballed and, in 1924 ignominiously towed to the breaker yard where her 30-year-old bones were dismantled for recycling.

Some persons, confused by the duplicative use of ship names had thought her career had ended on 8 August 1915, when a ship of this name was sunk in the Dardanelles by the British submarine E-11. This "Barbarossa," however, was an obsolete Turkish warship carrying 11" guns and escorted by destroyers on her way to help defend the passage against the Allied landing effort.

Berth deck of the troopship *Mercury*. U.S. Navy photo.

FRIEDRICH DER GROSSE

The senior member of the *Barbarossa* class was *Friedrich der Grosse*, which sailed from Baltimore for Bremen on 29 July 1914. The ship owed her name to the third king of Prussia (1712–1786), a contemporary of Catherine the Great of Russia and Maria Theresa of Austria, whose legacy to legal history is known as the Corpus Juris Fredericiani. Turned back in midocean by a radio message, like the *Kronprinzessin*, Captain Dierkes sought refuge in New York harbor. The ship languished at her pier until renamed *Huron* for wartime service as an American troop transport. She was a Vulcan-built ship of the original group, but had a much shorter life span than did the class name ship. Under her new, post–1917, name, she had one near-disastrous encounter in a convoy on the open ocean with another classmate, *Aeolus*, renamed from the *Grosse Kurfürst*. But both ships survived and after the war *Huron* was extensively rehabilitated, her boilers now converted to oil-firing, and equipped with a massive cargo

Friedrich der Grosse, built in 1896. Steam Ship Historical Society of America.

refrigeration system — all at a cost of some $3 million in 1920 (roughly $50 million today). She then joined the Munson Line, but was soon passed off to the Los Angeles Line as the *City of Honolulu* and, outfitted with a brilliant new coat of white paint, set out on her maiden voyage into the Pacific. She would never come back to her Long Beach pier.

On Columbus Day 1922, while returning to the mainland with a crew of 145 but only 73 paying passengers, and some 400 miles out of her namesake city, she caught fire from what her captain, Henry Lester, later stated was defective wiring in one of the cabins. Fortunately, the seas were calm. In fighting the fire, however, the crew used so much water that the ship developed a severe list to port so great that her lifeboats could not be safely lowered. Nonetheless, by the time the freighter, *West Faralon*, came near, she was righted sufficiently that all personnel could be removed.

The U.S. Navy transport, *Thomas*, which had been involved in ferrying American troops to and was now involved in ferrying them from Vladivostok, was fortunately near enough to relieve the freighter of its unusual burden of human cargo. The *Thomas* also had sufficient firepower to then

Coal barges refueling *König Albert* at Hoboken. Steam Ship Historical Society of America.

sink the burned-out hulk so that it would not become a hazard to navigation. *Thomas* had started out life in 1894 as HAPAG's 5,713-ton *Persia*, but was sold in 1898 to the Atlantic Transport Line as *Minnewaska*. Later that year, as the United States got ready to beat up on an almost defenseless Spain, she was acquired as an army transport and given a name to honor the Civil War "Rock of Chickamauga," General George Henry Thomas. The venerable vessel was broken up at the Boston Navy Yard in 1928 after an active life of more than 34 years.

KÖNIG ALBERT

After much pressure from Great Britain, and stimulated by Allied promises of long-coveted postwar territorial gains in the South Tyrol and along the Austrian-held Dalmatian coast, Italy entered the war in the late spring of 1915. Although not unexpected, this was a slightly perfidious and long-remembered violation of Italy's two-decades-old treaty of mutual support with Germany and Austria. Interestingly, for the next several months, it was a war against Austria only. For some months before, the tenor of Italy's relations with the other Central Powers had been moving slowly from closeness, to amity, to wariness, to distrust, and finally to hostility.

As early as 9 April 1915, some of the Italian ships in American ports had been ordered to stay there and not risk the return trip to Italy. In the meantime, from the very start of the war, quite a number of German U-boats had been reassigned to Austro-Hungarian control for Mediterranean operations. The Italian government rightly felt these warships would sooner or later be used against Italy. Yet, on 23 May, the day that a state of war was finally declared, there were two German ships still in Genoa harbor — one each of HAPAG and Lloyd. Both of them were promptly taken over despite the very limited declaration of war. It was actually a gunpoint transaction that had the fig-leaf appearance of a lease for some months. However, the German ships were as effectively cornered in Italian ports by British and French patrols as if they had been interned in the United States.

König Albert (1490–1568) was the last Grand Master of the quasi-religious Teutonic Knights, an order formalized under the aegis of Pope Clement III in 1211 to assist in the Crusades.[30] After a series of convincing conversations with Martin Luther, Albert formally dissolved the order in Prussia (though it continued in operation elsewhere) much to the distress of the then Pope and the Holy Roman Emperor. He then set himself up as the first Duke of Prussia and reigned, somewhat under the suzerainty of the kings of Poland, during a period of great religious turmoil and political unrest. In time, he became regarded as the prime figure in the evolution to prominence of the House of Hohenzollern.

Once taken over by the Italians, the NDL vessel bearing Albert's name was rapidly transformed into the hospital ship *Ferdinando Palasciano*[31] and would stay so marked for the balance of the war years. At the conclusion of hostilities the ship was sold to the Navigazione Generale Italiana and again renamed. As *Italia* she made several postwar trips between Genoa and New York before being detailed as a troop transport. For three years she carried Italian soldiers across to Suez and down the length of the Red Sea to Eritrea and Somaliland for service in former sergeant Benito Mussolini's increasingly convoluted and controversial East African adventures. In 1925, the 26-year-old, Vulcan-built ship made her last voyage — back to Genoa and the ship breakers where her career ended the following spring.

HAMBURG

The steamship *Hamburg*, built by Vulcan, was the second in the younger generation of the *Barbarossa* class. Initially intended to be christened *Bavaria*, a last minute change of name occurred at the time of her launching late in 1899. As in the case of the name ship, her originally intended trade route was from the ports of Europe to those of the Far East, where, as detailed above, since 1897 Germany had been among the several western powers holding extraterritorial privileges in China. Over the years of this duty for HAPAG she achieved some fame for her rescue of the crew of a foundering Chinese fishing boat on 30 October 1903, and some notoriety a few years later for colliding with, and sinking, the tug *Eolo* in the harbor of Naples. This latter event, a considerable embarrassment for the local pilot aboard the liner, occurred on 27 February 1910.

The first day of August 1914, however, found her also tied up at Hoboken. For a short three months she escaped the lengthy idleness of her sister ships and brought a small return to her owners by being chartered to the International Red Cross for one voyage to the Dutch refugee port of Rotterdam under the name of *Red Cross*. Back in New York by late October, she was now formally interned along with several of her sisters and other German-owned ships, until the United States marshals marched up her worn but latterly little-used gangplank on 6 April 1917. After the now ritual rehabilitation and once again assigned to the transatlantic passenger run, *Hamburg* was rechristened *Powhatan*, after the legendary Indian chief of early colonial days in Virginia. Under this new name she made a dozen crossings, taking more than 15,000 troops to France and then returning almost 12,000 after the armistice.

Hamburg enjoyed a better postwar life than *Barbarossa*. When returned to civilian status in 1920, she was chartered to the same Baltic Steamship Corporation of America that had also acquired the one-time *Barbarossa*, and given another new name, *New Rochelle*. As such she actually made one trip to Danzig, which was now a "free" city by terms of the Versailles treaty, but it continued to be a largely German enclave for economic purposes. The nearby port of Gdynia, just to the north along the gulf, was developed by the government of the newly established Polish Republic.

The new firm's bankruptcy then caused her to be rechartered to the United States Mail Steamship Company, an entity that gave her yet another name, *Hudson*, and then leased her to the United States Lines for further service between New York and Bremen. The process of bouncing around from owner to owner continued on an almost annual basis, with the

Hamburg/Red Cross/Powhatan/New Rochelle/Hudson attaining her final handle of *President Fillmore*, after America's 13th president, when she was acquired by the Dollar Line for service between San Francisco and the Far East. Four years of prowling the sea lanes of the Pacific with one "Round the World" cruise were enough. The much-named vessel, now in her 30th year, was sold to a West Coast firm of ship breakers in 1928.

GROSSE KURFÜRST

Described in her initial brochures as having "enormous carrying capacity" and "excellent passenger accommodation," the *Grosse Kurfürst* had a far more adventurous and longer career than any of her sisters. In Teutonic Europe, from the days of the Holy Roman Empire, the term "Elector" was an honorific applied to the several German princes and bishops who were entitled to elect the Holy Roman Emperor. The "Great Elector" was the vigorous Frederick William of Brandenburg (1620–88) who restored the Hohenzollern domination of Prussia after the disasters that befell almost all of Germany during the Thirty Years' War. The elector's namesake ship, however, was among those at sea which received the message about Erhard's illness and turned back to New York when a much greater European conflict opened. There the vessel had to wait for the fateful sixth day of April 1917, before coming back to life. But the fourteen-year-old *Kurfürst* had already made a name for herself.

Less than a year before the war broke out, on 9 October 1913, the 7,000-ton British ship *Volturno*, one of the three mediocre craft owned by the Uranium Line, caught fire while transporting 600 immigrants across the Atlantic to the New World. Ten ships from six different nations and under eight separate ownerships rushed to a mid–Atlantic rendezvous in answer to the recently adopted international distress call — sent out by the *Volturno*'s "wireless telegraph" in the Morse code's SOS, ··· −−− ···. One of them, the British tanker *Narragansett*, released some of her cargo of heavy oil onto the waters—a risky venture in the presence of a burning ship—but it calmed the ocean sufficiently that 521 passengers were able to be taken off the flaming derelict before she sank. *Kurfürst*, the second rescue ship on the scene, gathered in some 20 percent of the survivors.

Commandeered by United States' marshals along with close to two dozen other enemy passenger ships, *Kurfürst* became another U.S. Navy transport and was renamed for the ancient Greek god of the winds, *Aeolus*. In the New York area alone, the treasury agents seized 31 German-owned ships on 6 April 1917, and packed all their caretaker crew members

Grosse Kurfürst, **built in 1899. Steam Ship Historical Society of America.**

off to a detention center in the momentarily unused immigration and quarantine facilities on Ellis Island. After a six-month rehabilitation at the Brooklyn Navy Yard, *Aeolus* made a total of eight round-trips by convoy from her usual Hoboken berth to St. Nazaire and Brest.

The Austrian merchant marine had never been in the same league as that of the ships of the Hanseatic cities of north Germany, and most elements of it had already been sold when the going was good, pursuant to a more realistic appreciation on the part of Austrian officials regarding the likely length of the war. In addition, almost everyone involved on the Allied side recognized that this had become essentially a war against Germany, personified by its Kaiser, and not against his fellow-travelers. The United States, for instance, did not feel it necessary to formally enter the war against Austria until eight months after the declaration against Germany — to the Congress, it wasn't that significant. While Turkey formally severed diplomatic relations with the United States, a state of war never came into being, and no one on the west side of the Atlantic really cared about Bulgaria; most of them didn't even know where it was.

On 25 April 1918, during the third such voyage of the *Kurfürst* as an American transport, and only three days out of New York, the newly built USS *Siboney*'s rudder jammed, forcing that 11,000-ton ship to move suddenly out of her assigned position in the convoy. *Aeolus*, in order to avoid an imminent collision, altered her course so abruptly that she struck the neighboring transport, *Huron*, in an unfortunate "reunion" of old class-mates. A year earlier *Huron* had been *Friedrich der Grosse*, also tied up at the Hoboken pier. Though there were no casualties from this midocean impact, both ships were sufficiently damaged they had to return to home port, barely five days after departure. The three thousand doughboys aboard were given a 20-day reprieve of their assignment to combat while the damage was repaired.

In civilian attire once more at the end of the war, the *Kurfürst/Aeolus* was chartered to the Munson Lines and her boilers converted to oil-burning, during the course of which alteration four men were killed in an explosion. Assigned to the South American run between New York and Buenos Aires, in March 1922, *Aeolus* managed to ram and sink the British freighter, *Zero*, in the estuary of the Rio de la Plata but suffered little damage herself and did save her victim's crew. As poetic punishment for this mishap, she was passed off to the Los Angeles Steamship Company and received yet another name, *City of Los Angeles*.

Refitted once more in 1923, and now upgraded to turbine power, the new owners spent many hundreds of thousands of dollars in turning the aging German vessel into a more modern liner fit for the luxury trade of the Pacific Ocean. Unfortunately, after a dozen years on the Long Beach–Honolulu run, the much named *Kurfürst* was finally caught by the Great Depression and made her last voyage in 1937, with a skeleton crew, to a Japanese ship breaker. There were some who saw an ironic twist to the demise of this German-made, once American liner — she had now become scrap iron to enhance the Japanese war effort against China and, soon enough, the United States.

PRINZESS IRENE

This ship was named by NDL for the daughter of Princess Alice of Hesse who became the wife of Kaiser Wilhelm II's younger brother, Heinrich. Midway through her career, on 5 January 1910, during a voyage from New York to Bremen, the *Prinzess* lost her rudder. Undaunted, her captain radioed his problem, but continued on course managing to steer the ship by means of her twin screws. He reached New York harbor only 40 minutes later than scheduled. Modern airplanes, traveling at 30 times the speed, are frequently later than that. She did make one embarrassing run to New York in the spring of 1911, when she lost her way in the fog and

Prinzess Irene embarrassingly aground off Long Island. Steam Ship Historical Society of America.

ran aground on Fire Island. Fortunately little damage was done by the sandy bottom and she was soon towed free.

Fourth in age of the second group of *Barbarossa* class ships, she, too, was caught in New York when the message concerning Erhard's illness was flashed to German-owned ships around the world. When taken over by the American marshals on 6 April 1917, she was renamed — as befitted a younger classmate of the *Hamburg* — to bear the best-known name of Chief Powhatan's historic daughter, *Pocahontas*. Her wartime career against the land of her birth was only slightly more exciting than that of her class-mates. On the morning of 2 May 1918, the submarine *U-151* surfaced nearby and commenced shelling her with its two 105 mm guns. Though carrying weapons of her own, *Pocahontas* was considerably outgunned by the large U-boat and Captain Edward Kalfbus had little choice but to flee, though he did order his gun crew to return the enemy fire while the engine room crew drove the ship up to a record speed of 16.2 knots, measurably over her rated maximum, and left *U-151* well astern.

The attacking U-boat was one of a limited class of submarines that were designed to keep Germany's overseas commerce alive; they were, effectively, submersible merchant ships. Only two of the eight ships thus designed actually put to sea in such a capacity; only one actually made the round trip across the Atlantic. Most of them, including *U-151*, were converted to fighting ships after mid–February 1917, when unrestricted submarine warfare was resumed in the German-declared war zone of the waters around western Europe. They were large craft, 1,512 tons, with a surface speed of more than 12 knots. *U-151* survived the war and was turned over to the French Navy, who used her for target practice until 7 June 1921, when she sank off Cherbourg from too much accuracy in this abusive treatment.

After the war, *Pocahontas* made a few civilian voyages to Mediterranean ports, but in the early summer of 1922 was forced to tie up at Gibraltar when her machinery refused to function. At this point her crew was unpaid, and her owners, the United States Mail Steamship Company, was seeking protection from its creditors. North German Lloyd, however, still thought the ship had some value and later that summer reacquired ownership and had the inert hulk towed back to Bremerhaven. Here she was put back into good shape and renamed *Bremen*— the third ship of this name to sail under the company flag. This was not the transatlantic speedster of a decade later, but for the next eight years she plied the Atlantic profitably and made one daring and dramatic rescue.

The British freighter, *Laristan*, having lost its rudder and power and being buffeted by a January snowstorm on the North Atlantic, radioed frantically for help. On 26 January 1926, in the midst of the furious winter storm, the crew of the much larger *Bremen* managed to save six men from the sinking 4,293-ton ship, but were unable to retrieve the remaining 26 before the disabled vessel rolled over and foundered amid the towering seas.

Typical of a number of those who hungered to engage in the proverbial American "pursuit of happiness" was one member of this *Bremen*'s crew. For a subsequent voyage later in 1926, North German Lloyd hired an assistant cook named Hans Alfred Hemmerle, who had already served an apprenticeship under several famous German hotel chefs. He thought to see the world, courtesy of NDL, but on his very first voyage developed a crush on an American girl who was traveling home with her parents. Determined to pursue this romance, he left the ship in New York, but then found the young lady's parents to be an insuperable obstacle. Aground in the New World, he started working his way west as an itinerant short-order cook, reaching San Francisco in time to become an assistant chef at the opening of the famous Mark Hopkins Hotel. Summer trade was slow in the city and Hemmerle had found a friend who loved to spend time in California's then pristine Yosemite Valley. For the summer season of 1927, he found employment at the newly opened and luxurious Ahwahnee Hotel. He had arrived! For many years the errant sailor was a major figure in the famous "Bracebridge Christmas Dinner and Pageant," where he was joined by such other future local luminaries as Ansel Adams. In his later years, Hemmerle migrated back to San Francisco as sous-chef of the Fairmont Hotel; but his children and grandchildren all found summer employment with the Yosemite Park and Curry Company, then concessionaire for the Yosemite Park facilities.

Renamed *Karlsruhe* in 1928, in order to make way for the North German Lloyd's fourth and newest powerhouse to honor its home base of Bremen, the ageing princess was finally broken up four years later.

PRINZESS ALICE

Built (and at one time named) to be acceptable for the Far Eastern trade, the fifth ship in the second generation in the *Barbarossa* class was named and renamed twice before she was even ready for sea. Her HAPAG owners finally settled on the title *Kiautschou*, an alternative westernized spelling for the German treaty port of Tsingtao. Even so, Herr Ballin's staff was not content with her performance and, after less than four years on the job, sold her to North German Lloyd, who came up with yet another of their honors to Teutonic royalty in renaming her. The name *Prinzess Alice* was a tribute to the daughter of Queen Victoria, who became the wife of the short-lived Kaiser Friedrich III and mother of the then current German emperor.

Despite the difference in ownership, little else was done to improve her characteristics and *Alice* remained mostly assigned to the Far East run. Dawn of 1 August 1914 — the moment of warning for the start of the Great War — found her unprepared and vulnerable in the South China Sea. As did many another German merchant skipper when word was sent out "over the ether," the *Prinzess* made a run for the American-controlled port of Manila, where British supremacy of the seas forced her to spend the next 2½ years in frustrating idleness. With American entry into the conflict, the ship, uniquely undamaged by sabotage, was formally seized on 7 April 1917, and again renamed, though now to honor an early American lady. The *Princess Matoika*[32] was promptly sent halfway around the world for duty in the Atlantic as a troop transport. Earlier on that job than those ships which had been the victims of sabotage, she carried a total of 21,216 fighting men across the ocean in 1917–18 and a slightly smaller number back to the United States a year later.

Reconstructed after the war to a slightly lesser registered tonnage, the much named *Princess* worked the Atlantic one year for the United States Mail Steamship Company under the name *President Arthur* and was then transferred to the American-Palestine Line where she acquired yet another new name — *White Palace* — but never sailed anywhere.

In 1926, like her classmate *Friedrich der Grosse/Huron*, the *Princess* was sold to the Los Angeles Steamship Company, and refitted in San Pedro to be a luxury liner. A year later she was sent back again to sea duty in the Pacific but, with new, oil-fired boilers she now produced 11,000 horsepower and could attain a speed of 17 knots. Perhaps her final owners should have known better than to replace the sister ship of their burned-out luxury liner, *City of Honolulu,* with another *Barbarossa*-class vessel and reuse the same name. They got three years of service out of this vessel before she, too, caught fire on the night of 25 May 1930, while tied at her pier in Honolulu. It was the end! After a decent interval, the burned-out shell was sent on her final trip, empty of all but the boiler room crew, to the ship breakers of Osaka.

BLÜCHER

This HAPAG ship was named for the great Prussian hero of the Napoleonic Wars whose part was critical to their culmination at Waterloo. While making a trip to Brazil in the midsummer of 1914, she was caught in the port of Pernambuco where she stayed until seized by Brazilian authorities upon that nation's entry into the war in October 1917. Renamed *Leopoldina,* she did a minimal amount of war service for her new proprietors and was then turned over to the French as war reparations. Under the name, *Suffren,* derived from the heroic French admiral of the 18th century, she spent several years on the North Atlantic run from Le Havre to New York before making her final trip to the ship breakers at Genoa.

MOLTKE

Endowed with the name of two of modern Germany's great military figures, both of whom served as chief of the general staff for the same All

Highest, this final member of the *Barbarossa* class "enjoyed" a fate quite similar to that of *Blücher*. Two years younger that *König Albert*, near which she was berthed when war broke out, this HAPAG liner ended her seafaring days one year earlier. When leased (i.e., taken over) by the Italian government on 23 May 1915, she was renamed *Pesaro*, the titled name of Giovanni Sforza, first husband of Lucrezia Borgia, the celebrated daughter of Pope Alexander VI. She was managed by the Italian State Railways. With the settlement of the Great War, she was sold back to the German-controlled Lloyd Sabaudo Line for a final six years of transoceanic service on the New York–Genoa run. She went through her entire career, as did the *König*, without major misfortune or distinguishing events. *Moltke* generally plied the transatlantic trade while the *König* was often sent to Yokohama and other ports of the Far East.

14

The Heavyweights

When war broke out in the summer of 1914, HAPAG was the largest shipping firm in the world, and the German merchant marine had the second-largest floating tonnage while growing faster than that of any other nation. Other than the prosaic workhorses of the seas, whose careers are described in the previous chapter, HAPAG and Norddeutscher Lloyd also had several other large and well-equipped ships designed (and many of them thoughtfully named) to appeal to the increasingly lucrative American tourist trade. *Amerika, George Washington, President Lincoln, Cleveland, Pennsylvania* and others, as well as the second *Kaiserin Augusta Victoria*, had been in service for several years prior to the outbreak of the Great War and had successfully achieved their owners' planned result of attracting a large following of upper-crust Americans. There were also many slow and unsung but profitable freighters that served the war effort briefly as tenders for the major ships at sea.

However, the biggest of all prewar passenger liners were just coming into service when the black clouds of the Great War began to gather over Europe and the storm finally broke in midsummer of 1914. In making sturdy and profitable ships to the thousand-foot dimensions of their final products the German shipbuilding industry of those days showed itself to be twenty years ahead of the rest of the world — a further frightening reality to Great Britain that was to have an obvious impact on the reparations terms of the Versailles Treaty.

HAPAG's three prewar monster ships each carried 83 lifeboats; at least one part of the message from the *Titanic* disaster had been clearly understood. After the London Conference on Safety at Sea, the Congress of the United States had reacted to the *Titanic* sinking with legislation requiring the carriage of sufficient lifeboats for *every* person on board every ship that docked in American ports. Each of these monster vessels had, initially, three funnels that rose 69 feet (21 meters) above the upper deck. These massive metal chimneys were designed to provide an adequately enhanced draft for the massive coal-fired boilers below. So tall were these smokestacks, however, that they created balance problems for the ships when under way in the open sea, and were later cut down by three meters. *Imperator*, the first of HAPAG's final giant three, was so top-heavy that, in addition to having the funnels shortened, much of her upper deck fittings were replaced in lighter stock, and quantities of concrete were poured into her lower cells.

Chairman Ballin, with a mind toward greater commercial appeal, wanted to call the first of these colossi, *Europa*, a name that was finally used for a competitive but still German, Atlantic speedster a dozen years later. But his friend, the Kaiser, had become so fascinated by the huge ship that when he was asked to participate in its launching, on 23 May 1912, the ruler insisted that it bear a Latin name more suited to his personal, egotistical style. As *Imperator*, the big ship was the world's largest (until *Vaterland* came along a year later), but she spent very little of her life adding glory to the Kaiser's name.

On 31 July 1914, as the *Kronprinzessin Cecilie* was being ordered to turn back to the west from midocean to evade the justly feared British dragnet, a freshly remodeled *Imperator* (her funnels now shortened by nearly 10 feet), though fully booked for her transatlantic departure of 12 August at 9 A.M., was abruptly ordered, without the benefit of any mysterious code messages over the ether, to stay tied at the pier in her home port of Hamburg. She thus avoided becoming a wartime statistic, or anything else, but she had already become the talk of the shipping world. She stayed at home in Hamburg for the duration of the war, where she was unsabotaged and ready to serve new masters immediately upon the signing of the Armistice. The ship was used briefly in 1919 as a transport for the U.S. Navy, then became a British prize of war in 1920, and was ultimately acquired by the White Star Company.

These owners soon rebuilt the massive ship to burn oil as a fuel and gave her a new name, *Berengaria*, after the princess of Navarre who became wife to the English King Richard I and who had the further distinction of being the only English queen never to set foot in England. The big liner

Imperator on the ways in early April 1912. Hapag/Lloyd.

stayed on as a fixture of the North Atlantic trade for a dozen years, until the amalgamation of Cunard and White Star in 1934. Aging, and reduced in status with the arrival in service of a ship named for the consort of a British monarch,[33] the one-time pride of Albert Ballin's fleet caught fire at her pier in New York on 3 March 1938, and was severely, almost completely burned out. She was returned to Southampton without passengers and was soon sold for breaking up.

The second of this giant series was the enormous *Vaterland*,[34] launched from Blohm & Voss on 13 April 1913. At 58,000 tons, she was 8,000 tons larger than *Imperator*. *Vaterland* had made only five Atlantic crossings, and was due to sail on her third return to home port at noon on 1 August 1914. She was still tied up at Hoboken, though, along with an inordinate

Opposite: Five lower decks under construction for the forward section of the *Vaterland*. Hapag/Lloyd.

Vaterland, at anchor in Hamburg with the coastal steamer Cobra. Hapag/Lloyd.

number of other German-flag vessels, when Siegfried's message went out to signal the outbreak of the war. Despite one well-publicized bomb scare, the big ship stayed at Hoboken, afraid to venture out through the British cruiser patrol, while her crew largely evaporated into the American mainstream. She became a fixture of New York's western skyline until the spring of 1917. Nevertheless, this craft had an even more notable areer to come than the one she had had before the war — but it would not be for HAPAG.

With her registered 58,000 tons' capacity and being just shy of a thousand feet long, *Vaterland* was a huge and most distinctive vessel. When taken over by the United States Shipping Board on 6 April 1917, however, a new name had to be found; after all, the prior name referred to the enemy's homeland. The word "leviathan" appears several times in both the Old and New Testament. It refers to a frequently malevolent, but always

Opposite: The light well in the First Class dining room of the ***Vaterland.*** Hapag/Lloyd.

American troops preparing to debark from the *Leviathan* at the port of Brest. U.S. Navy photograph.

large, sea monster, which some authorities have equated to the Great Blue Whale — perhaps the creature with which Jonah became so familiar. Though also applied to a contemporary British battleship, this biblical name was now given to what had been the prewar world's largest operating passenger liner. As such, she became so famous under the flag of the United States that most who traveled aboard the ship never knew of her foreign lineage.

    With her huge carrying capacity and great speed (26 knots) this one ship could carry almost as many American soldiers to Europe as any four of the other ships seized from Germany put together. But before being used in the war against her homeland, the ship's machinery had to be repaired; some members of her caretaker crew had taken her original name seriously and were obviously still loyal to the fatherland. The process of sabotaging the machinery on these German ships was now found to be so widespread that many persons felt it had been a coordinated program

Leviathan leaving New York harbor in combat camouflage paint. U.S. Navy photograph.

initiated in anticipation of an American declaration of war. During her ten subsequent trips as a transport for the United States Army, she carried almost 200,000 men to Europe before the armistice, and then brought as many back home afterwards.

Still a relatively new ship, and undamaged by any wartime mishap, *Leviathan* was reconditioned for civilian service over the next three years and then turned over to the quasi-governmental corporation, the United States Lines. An interesting manipulation of data occurred in this process. Though figured originally with a registered tonnage of more than 58,000, when rebuilt to civilian use again, she was remeasured to a capacity of less than 49,000 tons — a whole major bracket lower — thus saving much money for her new owners in port entry and dockage fees. Under her second name, and with minimal competition in her size range, she continued in the transatlantic service for another 15 years, until — already shocked by the advent of two new and more efficient German speedsters, *Bremen*

The stator and rotor elements of a *Vaterland* steam turbine. Hapag/Lloyd.

and *Europa*— the competition of the equally-sized British *Queen Mary* and the French liner, *Normandie,* proved too much for the profitable operation of her now aging frame. On 6 June 1938, the great sea monster, once the pride of the German merchant marine, was broken up at Rosyth on the banks of Scotland's Firth of Forth. This was almost the same date of death as her slightly older sistership, neé *Imperator,* and came when another world conflict was clearly in the offing.

Bismarck, the youngest and largest of Herr Ballin's massive trio, was originally due to enter service in the spring of 1915 but, with the outbreak of war, this became a clear unreality. However, because to the minds of Germany's leaders the war was always going to last for only a few more weeks, for quite some time work was continued. At first the troops would be home "before the leaves fall," then surely "by Christmas." Therefore, the workers at Blohm & Voss were told to prepare the ship for a triumphal postwar world tour by the Kaiser and his extended family. It was a great thought, but by midsummer 1915, the dream was losing its immediacy and work was halted.

The project completely evaporated into the cold and inhospitable mists of the North Sea with the failure of Ludendorff's final offensive in the late summer of 1918. At the end of the war, with the Kaiser hiding among reluctant hosts in Holland, the ship was still unready for immediate commissioning. In an irony that the Great Chancellor, now 20 years in his grave, might have appreciated, *Bismarck* was assigned to the victorious British as war reparations— to help make up for the dozens of *Kaiparas, Fryes, Willerbys* and other harmless vessels that German raiders and U-boats had destroyed over the previous four years.

Further delayed in entering service for her new masters by a fire and then by political wrangling, the huge vessel — 956 feet in length with a beam of 100 feet and just shy of 57,000 gross tonnage —finally put out to sea on 10 May 1922 as the Cunard liner, *Majestic.* As such, she had an uneventful but relatively short 14-year career on the North Atlantic run. Her run came to an end when British yards were finally able to produce a bigger and faster ship. One is tempted to observe that the namesake of Queen Mary (King George V's consort, styled "of Teck" for the small German town that was her birthplace) finally did in the aging Bismarck. Laid up in Southampton on the English Channel, *Majestic* was briefly used as a training ship at the start of the next world conflict. While being refitted for the more urgent work of troop transport, however, she caught fire for a second time and sank. It was the end of the line. She had existed almost the same length of time from launch to breakup as her two older sisters.

Amerika from below, prior to launching. Deutsche SchiffartsMuseum.

AMERIKA

Slightly older and decidedly smaller than the *Vaterland/Leviathan*, HAPAG's *Amerika* had a much greater life (more than twice as long) and a far more eventful career, both as a German ship and then under the American flag. Built by the Belfast firm of Harland & Wolff in 1905, *Amerika*, like so many others, spent the first year of her life as the largest ship in the world at 22,225 tons. She was never in the same speed category as the contemporary royally named Express Steamers of NDL, but she very much lived up to Chairman Ballin's dictum about passenger comfort. The principal decoration of the drawing room was a life size painting of Kaiser Wilhelm II in a white uniform, by an Italian artist. However, since the Kaiser did not like white, a German artist was hired to redo his coat in red. Complete with flower shop, this was the first of Ballin's ships to bear the full imprint of the renowned Swiss-born hotelier, Cesar Ritz, regarding dining facilities. *Amerika*'s à la carte restaurant was open from early morning

Amerika, **built in 1905. Steam Ship Historical Society of America.**

until midnight. One of the big vessel's decks was named for President Roosevelt. Aboard was the first seagoing electric elevator, spanning five decks! Her maiden voyage of nine days from Hamburg to New York (with one stop at Cherbourg) ended on 16 September 1905, in a gala reception with spouting fireboats and thousands of people on small craft and lining the Hoboken piers to welcome the newest pride of the company.

Slightly altered by enhancements in 1907, the big ship added 400 tons to her rated burden, but was still not able to outrace the vastly more powerful, though only slightly larger, Cunard liner, *Lusitania*. The British ship had enormously larger (and proportionately greedier) engines, developing four times the total horsepower, with four massive bronze screws to *Amerika*'s two. In the meantime, HAPAG's *Kaiserin Auguste Victoria* had momentarily (in 1906) taken over the title of "largest ship in the world." *Amerika*, however, was not out of the racing headlines—in 1911 she engaged in a well-publicized transatlantic contest with the Red Star liner, *Lapland*. The HAPAG ship made first landfall after the U.S. at Plymouth, while the Belgian ship had to go on farther east, to Dover. Despite losing, *Lapland*, "enjoyed" the racial tiff.

The big German ship did strike one prewar blow, albeit unintentionally, for the Fatherland. Early on the morning of 4 October 1912, just four miles off Dover in the English Channel, the British submarine, *B-2*, was on maneuvers with other elements of His Majesty's Navy. She unwisely rose to the surface immediately in front of the big liner which, moving with all the momentum of her cruising speed, neatly sliced the small naval craft in half. While the big ship reversed her engines, lowered her boats, blew her whistle and fired rockets, the two halves of the submarine went down like rocks with the loss of all but one member of her crew. The severed pieces of the submarine were later salvaged from a depth of only 20 fathoms.[35]

Amerika's normal run was between New York and Hamburg, but there were occasional deviations and way stops at such ports as Boulogne, Cherbourg, Southampton, and, in late July of 1914, to the alternative harbor of Boston on the west side of the ocean. She was in the latter port when war broke out in Europe, and was advertized in newspapers of both New York and Boston as leaving for home on 1 August 1914. However, when news of Erhard's illness reached Boston, she never even got up steam to move from her pier. For 2½ years *Amerika* remained unpowered and inactive, and meantime had to be towed from the active dock area across the harbor to a mooring near the *Kronprinzessin* and some of her associates off Deer Island. There she stayed, a displaced casualty of war, until she was formally seized upon the United States' entry into the conflict. At that moment it was discovered that, like most of the interned German vessels, some of her most critical moving parts had been sabotaged by the caretaker crew. It was not until early autumn that the big liner could once again be placed into service. At the start of September, when Navy Secretary Daniels issued his General Order #320 which officially changed the names of all the commandeered German liners to something more fitting for their new ownership, *Amerika* became the less Teutonic-reading *America*.

Given her first sea trials at the end of September, it was found that she was now a faster ship. The repairs to her machinery made in Boston enabled the giant reciprocating engines to make three more revolutions per minute than previously. At the end of October 1917, *America* began her new transatlantic passenger work of transporting the growing American army to the battlegrounds of Europe. She was in the company of many old friends and competitors, some smaller, some larger, but almost all of them former German liners. On her seventh such voyage the convoy she was traveling in, which also included many freighters carrying war materiel, ran into a storm which limited visibility so much that an errant British freighter, *Instructor*, got mixed up. Despite efforts to avoid a collision, *America* rammed into *Instructor's* port quarter and cut the smaller vessel's stern free from the rest of the ship. The smaller piece that was sliced off the wandering cargo vessel sank almost immediately, and her 42-man crew had to rapidly abandon the rest of the ship, which went down within minutes. Amid the dark, the storm and the fear of lurking U-boats, only the 11 men who managed to get into a lifeboat were saved.

On her ninth voyage as a troop transport, so many cases of influenza broke out that the ship had to be thoroughly fumigated upon her return to Hoboken. (These cases were part of the worldwide epidemic that ultimately caused more American casualties than did the Kaiser's armed forces.) Then, on the night of 15 October 1918, after coaling had been completed and when the ship was almost fully loaded with troops for an early morning departure, she began to heel over to port for reasons never satisfactorily explained. As the human cargo was being settled into place, water cascaded in through the many portholes left open to clear residual toxic fumes from the ship. The coaling ports had also been left open, so the ship filled rapidly. She was soon resting on the muddy bottom, but her main deck was barely awash. The swift flooding of the engine room had doused the ship's electric generators and great confusion reigned in the dark as soldiers and crew struggled to find a way topside. In the end six men were drowned.

Somewhat more than five weeks later, after much of *America*'s cargo and upper deck equipment had been removed and divers had closed all the open ports, the liner was pumped clear and refloated. However, the damage to her interior was so great that it took three more months to get her back into a shipshape operating condition. By then the war was over but the big liner was now fit enough to make eight further round trips, returning American servicemen home. Decommissioned by the Navy on 26 September 1919, she was turned over, in company with the former *Kronprinzessin Cecilie*, to the War Department "to transport certain passengers from Europe to the United States." All this meant merely that she continued to be a transport, now with a different commander. Things were soon to become more interesting for the big German-built liner, though.

The complications of mixed loyalties under the various "empires" of Europe had meant that quite a number of the men fighting under the banner of the Dual Monarchy were in reality anything but Teutonic or Magyar. The ruling Habsburg family of Austria had originally been Swiss but, by the early years of the 20th century, their sway extended not only over the neighboring Magyars but also over nearby Bohemians, Bosnians, Croats, Poles, Rumanians, Serbs, Slavs, Slovaks, Slovenes and even Italians. Only a few of these nationalities really cared to risk their lives to keep Emperor Franz Josef and his family happily in power, as the questionable success record of the Austro-Hungarian armed forces, both on land and

De Kalb, America and *George Washington* (left to right) in convoy to France. U.S. Navy photo.

sea, had indicated since the start of the Great War. More inspired German troops were constantly having to reinforce or replace Austrian forces in the supposedly Austrian theaters of the war. For instance, it was a force of six German divisions (with Erwin Rommel as commander of the lead company) that brought on the crushing Italian defeat of Caporetto in 1917. In fact, given half a chance, many so-called Austrian troops deserted to the enemy in droves. One such alienated group included some 40,000 men of the "Czech Legion" who wanted — more than anything — to attain freedom for their own country, the former Bohemia, and had been seduced to change sides midway through the war by Russian promises of future help.

However, when the Russian promises turned out to be valueless, after the Romanovs were dethroned and the Treaty of Brest-Litovsk took that nation out of the conflict, the Czechs found themselves lost, stranded and friendless, swallowed up inside a nation locked in seemingly endless turmoil. First the Czar's Black Sea Fleet had mutinied, then the Army; the Mensheviks had deposed the Romanovs, then the Bolsheviks had overthrown the Mensheviks. It had all taken place in 1917. By the end of 1919, "White" Russians were fighting "Red" Russians, anarchy had set in and few persons anywhere could tell the good guys from the bad. To most westerners, it seemed that the White Russians were better than the Red, but by that time they had also lost the contest for popular support in their homeland. In the midst of this melee of anarchy, the Czechs were clearly identifiable and had also largely found their collective way across Siberia to Vladivostok. More than anything, now they simply wanted to go home.

America and that ubiquitous and long-lived army transport, *Thomas*, arrived at Vladivostok at the end of June 1920, and — along with the *Kronprinzessin* and a number of other vessels engaged in similar service — began to embark the wandering Czechs, replacing them for the moment with American and other "western" troops, landed there to "keep order" and cover the withdrawal of others. A few weeks later the meandering Czechs were safely delivered to the once-Austrian port of Trieste where they entrained for home on 8 August, and *America*'s wartime service was finally over. The continued presence of western troops on Russian soil ineradicably tainted future Soviet-American relations. Few westerners have cared to remember the British occupation of the White Sea port of Archangel, the French occupation of the Black Sea port of Odessa, or the American occupation of Vladivostok on the Sea of Japan. To the Soviet, and subsequently Russian, leadership, however, these occupations were a humiliating and never to be forgotten lesson in Western, and capitalistic aggressiveness.

Reconditioned to civilian attire by 22 June 1921, *America* began her career as a United States Lines passenger ship, sailing pretty much as before, to Plymouth, Cherbourg and Bremen. She was now the third-largest vessel in American service, outranked only by her German-built associates, the former *Vaterland* and the once and future *George Washington*. To do her job well as such, she now needed a major refit and was taken out of service at the end of 1925 to undergo a modernization in the yards of the Newport News Shipbuilding Company. Only one day before she was to be returned to her owners, a fire, starting in a paint locker, swept through her entire passenger area and did some $2 million of damage. Repaired again, *America* saw another five years of profitable service before two more modern ships under the American flag displaced the now 26-year-old vessel and sent her into the brackish waters of retirement.

Even then, *America* was idle but not finished. Though laid up in southern Maryland's tidal estuary, optimistically named the Patuxent River, she was recalled to duty with the start of another German-inspired

George Washington, built in 1908, doing transport duty for the United States in World War II. Steam Ship Historical Society of America.

war. By now, the United States Lines had another ship in being that had been given her good name, so the aging liner was again rechristened, to honor an American hero of the Mexican War, Edmund Brooke Alexander. Sent in early 1941 to serve as a floating barracks for construction workers at the newly acquired American Lend-Lease base near St. John's in Newfoundland, she was well suited to hotel duty but not nearly "up to speed." Her obsolete coal-burning boilers now limited her mobility and made her unsuitable for effective service as a troop transport. With the almost unanimous conversion of ships from coal to oil fuel in the years from 1910 to 1930, there were ever fewer facilities for handling coal-burning vessels— anywhere in the world. Still endowed with a sturdy frame and an efficient hull, *Edmund B. Alexander* spent most of 1942 being converted to oil-burning, having her twin funnels replaced by a single one and getting her cruising speed tuned up to her original 17 knots. Once more fit to cross the ocean under wartime conditions, she carried American servicemen to combat in Italy and France until the spring of 1945, and then began the more pleasant task of bringing them, along with a number of newly acquired dependents, back home again.

A rare picture of President Woodrow Wilson and Franklin Delano Roosevelt, Assistant Secretary of the Navy, standing on the review platform in Washington. (Left to right) Major General George Bennett, USMC; Admiral William S. Benson, USN; Roosevelt; Brigadier General Wendell C. Neville; Wilson; Mrs. Wilson. U.S. Navy photo.

At the end of May 1949, the 44-year-old vessel was again "put out to pasture," back in the lower Patuxent River. Two years later she was towed to another berth for moribund ships in the lower Hudson River and, early in 1957, sold to the Bethlehem Steel Company for scrap. By that date, *Amerika* had become one of the longest-lived passenger ships in history.

George Washington

Built along very similar lines to *Amerika*, the Norddeutscher Lloyd liner *George Washington* had a somewhat similar, but not quite as lengthy career. Slightly larger than *Amerika*, she was Germany's largest ship until the launching of *Vaterland*; in the interim, only the British-built *Lusitania* and *Mauretania* were larger. With considerably more powerful engines, she could make 20 knots in a pinch, two more than the older sister ship.

She was launched from Blohm & Voss on 10 November 1908, and placed in the Bremerhaven–New York service. She evaded enemy patrols and arrived in New York safely, exactly on schedule on 2 August 1914, to make a total of 19 German ships trapped in New York harbor.

After being taken over by the United States in April 1917, *George* was refitted and began wartime duty as a troop carrier in December 1917. During the next two years the 25,570-tonner made a total of 18 round trips. On some of her voyages, she carried distinguished passengers, such as President Wilson on his way to the Versailles peace negotiations in early December 1918. Though there was no longer any danger of hostile action, on this particular voyage she was escorted into harbor at Brest by nine American battleships and a host of lesser warships headed by the newly commissioned USS *Pennsylvania*, later to be the flagship of the American Pacific Fleet and a victim of the ministrations of *Taiyo Maru* in 1941 (see Chapter 20). One of the lesser-known dignitaries among the 7,000 men who went overseas to combat when *George* left New York on 29 March 1918, was 1st Lt. Harry S Truman of Battery D, 129th Field Artillery of the 35th Division.

George Washington never had to undergo a change of name for her service in the Great War; the North German Lloyd people had given her a good enough handle at the outset. After bringing her share of servicemen and dignitaries back home, she was acquired by another owner — the semigovernmental United States Lines. She then served a profitable further ten years on the transatlantic run until hard times and competitors with more modern motive power caught up with her and she, too, was mothballed in the lower reaches of Maryland's Patuxent River. Another ten years and another war saw the 31-year-old liner recalled for active duty. Briefly acquired by the Army Transport Service under the name *Catlin*, to honor a Marine Corps general, her aging engines no longer gave her the speed necessary to escape the new generation of U-boats.

Nevertheless, the British, facing another mass destruction of their civilian fleet at the hands of their enemy's modern undersea fleet, tried her out under the 1940 Lend-Lease program. One voyage to Newfoundland, however, served to convince the Royal Navy brass that *Catlin* was not for them and she was returned to mothball status. A ship in being, though, has a lot more immediate value than a ship on the drawing boards, and a six-month refit and major facelift can do wonders for anyone, even an ocean liner. On 17 April 1943, once again *George Washington* after conversion to oil-burning at the Todd yards in Brooklyn, she was back up to her original cruising speed of 19 knots and used on numerous transatlantic runs taking American servicemen to combat in Italy and England.

The end of the Second World War meant the end of the line. *George Washington* was laid up in 1947, somewhat damaged by a fire, and finally scrapped at Baltimore in mid–February 1951.

15

Presidents and Cities

HAPAG's midsized liners came in pairs. They were named primarily to cater to the growing American tourist traffic, much of which had ancestral roots in Germany. Its original set of midsized (11,000 GRT) liners was named for two American presidents who were well served by expatriate Germans; the line's second team (16,500 GRT) was named for the principal cities, at opposite ends of the State of Ohio, wherein resided many Americans of German descent. The older pair came with slightly more tonnage and an unusual six masts for handling cargo, but — given their less demanding engines and fuel needs — only one smokestack. These were also the last German-owned ships to be built in non–German yards. Coincidentally, these two were also rejects from the British Wilson Line, which had ordered them and then, beset by financial difficulties, sought to get out of their purchase contracts before the ships were completed. Harland & Wolff made arrangements to sell the already launched *Scotian* and *Servian* to Herr Ballin's line.

Thereupon, both were completed in mid–1907, the one as *President Lincoln* and the other as *President Grant*. These two ships had very distinctive silhouettes, with a bridge structure forward of and clearly separated from the first-class cabin quarters amidships. Other than *President Grant*'s 1911 collision with the Wilson line's freighter, *Tasso*, in a midwinter fog off Dover,[36] these ships had relatively uneventful prewar careers. Both were caught in New York at the start of the war, and both were taken over for use as American transport ships. Actually, *President Grant* had put to sea and was 430 miles east of New York when she received the message about Erhard's illness. Captain Meyerdiercks immediately turned back to safety but found the company's Hoboken facilities so crowded with other ships that he had to disembark his passengers at South Brooklyn.

From the time of seizure the two ship's fates took different courses. On 31 May 1918, *President Lincoln* was sunk, 53 years after the assassination of "the Great Emancipator." The ship's assassin, *U-90*, caught the liner two days' sailing west of France, fortunately on the return voyage and largely empty.

Commissioned on 2 August 1918, *U-90* was one of the last class of submarines that actually put to sea. With a gross tonnage of 1,165 and an overall length of 216 feet she could navigate at more than 15 knots while on the surface, and at a respectable 8.6 while submerged. German underseas technology had perforce made remarkable strides during the war years. She survived the reactive encounter with *President Lincoln*'s escort vessels making it safely back home, but was turned over to the British only nine days after the armistice and very soon broken up at Borrowstounness (pronounced Bo'ness) on the Firth of Forth.

The major motive power for U-boats (of all nations) in the Great War, as well as its sequel, was the diesel engine. These units powered the ship while on the surface and also recharged the immense batteries for the electric motor used while submerged. Interestingly, while Rudolph Diesel's engine is today well known to be most efficient and effective when operated at a high rate of revolutions (rpm), up until the time their 53-year-old inventor drowned in 1913, he steadfastly forbade such operation. The snorkel, however, which enables a submarine to "breathe" while just below the surface and thus save use of its batteries, was an invention that came along during World War II.

President Grant (due to sail for home on 30 July 1914) stayed put at Hoboken like most of her associates and made out considerably better than her sister ship. After her wartime service against Germany, she was considerably refitted at Newport News. One set of her cargo masts was removed, and to enhance cabin capacity, her superstructure was filled out (very much altering her original silhouette) by connecting the bridge with the passenger quarters. After the spring of 1924 she spent seven years sailing for the United States Lines on the same run on which she started her life — New York to Hamburg. The United States Army took her over again in 1931. She reverted a decade later to navy control and became a wartime troop transport. In 1945, she was refitted briefly as a hospital ship. Used for another five years on the transatlantic run as a transport for servicemen and dependents of American occupation forces, she was laid up in storage through the Korean crisis and finally scrapped in 1952. Incidentally, another *General Grant*— along with *Admiral Farragut, Stonewall Jackson* and *Robert E. Lee*—was among the numerous British monitors assigned to the Dardanelles campaign in May 1915.

HAPAG's *Cincinnati* was launched from Herr Schichau's yards on 24 July 1907, and her sister ship, *Cleveland*, from Blohm & Voss just two months later. Norddeutscher Lloyd also had two vessels of very similar design and which received more appropriately Teutonic names. *Prinz Friedrich Wilhelm* was launched from Tecklenborg on 21 October 1907, and *Berlin* (see Chapter 9) was launched from Weser on 7 November 1908. All four showed twin stacks, but the HAPAG ships had two cargo-handling masts forward as well as aft, while the NDL ships carried only one each. Their gross registered tonnages were roughly equal—just under (or just above) 17,000, despite the typically much greater difference in power and speed. *Cincinnati*'s twin screws were driven by 11,000 horses, while *Cleveland*'s had 500 more; the *Prinz*, however, was driven by 14,190 horsepower and could make a good two knots more speed than the HAPAG ships, while the largest of the group, *Berlin*, was driven by 16,000 horses.

Cleveland, whose maiden voyage to New York in the spring of 1909 was an event of some note, was the largest ship ever built by Blohm & Voss. She also had the distinction of being named at her launching by an American-born German countess, the former May Loney of Washington, D.C. Along with the by now familiar electric elevators, this ship was distinctive in having been outfitted with circular staircases that observers felt were much easier to mount in times of heavy weather than the traditional nautical companionways. Reflecting Herr Ballin's influence, her promotional brochures also noted that "The saloon, lounge and smoking rooms— for there are two in the second class— are better than first class on many of the liners built but a few years ago."

They all made their maiden voyages to New York—HAPAG's from Hamburg, and the *Prinz* and *Berlin* from Bremerhaven, at the mouth of the Weser. Thereafter, the HAPAG ships stayed on a similar pattern of transatlantic crossings in the warmer months of the Northern Hemisphere until 1913, when both began regular stops at Boston on the west side of the ocean. However, in a sign of many such events to come, on 19 October 1912, *Cleveland* departed New York for a 'round the world cruise that included an 18-day stay in India and, for its passengers, a trip across the United States from San Francisco to New York by rail. The ship then made a second such trip on the reverse route. All this was advertised as costing no more than $10 per day.

HAPAG's *Cleveland*, built in 1908. Steam Ship Historical Society of America.

Cincinnati completed her maiden voyage on 6 June 1909, two months after that of the *Cleveland*. Her promotional literature pointed out that the ship was 600 feet in length with a beam of 65 and was 50 feet from her main deck to the bottom of her holds. She was rated at 18,000 gross tons with accommodations for a total of 3,250 passengers. She had two cabin hospitals, a gymnasium, a bookstall and even a dark room for photographers.

HAPAG's pair of Ohio cities could be deemed to have had a spicier career after being taken over from the Germans. *Cincinnati*, carrying a distinguished list of passengers, was halfway to Europe when the message about Erhard's illness was broadcast. At first her captain thought to run for the Azores but, fearful of the British cruiser patrols operating from Gibraltar, decided to turn back to the west. Three days later everyone arrived safely in Boston. Two and a half years later, she was renamed USS *Covington* after being formally seized, and was one of the two American troop transports to be sunk while on that duty. On 1 July 1918, *U-86* spotted her off the coast of Brittany and slammed a torpedo into her port side which sent her slowly to the bottom. Before the ship finally sank the next afternoon, Captain Hasbrouk managed to save all but six men from her manifest of 776.

U-86 was very similar to, but a slightly older ship than the *U-90* (mentioned above). She was commissioned at the end of November 1916, and surrendered on 20 November 1920. She never had the final indignity of being broken up in the hands of the enemy, for she sank in heavy weather in the North Sea en route to Bo'ness.

Cleveland on the other hand, sat out the war in Hamburg, and was belatedly sold to Swedish interests. Delivery, however, was impossible so the sale was never consummated and the big ship remained tied up and available to be handed over to the Allied forces early in 1919. Briefly renamed *Mobile*, she was a postwar American transport, and, having completed this function under charter to the White Star line, was sold to the Byron Steamship Company, a Greek-owned firm, which renamed her *King Alexander*, after the then reigning monarch of that country. After two years on the run from Piraeus to New York, she was sold back to American interests and got her maiden name back, but was then registered under the flag of Panama because almost everyone's passengers preferred to enjoy an occasional alcoholic drink.

The now commonplace practice of foreign registry for American-owned vessels dates from these years. In a gesture responsive at first to unrealistic regulations — both commercial and governmental — after 1919 a great number of American-owned vessels quickly found their way into offshore registration. This began to occur about the same time and for some of the same reasons that American business firms evolved the practice of incorporating under the laws of the State of Delaware where fewer questions are asked and fewer paperwork strictures pertain. Among the effects of America's idealistic but ill-considered and unrealistic Volstead Act was a strong incentive on the part of many such owners to seek economic refuge in logging, for the record, their ships under the laws of Liberia or Panama. Both of these nations have never really cared much what an owner did with their ship, how much the crew was paid, or how safely the vessel was equipped, managed or manned, as long as they paid the necessary fees. Nonetheless, while these ships were docked in American ports, Prohibition laws obtained.

Happily, perhaps, at the end of her life *Cleveland* managed to get back to where she started. On 26 July 1926, HAPAG bought her for the second time and put her again on the Hamburg–New York run. This was not the final bit of ironic nostalgia for the 26-year-old liner, however — on 1 April 1933, she went back to Blohm & Voss, this time for scrapping.

While HAPAG's *Cincinnati* had fled to Boston at the outbreak of hostilities, and their *Cleveland* was trapped at home, NDL's *Prinz Friedrich Wilhelm* was on a pleasure cruise off Norway and was forced to take refuge from the much-feared British warships at Odda, deep in the Hardanger Fiord, some 100 kilometers inland from Bergen. In the meantime (as noted in Chapter 9) *Berlin* was at home being outfitted for service as a naval auxiliary.

The *Prinz* had some interesting prewar experiences. On a westbound crossing in late March 1909, Captain Prehn received a radio message warning of the presence of ice off the Grand Banks. Early the next morning his lookout sighted a record-sized berg, estimated to have risen more than 400 feet above the water and to have been over 1,000 feet long. Less than a year later her steering gear failed, but Prehn was able to bring his command into port safely, as other captains had done in similar cases with twin-propellored ships. In early December the next year (1911), even though beset by extremely heavy seas, the *Prinz* managed to outrace — by more than three hours — HAPAG's *Kaiserin Auguste Victoria* in an almost simultaneous passage from Cherbourg to New York, during much of which crossing the two ships were in close sight of each other.

After almost two years of idleness in the fiord at Odda, the crew of the *Prinz Friedrich Wilhelm* became inspired to strike at least some sort of blow for the Fatherland. They got up steam one night and managed to sneak the ship out of her refuge deep inside the mountainous Norwegian coastline. With all hands thinking they were doing a great thing for their Kaiser's cause, they made a speedy southward run for home, but as dawn broke they ran the *Prinz* hard onto a shoal in Danish waters.[37] The difficult salvage operation that ensued was hardly helpful to the war effort and concluded with the *Prinz* being laid up at Kiel, where she stayed until handed over after the war.

Chartered in 1920 to the Canadian Pacific, then bought outright the following year, she was refitted to a slightly greater tonnage and, on 2 August 1921, formally renamed *Empress of China* — for all of ten weeks. Before the new empress could make her first voyage, she was renamed the *Empress of India*, one of the fulsome titles of the British Crown (along with Defender of the Faith). Perhaps it was a more appropriate title in view of the more overt revolutionary turmoil astir in China at that time.

After making three round trips from Liverpool to Quebec she was again renamed — now as *Montlaurier* in a tribute to the late Prime Minister of Canada, Sir Wilfrid Laurier.[38] That lasted for barely two years until she developed a steering problem on 26 February 1925, and ran hard aground again, this time onto the less forgiving shoals off Queenstown (Cóbh) in southern Ireland, an event that resulted in considerable bad press. Patched up and refloated, the ship was haltingly towed to a Liverpool dry dock for repair, where it became clear that another name change would be helpful to future passenger good will. Before that could happen she caught fire and was badly damaged. Her owners then seemed to develop a problem in decisiveness; named *Monteith* in mid–June 1925, two weeks later she was being called *Montnairn*. Despite the tendency of their personnel to credit ships with animate personalities,[39] in fact all these fabrications of human engineering perform whatever the elements and their human controllers combine to bring about. Thus, in her last incarnation, the ship's misfortunes seemed to be over, and the much-named, German-built, Canadian-owned liner ran uneventfully between Canadian ports and those of north Europe until the Great Depression did her in and she was broken up in 1930.

16

Lesser Players at War

HAPAG's "P" and "B" classes were a fairly nondescript lot, playing — with one exception — no major part in the history of steamship operation and contributing very little to either side during the Great War. HAPAG built ten ships under these titles, all of them meant for the Hamburg–New York traffic. The classifications of these ships came about because all of them were originally supposed to bear names beginning with the letters "P" or "B." As passenger liners they were all plodders, with enormous steerage capacity for the westward crossing and little to offer the upper-crust patron in either direction. The pilot models of each class were made in Belfast by Harland & Wolff, where the first "P" ship, *Pennsylvania*, slid off the ways on 10 September 1896, to be followed some 14 months later by the first of the "B" class, *Brasilia*. Thereafter, the remaining craft of the "P" class were all made in Germany, while Harland & Wolff made only one other "B" class vessel, *Belgia*, in 1899.

Pennsylvania, at 13,335 GRT, was another "largest ship in the world" at the time of her delivery. With her plodding 13-knot speed, it was note-worthy, in a wry sense, that she managed the dubious distinction in the fog of early spring in 1910 of striking the German schooner, *Gertrud*, amid-ships at the mouth of the Elbe. From this disaster the liner's people man-aged to save only one member of the offended craft's six-man crew. This, perhaps, was by way of evening the score for her having rescued the crew of the Norwegian bark, *Bothnia*, several years earlier. Caught by a mid–season hurricane in the autumn of 1902, the 13 men aboard the sailing ship had struggled for more than two weeks to keep their foundering ship above water. Fortunately, when it finally went under, the big steamer was at hand.

Interned in New York harbor during the early years of the Great War, *Pennsylvania* was renamed *Nansemond* for her brief service as a troop transport. Her last tour of duty ended early in 1920 and, after four years of further idleness in the lower Hudson River, she was broken up in 1924. During that four-year period, the United States Shipping Board had more than 250 ships idle in several estuary waters of the East Coast, mostly in the lower Hudson, the Patuxent and the James. At the end of this period, an intensive survey found that, to no one's great surprise, many of the ships had been seriously vandalized.

Pretoria, the second ship of the "P" class, was built by Blohm & Voss and made her opening voyage to New York in midwinter 1898. As were all ships of her class, she was soon rebuilt to a different displacement and did not long survive the end of the Great War. Interned at Hamburg for the duration and handed over among the spoils of war after 1918, she was sold for breaking up in 1921. About the only noteworthy event of her plodding career was a collision off the Dutch island of Texel in October of 1908. Pretoria survived almost undamaged, but the much smaller *Nipponia*, also a German-registered vessel but engaged in the Far Eastern trade, was a total loss in both ship and crew.

Not all ships of these classes were still in German hands when the Great War broke out in the summer of 1914. *Brasilia* had been sold back to its builders early in 1900 and then taken over by the British-owned Dominion Line. Rebuilt and remeasured to 800 tons smaller capacity and then renamed *Norseman*, she stayed on the North Atlantic run, with accommodations for steerage passengers only, for the next ten years. In mid–1910 she made the first of several trips halfway around the world to Sydney. Still under British ownership and while employed as a supply ship for the war effort against Austrian and Bulgarian troops in the fighting north of Salonika, she was torpedoed on 22 January 1916. Beached near Kudros after much heroic effort by her crew, she was deemed not worth the effort of repair and abandoned where she lay. At the end of the war, an Italian firm of ship breakers took her apart on the spot and salvaged the remains for their scrap value.

The warship that did her in was *U-39*, launched just two months after the war started and with a submerged displacement of 878 tons. This was one of the last of a class that were regarded as very good sea boats, with four 50 cm torpedo tubes and armed (after a midwar refit) with one

Graf Waldersee, **as turned over to the victorious Allies in 1919. Steam Ship Historical Society of America.**

45-caliber deck gun of 105 mm. At the time she struck *Brasilia*, *U-39* was under Austro-Hungarian control. This was one of the numerous German undersea craft that got as good as they gave. Towards the close of the conflict some 28 months later, she was disabled by aerial bombs off the northwest Spanish port of El Ferrol on 18 May 1918 and forced to seek shelter there, where she was interned. Surrendered to France after the war, *U-39* was broken up at Toulon late in 1923.

Similarly, the other ship built by Harland & Wolff, *Belgia*, was sold to the Atlantic Transport Line before her completion late in 1899. Rebuilt to be primarily a cargo vessel with steerage only accommodations, her GRT rating was reduced by a thousand tons and she was briefly renamed *Michigan*. Soon transferred, like *Brasilia*, to the Dominion Line, as *Irishman* she stayed on the North Atlantic run for two dozen uneventful years until sold to a Dutch firm of ship breakers at the end of 1924.

The steamer *Graf Waldersee* was originally to be called *Pavia*, in keeping with the name pattern of other vessels in this class, but the commander of all the European forces in China at the time of the Boxer Rebellion just could not be ignored as a German hero. Alfred von Waldersee (1832–1904) of Mecklenburg-Schwerin succeeded the elder von Moltke as

Chief of Staff in 1888 and was created Field Marshall in 1900. The family tradition continued with his son who was Deputy Chief of Staff in 1914, and his grandson of the same name who fought at Stalingrad but managed to avoid being captured in the subsequent debacle. Despite having such a prestigious and distinctive name, the ship's life was similar to those of most of the others in this class—drab. Rebuilt to handle even more steerage passengers, and re-measured to a greater displacement, she was caught in her home port at the start of the war, handed over as reparations, found uncompetitive in the postwar world, and broken up in 1922.

Patricia, the final ship of this class to be launched and completed, lived an almost carbon copy life of the two-month-older *Graf*. She did achieve one momentary distinction, though it was dubious. In a dense fog on 2 January 1910, while inbound from New York, she collided with and sank the *Elbe V* lightship. In this act, she did better than *Pennsylvania* near the same locale and managed to save the entire crew.

Besides inspiring the opening line for an off-color limerick, the steamship *Belgravia*, of HAPAG's B class, was gifted with twice the life span of her sisters and saw service for Germany's enemies in both World Wars. Her days afloat terminated in the narrow waters between Japan's northern island of Hokkaido and the Russian-owned island of Sakhalin, where she became mistakenly the target of an American submarine.

Between launching and sinking, this ship spent most of her life in Russian hands. After a refiguring in 1905, she was sold to the Czar's navy, then trying desperately to rebuild both ships and personnel after the drubbing its obsolescent fleet received from the newer vessels and superior marksmanship of Admiral Togo's fleet at the battle of Tsushima. Renamed *Riga*, she worked out of the Black Sea port of Odessa until the mutiny of the Russian Navy in 1917. When the dust finally settled from both revolutions of those sorrowful and trying years, she bore the Soviet-style name of *Transbalt* and was equipped as a hospital ship for three years. Thereafter returned to humbler status as a freighter operating out of Vladivostok, *Transbalt* had the misfortune of being mistaken by the USS *Spadefish* for one of the few sizeable Japanese merchant ships remaining afloat in the closing weeks of World War II.

Interestingly, in the official records cited by the "Dictionary of United States Fighting Ships," one can read only that *Spadefish* was operating at that time in the waters of La Perouse Strait off the northern end of Hokkaido. The record states that on 12 June, she sank a "motor sampan"; on 14 June she sank the passenger-cargo steamer *Seizan Maru*. Nowhere, however, is there mention of her sinking the very much more substantial Russian-owned *Transbalt* on 13 June. It was a much larger vessel than either of those enemy craft torpedoed on the proceeding and following days.

BULGARIA

The months of January and February 1899 were among the coldest and stormiest in the records of North American and North Atlantic weather recording. Ships from Europe were arriving in New York, days later than scheduled and then covered with ice and replete with tales of monstrous seas and dreadful, freezing winds. On 12 February, half a dozen people were reported lost on ice floes in Lake Michigan; the same day an avalanche near Georgetown, Colorado, carried two dozen miners to their deaths. Parts of New York harbor were frozen over, as was most of Narragansett Bay, Nantucket harbor and dozens of lesser-known seaside localities in New England — including Bar Harbor, in Maine, though the event escaped the notice of the local chamber of commerce.

In the midst of these accounts of a fearsome and seemingly endless winter came a cabled report from Ponta Delgada in the Azores that the tanker *Weehawken* had arrived there with 25 extra passengers who had been taken from HAPAG's liner *Bulgaria*. That vessel was reported as last seen on 5 February, drifting helplessly some 800 miles away. Captain Gustav Schmidt, one of HAPAG's most experienced skippers, had taken his almost new, 500-foot, 8,000-ton vessel from New York on 28 January with a manifest that included 47 paying passengers, a crew of 75, 15,000 tons of grain, and an unusual cargo of 107 horses penned in a special enclosure built on the deck above her forward hold.

The day after *Weehawken*'s report, 13 February, HAPAG's main man in New York, general agent Emile Boas, stated that two other steamers were reported to be standing by his line's stricken freighter. In the meantime, the Cunard liner, *Pavonia*, also in midocean, was the object of similar concern. Oceangoing tugboats were dispatched from Delgada to the aid of both vessels. The tugs soon returned to port, though, because the continuing high seas prevented their own safe maneuvering and threatened to overwhelm their relatively low freeboard. In a subsequent statement, the captain of the *Weehawken* said that because of her severe list, *Bulgaria*'s cargo appeared to have shifted, but that due to the ship's 11 secure watertight compartments, in his opinion this was not, in itself, a serious enough matter to cause the ship to founder.

While the outside world waited for real news in those pre-radio days, one of the rescued passengers, John Hill, stated that just before he left the ship for safety aboard the tanker he heard the chief engineer of the *Bulgaria* say that the ship could last only another four hours; therefore it must have foundered on the night of the 5th. Pressed for more information back in New York, Agent Boas announced only that *Pennsylvania* would put into Plymouth, England, to retrieve and continue the voyages of some of the passengers from the company's *Pretoria*, which had also been badly battered by the stormy weather and forced to seek unscheduled shelter.

On 18 February, Captain Simpson, of the British steamer *Koordistan*, arrived in Bremen and reported that he had seen *Bulgaria* with other ships standing by. He stated that her rudder was beating helplessly and she had such a heavy list to port that her main deck was level with the water and her port side lifeboats were missing. On the 22nd came a report from Baltimore where the British steamer *Vittoria* had just arrived. Captain Wetherall stated that he, too, had been near *Bulgaria* and had picked up four members of her crew, including the second mate, Otto Scarges. Lucky to be alive, Scarges told reporters that his ship's troubles had begun on 1 February when the "hurricane" became so severe that it was impossible for the ship to make any headway and the steering gear was carried away, along with the ship's flying bridges.

"Sea after sea swept over us," Scarges said, "smashing in the doors of the cabin and deckhouse, flooding the main deck, washing in the awning deck, and creating havoc and disorder all over the ship. To make matters worse, one hundred horses stabled on the upper forward deck stampeded, and in their fright made a wild dash, trampling each other to death. This state of affairs lasted until all but about twenty had been killed or drowned in the wash of the waves. Then the butcher of the vessel, with a number of seamen, went into the pen and tried to quiet the beasts that remained. This failing, as did the attempt to force the frenzied animals overboard, their throats were cut. Before the maddened animals were dispatched, however, the butcher had both his legs broken, and one of the seamen was badly injured.

"Any idea that our troubles were over was soon dispelled when it was found that the vessel was leaking. All the hatch covers had been blown off, and before they could be replaced four of the seven holds filled, and all had considerable water in them. The cargo next shifted, listing the steamer heavily to port. In addition, the carcasses of the dead horses washed aport, adding to the heavy list.

"Then, for seventy-two hours, passengers and crew worked like slaves, throwing the cargo overboard to lighten the ship, but it was of little avail. Inch by inch, foot by foot, the ship settled, and as she sunk [sic] deeper the waves washed with greater force and freedom over her. One wave carried away eight of the lifeboats from the low-lying port side, and with

Woodcut of *Bulgaria* returning under her own power to Hamburg. *Illustrierte Zeitung*—9 March 1899, page 305.

them went much of the hope from the hearts of the passengers and crew…." There was more.

All this gloom and uncertainty notwithstanding, on 24 February, Captain Schmidt was finally able to bring his charge into port at Punta Delgada under her own power and reported only one casualty with all remaining personnel safe on board. He stated that two days after Scarges and three other men had been swept away in an open boat and fortuitously picked up by *Vittoria*, the weather had eased. On the morning of the 9th, the crew was able to toss overboard the remains of the horses, but the swells remained high and there were still several feet of water in the holds. Schmidt had asked the British steamer, *Antillian*, to stand by and take *Bulgaria* in tow, but that effort was unsuccessful as the three-inch manila hawser parted repeatedly. Meanwhile, at last, the ship's pumps began to make headway against the water, particularly the 14 feet of it in #4 hold, and the crew finally managed to repair the steering apparatus with a makeshift tiller. On 15 February, Schmidt thanked the *Antillian*'s captain for his kindness and concern, but said that he felt *Bulgaria* was once again seaworthy and could proceed on her own.

The next day from Berlin, Kaiser Wilhelm sent a message to Albert Ballin: "With deep gratitude to God, who has so marvelously saved the ship and crew, I want to express my warmest congratulations on the saving of the *Bulgaria*. Captain Schmidt, like a true German seaman, and with a firm trust in God, victoriously carried on a life-and-death struggle for

Bulgaria Captain Gustav Schmidt. *Illustrierte Zeitung*— 9 March 1899, page 305.

twenty-four days against the ocean, assisted by a crew gallant and self-sacrificing, devoted to duty. As a mark of my recognition of his services, I bestow on Captain Schmidt the Cross of Commander of the Hohenzollern Family Order. You will communicate to me, the names of the crew who are deserving of distinction."

With all flags flying, *Bulgaria* made it back to Hamburg by early March and to a hero's welcome, complete with parade. The local newspaper reported the arrival and the ship's near escape in great detail. "... Then the crew proceeded to the 'Grundsteinkeller' of the City Hall, where two long tables were set for the crew and the other invited guests. Herr Moormann (not otherwise identified) gave a toast to the Kaiser emphasizing particularly the interest of the Kaiser in the sea and the creation of a great and mighty war fleet."[40]

A dozen years later, in 1913, *Bulgaria* was briefly transferred to nominal Austrian ownership, as *Canada*, to escape the ravages of a rate war on transatlantic fares being led by the Canadian Pacific. When Chairman Ballin's ministrations finally put an end to such commercial destructiveness later that spring, the ship was officially returned to HAPAG and resumed her original name. That pro forma transfer, however, was nothing like what happened when she, too, was caught in the harbor of Baltimore by the start of the Great War. Renamed *Hercules* for wartime service under the American flag, she was optimistically christened *Philippines* at the war's end, but — with the enormous glut of shipping after the war[41] — she never made a further voyage and was broken up in 1924.

❖ ❖ ❖

There were two similar ships, not of the "P" or "B" class, but of comparable tonnage and speed, built for Norddeutscher Lloyd. Though slightly faster than the "P" and "B" vessels, neither of them achieved much distinction during their lives under different flags. *Rhein* was launched from Blohm & Voss in 1899, sailed for 15 uneventful years on the transatlantic and transpacific runs, but was tied up in Baltimore when the war broke out in Europe. Seized and refitted by the U.S. Navy under the name of *Susquehanna*, she made eight round-trip transatlantic runs as a troop transport and was then chartered to the short-lived United States Mail Lines where she followed a very similar fate to the very similarly aged *Barbarossa*. In 1928, after a few voyages between New York and Bremen, she was sold for breaking up in Japan.

Rhein's sister ship was named for another German river, a tributary of the Rhine, the Main. In her later years she was mostly used on the Bremerhaven to Baltimore run, but on her second voyage to New York, in late June 1900, she had the misfortune of being tied up at Hoboken when the great fire swept the entire warehouse area and spread into the several vessels that were immobile alongside the piers. While *Kaiser Wilhelm der Grosse* escaped serious damage, *Saale* was completely burned out and both *Bremen* and *Main* badly damaged. *Main* ultimately sank, due to the ministrations

Main, almost the last of her class, built in 1900. Steam Ship Historical Society of America.

of New York's fire boats, but fortunately in shallow water. She was raised and towed down the coast for rebuilding at Newport News. Back in service by the end of 1901, she plied the Atlantic uneventfully until the outbreak of war found her at anchor in the Flushing Roadstead. In April of 1915, the Dutch authorities found she was sending coded wireless messages to Zeebrugge and ordered the ship to leave or be interned. The captain opted to depart for the Belgian port of Antwerp. Handed over, finally, to the victorious French, *Main* did not fare well in the competition of the postwar world and was soon out of service and broken up.

❖ ❖ ❖

A total of 2,053,347 American fighting men went to Europe in 1917–18, about half to Britain for further training and thence across the Channel to the front. A slightly greater number went directly to the war in France. Those going to Britain were largely carried in the 49 British passenger vessels that were in the transatlantic service; despite the wartime sinkings, Great Britain still possessed by far the largest merchant fleet in the world. Those 43 ships that went directly to France were all labeled "American," but only a few were really born that way — the *Siboney* carried a total of 55,169 men to Europe and the small but fast *Great Northern* and *Northern Pacific* carried a similar number. The overwhelming majority were vessels formerly of HAPAG and NDL, and they carried the lion's share of American troops into battle against the Kaiser and his allies.

Before the war was over, *Leviathan*, at more than 12,000 men per 27-day round trip had carried a total of 192,753 soldiers and auxiliaries; *Mercury*, 39,463; *George Washington*, 83,350; *Agamemnon*, 78,249; *America*, 86,801; *Powhatan*, 30,087; *Huron*, 41,658; *Pocahontas*, 43,141; *Princess Matoika*, 34,937; *Madawaska*, 34,937; and *Susquehanna*, 34,911, to cite but a few.[42] Clearly, without these ships, the American manpower and munitions that helped win the Great War would have been vastly slower in arriving.

PART FOUR

17

The Stay-at-Homes

The label "express steamers" was a generic title for the faster German ships that began to enter the North Atlantic service in 1881, with the commissioning of the Norddeutscher Lloyd's initial "Schnelldampfer," *Elbe*. Sixteen years later, in 1897, Teutonic engineering produced the *Kaiser Friedrich*, named to honor the father of Germany's then reigning monarch. A gentle and tragic figure, married to the daughter of Britain's Queen Victoria, he died of throat cancer after ruling for only the 99 days following 9 March 1888. The ship was built to very nearly the same external dimensions as the slightly later *Kronprinzessin Cecilie* and her classmates. However, because its engine and boiler room ensemble produced less power and speed, and consequently demanded less fuel, the vessel required only three stacks.

Launched in the same year as the *Kaiser Wilhelm der Grosse*, but from the Schichau yards, *Kaiser Friedrich* was completed the following spring and sent out into the Baltic for sea trials. As it turned out, because of the lesser horsepower from her smaller quadruple expansion engines, she was unable to make more than 19 knots. When the ship failed to come up to the requisite 22-knot speed that had been specified in the order from the prospective owners and which had easily been met by her four-stacked sisters, Norddeutscher Lloyd refused to accept her. Schichau promised to go back to their drawing boards and make good on their commitment. Thus assured, on 7 June 1898, *Kaiser* was sent on her first commercial voyage — to New York — after which she was returned to Danzig (modern Gdansk) to see what the builders had come up with that might enhance her performance.

The alterations completed, three months later *Kaiser Friedrich* was back at sea, but showed only a slight improvement in her speed. During three voyages to New York over the balance of the year she never managed to attain more than 20 knots. Herr Wiegand of NDL remained quite unhappy, still refusing to authorize the final payments, and in January 1899 the big ship was again sent back to Danzig. The shipyard lengthened her three funnels by some four meters in an attempt to enhance the draft of the boilers and asked NDL to try again. This time the *Kaiser* managed to break the 20-knot barrier, but was still not up to her promised performance.

In June, North German Lloyd returned custody of the boat to the builders and demanded all their money back. In response, Schichau went to court to enforce payment of the balance due. Lloyd resisted their demand. By demonstrating with Schichau's own reports the failure of performance to meet promises, NDL won, much to the embarrassment of the famous company of builders. Schichau (now managed by the son of the firm's founder) was thus firmly stuck with a vessel that had been broadcast to the whole world as defective. The *Kaiser* was laid up in Bremerhaven while her builders got a very public black eye; for several years the Schichau yards did little civilian business. There were compensations for the misfortune, however; the busy ways at Danzig were fully occupied with orders for increasingly large and sophisticated warships that Grand Admiral Tirpitz and his headstrong Kaiser had wrung from a skeptical and reluctant Diet. One hundred sixty-one such vessels were launched at Danzig before Schichau received another order from either Norddeutscher Lloyd or HAPAG.

On 1 May 1912, the builders finally unloaded their white elephant. A newly formed Compangie Sudatlantique, operating out of Bordeaux and intending to compete with Hamburg-Süd, acquired the big ship and engaged the competitive Hamburg firm of Blohm & Voss to refit her with new boilers. Under her new French owners and with the new name of *Burdigala*, the former *Kaiser Friedrich* made a series of trips to ports in South America. But she was still an expensive and nonperforming pariah; after barely a year of such duty, she was again laid up, this time at her new home base of Bordeaux.

Six months after the outbreak of the Great War, the not-so-speedy express liner was again placed into service. With Great Britain's promise to safeguard France's northern and western coastlines from naval assault by Germany, almost all the French Navy had been reassigned to duty in the Mediterranean Sea. As an armed transport for the French Navy, *Burdigala* was at first to bring troops from French overseas possessions in Africa and elsewhere to close the gaps between the several French armies as the massive right wing of the Wehrmacht punched through toward Paris.

Several years earlier the German army had adopted a system whereby reservists took preassigned places in existing regular regiments that had strong and full-time cadres. The French retained a system that organized older classes of reservists into their own units. As a result, when mobilization was announced for both major belligerents, the Germans had a much larger force of men already in fighting order. As the weeks of war went by, however, the French Army grew much faster than Germany's. Thus *Burdigala*— once the western front had stabilized — was used to carry men and munitions from Toulon and Marseilles to the battlegrounds north of Salonika against Austrian and Bulgarian forces.

On this wartime assignment, the 12,500-ton outcast met her final nemesis— a mine field some 150 kilometers east-southeast of the major Greek port of Piraeus. The mines had been set from the German *Unterseeboot U-73* between the islands Mikonos and Tinos, in the center of one of the busiest passages of the Aegean Sea. Thus it was that on 14 November 1916, a German warship brought an end to an unloved but German-built passenger ship.

A sister ship of the *Kronprinz* (of Chapter 7) and the *Kronprinzessin* (of chapters 10 and 11), *Deutschland* was laid down as hull number 244 in the Vulcan yards, launched on 10 January 1900, and completed at the end of June. On her very first crossing of the Atlantic, she attained a highly publicized record speed of 22.42 knots and did better (with the help of the Gulf Stream) on the return trip. A year later, she beat even that pace, making the eastward trip at a speed of 23.51 knots. This performance by the HAPAG ship rubbed salt into the North German Lloyd's wounds received from the poor performance of their Schichau-built *Kaiser Friedrich*. However, this was the only HAPAG liner ever to hold the Blue Ribband prize; furthermore, her drive system was not quite in balance and the heavy vibration induced by high speed rotation of her twin propellers resulted in considerable passenger discomfort, particularly among those quartered towards the ship's stern.

The coveted prize came at further cost. On 22 April 1902, that annoying and persistent shuddering shook the ship's stern so badly that her rudder and stern post became loosened and fell completely off. Fortunately, though, she was able to continue her passage by steering with her twin propellers. Upon her return to Hamburg, she was taken into the yards of her

Deutschland, built in 1900. Steam Ship Historical Society of America.

builder's competitor, Blohm & Voss, for major alterations to her engines and drive shafts in the hope of more evenly balancing the kinetic forces developed by the various elements of her multiple pistons and propellor blades. Back at sea several months later, though eased, the vibration problem was still not solved; the engines remained excessively noisy and continued to cause much objectionable pulsation. For passenger comfort — a high priority with Chairman Ballin — the line was forced to operate the ship at considerably less than her designed and most efficient speed.

Speed or no speed, on 16 October 1907, while making the final approach to her mooring, *Deutschland* came to a complete halt crosswise off the end of her Hoboken pier. The tide went out and she grounded in the mud with one cable attached to land, but unable to move further even with the continuing aid of seven tugboats. Captain Kämpff later complained that his ship was normally serviced by twice as many such craft when she came into harbor and that a strike on the part of some tugboat crews was the cause of his mishap. In any case, the passengers, all set to disembark that evening, found themselves guests of the line for a further night, until the next high tide could free the ship from her sticky and embarrassing predicament.

In 1910, HAPAG sent the ship back to Vulcan for a complete redo. The massive engines that had generated almost 38,000 horsepower were replaced with far less powerful ones, producing only 15,000 horsepower and capable of driving the ship at only 17.5 knots. No longer a potential speedster, at least and at last the vibration was gone, allowing the ship's

Aboard *Deutschland* approaching HAPAG pier in New York harbor. Steam Ship Historical Society of America.

owners to feel that their 16,700 ton vessel could be used without fear of perpetual passenger complaints. In 1911, she was painted white, renamed *Victoria Luise* after both the wife and the youngest daughter of Kaiser Wilhelm II, and put into service as a luxury cruise ship.

The ex–*Deutschland*'s happy civilian life — taking tourist trips to experience the midnight sun near Norway's North Cape in the summer and around the numerous islands of the Mediterranean in winter — did not last long. On 3 August, as the British ultimatum was on the verge of expiration, she was commandeered by the German admiralty and refitted once again, now as an auxiliary cruiser. But even this duty evaded her. At that point, the Admiralty inspectors determined that the ship's boilers were not capable of the required level of performance for a Hilfskreuzer. The once widely touted liner remained laid up and neglected in Hamburg for the duration of the war. After the armistice, her rusted paint and unmaintained hull caused the ship to be deemed of such little value that the Allies refused to count her tonnage as part of the war reparations exacted from Germany.

Her German owners still had hope, however, and in 1920 HAPAG took *Victoria Luise* back to Vulcan for a long overdue general overhaul. On 27 October 1921, slightly reduced in tonnage, the newly renamed *Hansa* made her first transatlantic voyage. She was no longer recognizable as a member of the famous Express class—her forward pair of funnels had been removed as part of this final great refit. Once again, though, despite the immense effort that had been put into making her useful, the ship remained unprofitably jinxed. HAPAG had suffered enough; she was laid up again in the fall of 1924 and sold for scrap the following spring.

AFTER THE WAR WAS OVER

With a world-class chain of hotels, two largely double-tracked transcontinental rail lines, and fleets operating on both the Atlantic and Pacific oceans, the Canadian Pacific Railroad had, by the start of the Great War, become established as the most ubiquitous transportation system on earth. Albert Ballin's HAPAG may have had the largest armada of merchant ships, the Czar's railroad across Siberia might have been longer, but the firm put together under the leadership of American-born Sir William Cornelius Van Horne and his handpicked successor, Sir Thomas George Shaughnessy, had longer tentacles.[1]

Almost simultaneously with laying its transcontinental rail lines, the first of which began full operation in 1886, the CPR got itself into the hotel business—in order, initially, to reap maximum benefit from the spectacular scenery along its main line in the West. Actually, the CPR's first three mountain hostelries had initially been planned as eating facilities only, in the style of Fred Harvey's emporia along the line of the Santa Fe. This was a means of avoiding having to haul heavy dining cars over the steep mountain grades, some of which reached 4 percent until a massive rebuilding and tunnel program was initiated in 1907. With that issue taken care of the railway went to sea with a series of ships named for various princesses and empresses. The younger ladies were generally found in the Pacific Coast trade, operating from Vancouver south to destinations in California and north to Alaska. The larger and more exalted empresses were engaged in the transatlantic and transpacific trades. They carried the company flag pretty much around the world.

There were six empress ships altogether — but seven names. One ship —*Kaiserin Auguste Victoria*, the subject of this immediate discussion —

Opposite: Around the World in 110 days on the ***Victoria Luise***. HAPAG/Lloyd.

went through life under six different names. In this regard she was some-what like European royalty, one of whose members she was initially named for, and included among her titles *Empress of China* and *Empress of India*. The other ships bearing such titles included *Empress of Russia* and *Empress of Asia*, built to the order of the CPR in Glasgow in 1912 as sister ships destined for the Pacific trade. An older pair, built by the same Fairfield yards in 1906, bore the names *Empress of Britain* and *Empress of Ireland*; the latter was tragically rammed by the Norwegian steamer, *Storstad*, in thick fog in the St. Lawrence river and sank with a loss of 1,024 lives. (The story of one other *Empress*, of both China and India, is noted in Chapter 15.)

Kaiserin Auguste Victoria weighed in at 24,581 registered tons when launched at the end of August 1905. Already an empress, albeit of Germany, the *Kaiserin* completed her maiden voyage the following May. With an overall length of 705 feet and breadth of 77, she was similar in many ways to the contemporary *Amerika* and held the title of "the largest ship in the world" for the next year. This was the second of Herr Ballin's ships to bear the distinctive and well-promoted stamp of Cesar Ritz in her passenger amenities. The originally intended name of this hull was *Europa*, a name that was later used for one of NDL's famous postwar pair of speedsters.

One notable tragedy marred the *Kaiserin*'s prewar civilian career. On the evening of 24 February 1909, as members of the crew were boarding the ship in Hamburg preparatory to sailing for New York the following morning, the upper gangway attachments came loose and 27 persons tumbled 40 feet down into the "drift ice" between the ship and the dock. All of them sustained serious injuries, several were badly crushed, and ten were killed outright.

The year 1910 was a bad year for the *Kaiserin*. On 15 January, while under the command of Captain Johannes Ruser, she docked at Plymouth after encountering such heavy weather that she was delayed in completing the crossing and a "huge wave broke aboard and swept away about fifty feet of rail on the port side of the upper promenade deck." On a westward crossing in late June, with some 600 passengers, her port engine's drive shaft broke in midocean leaving the ship to continue the voyage with the use of only one engine. Continuing on, the aptly named Captain Harrassowitz was able to make no more than ten knots and reached New York three days late. Repairs at Newport News delayed her return voyage by two weeks.

The start of the Great War, however, found the *Kaiserin* safely at home in Hamburg, but she might almost as well have been in New York, Baltimore or Boston with her peer group. She spent all the war years laid up and on 23 March 1919, was handed over intact to the British government among the spoils of war. At first, she was used to return American servicemen to the United States; after that chore was completed in 1920, the big ship was chartered to the Cunard line. Then, in the spring of the following year she was sold to the Canadian Pacific which promptly sent her back to Hamburg for a complete refitting, including a change to oil-burning boilers. For the following eight years, the ex–*Kaiserin*, now a more English-sounding *Empress*, ran between Southampton and the northern ports of the New World before falling victim to the worldwide economic slump that set in at the end of 1929. The next year, the now aging *Empress* was sold to a Scots firm of ship breakers, in whose hands she burned, sank, was raised, broke apart, and was finally scrapped in mid–1931.

PART FIVE

The Second Wave

18

Möwe

What follows is not truly a part of the same story as the big-name ships that were the subject of prewar planning on the part of the Admiralstab. Starting from their home ports soon after the last famous Hilfskreuzer had been "retired" from combat, these German ships were conspicuous for their anonymity and were outfitted in the greatest secrecy. Only one of them was treated to a personal visit from the Kaiser before setting out to sea. This second effort to hamper their enemies' overseas lifelines did not stem from any "grand plan." Those few Hilfskreuzer that were loosed on the mostly British commerce in August of 1914 were meant for the task and, along with the naval warships *Karlsruhe*, *Dresden*, *Konigsberg*, and *Emden*, did their "thing" more or less according to plan. Operating on more of an ad-lib basis, this second effort derived its considerably greater success (for the costs involved) from the experiences of, and problems encountered by, the first generation of Hilfskreuzer.

Just as in the Royal and the U.S. navies, the German used the same names serially. For example, the American battleship, *Maine*—the one which exploded in Havana harbor sparking the Spanish-American War — was merely the first of three "modern" battleships of that name. As noted earlier, there were also a number of major German vessels, both naval and commercial, that bore the same name, simultaneously, adding a measure of confusion for the unwary. Among the warships that received this treatment were a number of smaller craft, the originals of which were mostly commissioned as gunboats for overseas duty.

SMS *Eber*, a bit player in the *Cap Trafalgar* saga, was the youngest of the *Iltis* (European polecat) class that also included *Jaguar*, *Tiger*, *Luchs* (Lynx) and *Panther*, all laid down in the years 1897 to 1902. One of these gunboats achieved considerable, if fleeting, prominence three years before the Great War began, when it became the pawn in the most notorious of Kaiser Bill's bellicose posturings. Agadir is a small, generally ignored port on the Atlantic at the end of the Atlas Mountains in western Morocco. A German trading firm, Mannesmann Brothers, contended they had some interests there but the French had already established a military outpost some miles inland at Fez and claimed the whole region as theirs. While German Foreign Minister von Kiderlen-Wachter protested that his country's rights superseded those of France, the Kaiser went behind his minister's back and ordered *Panther* to take up station in the port of Agadir. The affair became increasingly critical for the underdog French until a speech by the heretofore assumed pacifist, Lloyd George, made it clear to the German ambassador in London, Count Metternich (a grandson of the famous Austrian Chancellor), that the *Panther* would stay afloat longer if it left. Fearful of calling the British bluff, the Kaiser complied. A few minor colonial territorial adjustments were made at the expense of the African locals and in the end, Metternich was the biggest casualty of the affair; after ten years at the Court of St. James's he was recalled for having so underestimated the unanimity of the British will to stick up for French interests.

Eber's fate has already been mentioned, and *Panther*—having survived the war but no longer deemed dangerous by the victorious Allies—remained in German hands until its breaking up at Wilhelmshaven in 1931. In midsummer of 1914, all but the boar and the panther were assigned to the Far East Squadron; they, along with some other German vessels, were scuttled on the approach overland of the Japanese armed forces which overwhelmed the German naval base at Tsingtao in late September 1914. The memory of these ships, however, survived. A Great War use was found for the name of one of them, an older German gunboat, *Möwe* (Seagull). The next vessel to bear this name, plus two *Wolfs*, one *Greif* (Griffin) and a *Meteor*, were to form the more effective second wave of German Hilfskreuzer surface raiders.

In the days before the Great War, not one of these civilian ships was anything to boast about. The very opposite of their predecessors, they were unknown, anonymous, pedestrian commercial vessels. Their speed was plodding, their cargo capacity mediocre, and their prior peacetime records inconsequential, but they were far more successful at their wartime task than the more famously named and advertised merchant ships which preceded them into war. Part of the reason for this greater success was that very inconsequentiality. They were nothing like the big time Hilfskreuzer of the first wave. The second wave of surface raiders were small, slow, unimpressive, nondescript vessels—but equipped with the means to adopt numerous and varied disguises.

The idea for this kind of ship—to dupe the unwary passing skipper into thinking her harmless—was the brainchild of a 30-year-old reserve officer, Oberleutnant-zur-See Theodore Wolf, who was to be lost overboard from *U-73* on 16 January 1916 before he could enjoy knowing all the fruits of his dream. He recommended a plan that was simplicity itself: using ships of about 4,500 gross registered tonnage, with a working crew of about 150, with cruising ranges in the order of 38,000 nautical miles, and—in the greatest difference from the earlier Hilfskreuzer—supplied for an endurance at sea of at least four months. Speed was the least of Wolf's criteria.

The most notable of the second wave of German surface raiders was the second Seagull, which carried a good name from the past. The original had been another of the gunboats built by Herr Schichau in 1879 and stricken from the list of active ships 26 years later; it was kept afloat as a storage hulk at Tsingtao. On the approach of the Japanese forces in September 1914, she, though essentially valueless, was also scuttled.

The Hilfskreuzer, however, was a much newer vessel. She had been the 4,788-registered-ton fruit-carrier, *Pungo*, built for the Hamburg-based Laeisz Line in 1914; as a warship she was rated at 9,800 tons displacement. Barely 400 feet in length, this seagull was a dumpy 47 feet in width and drew 24 feet when loaded. *Möwe* had four holds, four watertight compartments, four decks, five boilers, but only a single triple-expansion engine. Having, fortunately as it turned out, been designed before the Admiralty's edict of 1913 went into effect, she had only one screw and was capable of only 13.3 knots. However, with a capacity of 3,441 tons of coal, she could cruise at sea for 30 days without refueling—at a sedate and economical 12 knots. This was the ideal vessel for the plan that had now been approved at the highest levels of the Admiralstab.

On 29 December 1915, after a hurried 24 days of conversion to this wartime function, the former *Pungo*, now *Möwe*, put to sea from Wilhelmshaven in company with *U-68* and under the command of 36-year-old Korvettenkapitän Nicholas Burggraf zu Dohna-Schlodien,[1] who had been entrusted on 1 November 1915 with implementing the original plan advanced by Oberleutnant Wolf. She carried a well-disguised armament consisting of four six-inch (155 mm) guns (600 rounds), one gun of four inches (200 rounds) and three hundred mines. In addition she had two 12-inch torpedo tubes which were rigidly mounted forward, a primitive design feature which meant that the whole ship had to be aimed at any target before launching a "fish." *Möwe* was manned by 11 other officers and a crew of 223 men. On the third day after sailing from Wilhelmshaven, the dowdy little steamer was a few miles off John O' Groat's House, the northeasterly tip of Scotland, where the bulk of her mines were set in the Pentland Firth, an east-west waterway at the southern entrance to the principal base of the British Grand (Home) Fleet at Scapa Flow.

Five days later, on 6 January 1916, the aging pre–Dreadnaught battleship *King Edward VII*, armored almost solely to resist above waterline attack, sank after striking one of these mines. Again, the Admiralty's First Lord[2] was embarrassed to feel obligated to withhold this distasteful news from the public. *Möwe*, however, was just "getting up to speed." Having lightened herself of most of her mines and thus riding a bit higher in the water, she continued westward into the North Atlantic and set a leisurely course to the south around Ireland. Before the month of January was over, *Möwe* had surprised and sunk nine more British ships, all merchantmen, with an aggregate tonnage of 35,669.[3] Continuing into February, the raider accosted another five British vessels and one French, putting another 21,850 tons of enemy shipping under the waves and out of the war.[4] The immense tonnages of mostly British merchantmen sunk during the war is better appreciated as a percentage of the whole. Overall, during the entire war, only about ten percent of England's merchant marine was sunk. Like all statistics this one is more impressive to those who were part of the 90 percent than those who had to suffer from enemy action.

The wide seaway of the North Atlantic was the prime hunting ground for all German naval craft, both surface and submersible. The wartime requirements of the western Allies meant enormous business for American manufacturers, but the materiel thus purchased then faced the hazard of an ocean crossing before it could be used. German naval strategy evolved during the war, from the sheer brute challenging of the Royal Navy that Bismarck had so wisely opposed, to one of much greater subtlety — starving and bankrupting the English, who had to import most of their foodstuffs as well as manpower and munitions.

The system of convoying, with a number of merchantmen escorted by several faster armed craft, was partially instituted earlier in the war but never completely effectuated. As a result, some ships, particularly those with less valuable cargoes or not carrying personnel, were often allowed to proceed on their own. Those ships furnished the bulk of the 10 percent mentioned above. As a result of the depredations made by raiders like *Möwe* and the intensified submarine campaign that came in 1917, convoying became a more universal requirement and, while total movement became slower, shipping losses dropped dramatically. In the sequel conflict a generation later, the use of land-based air cover also worked to diminish the effectiveness of undersea craft.

At this point in her career, the Hilfskreuzer with the innocent name of "Seagull" had been at sea longer than she was designed for, thanks to the replenishment of her supplies by removal of perishable foodstuffs from some of her captures—a process that prevented her crew from experiencing the debilitating ravages of scurvy, which had afflicted those aboard the *Kronprinz Wilhelm* and the *Prinz Eitel Friedrich*. But fuel — the bugbear of all Hilfskreuzer — was on the wane and so she turned north again, making for home around the northern tip of the British Isles. She returned safely to Wilhelmshaven on 4 March 1916 to refit and begin a second phase of her remarkable career.

Heartened by the sinking of *King Edward VII*, and because there were almost no German vessels at sea and thus at risk, the Kaiser's Admiralstab determined that the sleeping hazard of mine sowing was a profitable way to hamper the actions of the enemy's fleets, both naval and merchant. Three months later, on 12 June, *Möwe* was dispatched through the Kiel canal into the Baltic Sea, this time under the name of *Vineta*. This was the name that had been briefly applied to Hamburg-Süd's *Cap Polonio* before she was found unsuitable for war purposes. It originally derived from that of a legendary city on the Baltic island of Wollin that was "devoured" by the sea. It was applied to two warships of the Imperial navy, one commissioned in 1864 and a cruiser commissioned in 1899. Under this name, the *Möwe* managed only to eliminate one enemy ship, capturing on 27 June and taking back with her the 3,326-ton British vessel, *Eskimo*. She did lay all her mines, however, though no result of military value was ever credited to them.

Returning to home port once more on 24 August, *Möwe* was again refitted and, on 23 November 1916, put to sea for a third, and much longer cruise, but in warmer waters. Before she returned to Kiel on 22 March 1917, she did in an additional 21 British steamships with an aggregate tonnage of 111,100. In addition, she accosted and sank three sailing vessels, one British and two French, a 2,586-ton Norwegian freighter, and the Japanese ship, *Hudson Maru*. By the time she got home, 120 days after setting out, she had accounted for a total of 25 ships and 123,256 tons of hostile shipping. The most useful inclusions in her "haul" were the 4,652-ton *Yarrowdale*, which was taken whole early in the voyage and sent into Swinemunde to be outfitted as yet another auxiliary cruiser, *Leopard*; and the 4,992-ton *Saint Theodore* which soon became the auxiliary *Geier* (more about both of which below).

The most momentous part of *Möwe*'s third voyage occurred on 10 March, when her skipper took on the much larger British freighter *Otaki*. That ship, with a rated civilian capacity double that of the raider, had long been armed pursuant to First Lord Churchill's edict of early 1914. When the disguises were dropped, much to the surprise of Captain Dohna-Schlodien, the bigger ship fought back. There were several casualties on both sides before the superior training and armament of the German crew won the day by holing the *Otaki* at the waterline repeatedly and finally sinking her.

Leopard, the one-time British-owned *Yarrowdale*, and the unwilling "child" of the "Seagull," was outfitted with five guns of 15 cm (six inches) with 600 rounds, four guns of 8.8 cm, and two torpedo tubes with a total of twelve "fish." Her 14 other officers and 304-man crew were under the command of Korvettenkapitän Hans von Laffert, a 35-year-old native of Dresden. As outfitted for wartime her registered commercial tonnage of 4,652 became a displacement of 9,800, though her overall dimensions were not much different from those of her captor, *Möwe*. She had two boilers to drive one triple expansion engine with 2,400 horsepower and a speed of 13 knots. When outfitted under German management as another Hilfskreuzer, she carried 4,500 tons of coal, enough to keep moving for three months at sea, or for 26,000 miles at 11 knots. In one respect, however, she was three up on her "parent"; she had seven watertight compartments, which gave her considerably better flotation in case of any adverse encounter.

Leopard left Wilhelmshaven on 10 March 1917, but got only as far as the Faroe Islands at the northerly and of the North Sea in her attempt to circle around Great Britain and break out into the Atlantic Ocean. On 16 March, HMS *Achilles*, a modern British cruiser accompanied by the converted auxiliary vessel, *Dundee*, spotted the raider and put an end to her career before it had even started. Captain von Laffert went down with his entire crew. Not a man was saved from the freezing sea.

The original *Geier* (vulture) was a gunboat of the *Bussard* class, launched on 18 October 1894. After leaving Tsingtao she had a short and unproductive wartime career in the Pacific and was interned at Honolulu on 7 November. Taken over by the U.S. Navy on 6 April 1917, she was renamed *Carl Schurz* and met her end when rammed off Cape Lookout, North Carolina, by the SS *Fruita* on 21 June 1918. Originally the British-owned *Saint Theodore*, the second *Geier* was adapted at sea from extra armament carried by *Möwe*. She had been captured intact on 12 December 1916, and was very highly valued because of her cargo of 7,360 tons of the finest Welsh coal. A ship of very similar dimensions to SMS *Leopard* and to her captor, she was given a prize crew of two officers and 46 men under the command of Korvettenleutnant Friedrich Wolf[5] and armed with a pair of six-inch guns loaned from *Möwe*. Her career was somewhat more productive than that of *Leopard*, but lasted not a great deal longer. At the very end of December she sank the small British sailing vessel, *Jean*, and on the third day of the new year of 1917 she did in the considerably larger Norwegian barkentine, *Staut*.

Traveling largely in company with her "parent," *Geier* was seriously undermanned for her needs, therefore some members of her original crew had been kept aboard to ensure sufficient manpower to do the dirty work of shoveling coal below decks. They made a very reluctant black gang, however, and — as with the German crews on those ships interned in American ports — they hardly cared to keep the ship's engines in good order. On 14 February, though the boilers and engines remained operable, the unoiled bearings on her main shaft ground to a sticky paste and her propulsion apparatus seized up, rendering her motionless not far from the island of Trinidad. Captain Dohna-Schlodien had little choice but to retrieve his prize crew, remount his loaned armament and sink the immobile and now disabled vessel.

The career of the profitable "Seagull," however, was far from over. After her third and final voyage as a raider, under two names, she was again renamed — *Ostsee* — and reverted to the more pedestrian task of mine laying in the Baltic. With the closing of the Eastern Front against Russia in 1917–18, however, this was not much of a challenge and she returned home with nothing to report.

At the end of the Great War, the one-time fruitship *Pungo* was still a young vessel, barely five years of age when handed over to the British as war reparations. They gave her yet another handle, *Greenbrier*, and she served under these foreign masters until sold back to German ownership in 1933. Renamed again as the freighter *Oldenburg*, the increasingly venerable vessel was once more playing a wartime role for the Fatherland when a British submarine slammed a torpedo into her engine room off the coast of Norway on 7 April 1945, and sank her in shallow water. Finally, in 1953, the aged and now very rusty bones of the *Pungo/Möwe/Vineta/Möwe/Ostsee/Greenbrier/Oldenburg* were pulled from the sands and broken up for their salvage value.

19

Eagles, Meteors and Wolves

The North Sea was far from being a British lake, though Admiral John Jellicoe of the Grand Fleet and Vice-Admiral David Beatty of the independent battle cruiser squadron often tried to act as if it were, and certainly talked that way for home consumption. Nonetheless, British cruiser patrols covered most of its surface with regularity, though never completely, given nights and recurrent bad or foggy weather. Occasionally they could spot and destroy a U-boat, particularly when caught at recharging batteries on the surface, and they had a stroke of exceptional good luck in coming across *Leopard*. But still there were several German raiders that slipped past the patrols and made it to the open sea southwest of Iceland to where they could disrupt the Allies' economic lifeline from North America.

Four days before Christmas 1916, a full-rigged ship set sail — literally — from Wilhelmshaven. This traditional act was not really necessary, since the *Seeadler* (white-tailed gray sea eagle) could make up to nine knots as a motorship and carried 2,100 tons of oil for her diesel engines. Her skipper, however, was a sailing ship aficionado from Dresden, Graf Felix von Luckner,[6] who had previously been a watch officer on the aging battleship, *Kronprinz*, a bit player in the confused sea battle off Denmark's Cape Jutland on 31 May 1916. This elegant vessel had started out the war as the American-owned *Pass of Balmaha*, a three-masted full-rigged ship bound for Archangel with a cargo of wheat, but had been captured in the North Sea by a U-boat and sent into Hamburg. Once safely at large on the ocean and in part because of the elegant but innocuous-looking full rigging (which gave eloquent justification to her name) the *Seeadler* had quite good luck with more of her kind. Of the 16 ships she accosted as she sailed down the Atlantic and around Cape Horn into the Pacific, all but three were sail-powered only, for an aggregate capacity of 20,127 tons put out of the war. Three steam-powered British freighters, aggregating 9,972 tons, also fell victim to the "Sea Eagle." With the exception of a French vessel, the 1,833-ton *Cambronne*,[7] which was sent off to Rio de Janeiro with a boat load of prisoners, all of these ships ended up on the bottom.

After sending a total of 29,973 tons of enemy shipping to their watery graves, which included three American sailing vessels nabbed in the South Pacific, Luckner headed his "Sea Eagle" west for the Society Islands, a French "protectorate" of which Tahiti is the principal member. Anchored off the small windward island of Mopelia (on modern maps as Maupihaa), in the darkness early on 2 August 1917, a huge wave tore the ship loose from her anchors and swept her up onto the barrier reef. It was an unromantic end for the *Seeadler* and her voyage. It was not the end for Luckner or his crew, however.

Teaming up with five of his men, the venturesome skipper promptly outfitted the largest of *Seeadler*'s boats with a machine gun, some rifles and revolvers and half a ton of gold. He christened the pinnace yet another *Kronprinzessin Cecilie*,[8] now the smallest ship in His Majesty's Navy, and headed off to see what havoc he could wreak in the direction of New Zealand. Unfortunately, three weeks later and some 2,000 miles to the west, though well-armed he was out-bluffed by the unarmed local police on Fiji and ended up in a New Zealand prisoner-of-war camp. In the meantime, the rest of his men spent five unhappy weeks ashore before accosting — and overwhelming — the crew of a small, barely seaworthy interisland schooner, *Lutèce*, who made the mistake of calling at their lonesome hideaway. They renamed the ship *Fortuna*, and, in another feat of excellent seamanship but without their famous skipper, the company sailed away to the east. A month later, on 4 October, the Germans had managed to bring this leaky and almost derelict vessel some 3,000 miles to the Chilean outpost of Easter Island. The woebegone craft had eluded various elements of the Royal Navy and finally sank just offshore. Subsequently the Germans were taken to the mainland and interned.

The 1,912-ton Currie line freighter, *Vienna*, had the misfortune of being trapped in Hamburg by the unexpected outbreak of the Great War.

The formerly British vessel then enjoyed the further distinction of being the first cargo ship converted to wartime duties for her new masters. Armed with two 88 mm guns (600 rounds) and a hold full of mines, the freshly commissioned SMS *Meteor* (also the name of the Kaiser's yacht) went to sea at the end of May 1915, under the command of 35-year-old Korvettenkapitän Wolfram von Knorr.[9] Her first voyage lasted only a few weeks, occupied mostly in mine-laying off Moray Firth and the port of Archangel. The voyage did result in the capture and destruction of three small freighters, however: two Swedish and one Norwegian — hardly a notable achievement in view of those nations' neutrality in the conflict then raging.[10] By the end of June, the *Meteor* was home again.

Re-equipped with more guns and two torpedo tubes, as well as a new commander, *Meteor* went out again on 6 August. This voyage was even shorter. After doing in two small freighters, one British and one Danish, on 8 August, the *Meteor* saw a British cruiser patrol come over the horizon the next morning. Korvettenkapitän Curth Hermann ordered his ship to be scuttled, and everyone took to their boats. It was over. Captain and crew were picked out of the water and spent the next 40 months in a British POW camp.

HAPAG's *Belgravia*, the second ship of this name,[11] was a product of the Belfast yards of Workman, Clark and Company. She was launched in 1908 with a displacement of 12,900 tons and a registered cargo capacity of 6,648, and placed into the transatlantic service. After conversion to auxiliary cruiser status (a process completed by the end of 1915) her name was changed to *Wolf*, in honor of the Oberleutnant. Her skipper was the still eager Curth Hermann,[12] previously a gunnery officer on the battleships *Oldenburg* and *Ostfriesland*. The ship was well-armed for a lengthy voyage and could have been at sea for four months, if powered as advised by the Argentines—"economically." She left port on her raiding voyage on 14 January 1916 but never got out of sight of land. While outward bound from Hamburg she ran onto a sand bar off Neuwerk where the wave motion broke her keel. Her nine watertight compartments did not save the ship from a disastrous settling into the sand, though the moribund vessel stayed upright and was visible from land. By the end of February it became obvious that this craft was a lost cause and she was formally decommissioned. Ultimately refloated and once again made seaworthy, she was turned over to France in 1919.

❖ ❖ ❖

A second *Wolf* had the longest active life and was the most successful of the entire nautical array of the Fatherland during the Great War. This may appear to be an overly bold statement, but there is no way to disprove it, for this *Wolf* was clearly the most successful of all surface raiders. The records of many U-boats (which might have been better) went down with the ships themselves; half of them never returned home to report. Starting out life as the Hansa Line freighter *Wachtfels*, a single-screw steamer of 5,809 tons, she was taken over by the admiralty at the start of the war as the support ship *Jupiter*. With the de facto bottling up of the High Seas Fleet, this task never came into being and the one-year-old ship stayed in port until her eminently desirable characteristics for the kind of raider described by Oberleutnant Wolf brought her to the fore early in 1916.

In this final effort of surface raiding, everything was done right. As originally built, the vessel had a top speed of only 13 knots (she cruised most efficiently at 11), was 419 feet in length by a dumpy 56 in breadth, and had a fully laden draft of 29.6 feet. Her single funnel served one triple expansion engine. However, when equipped as a raider-mine layer, she had an even greater depth and consequently less speed.

Having changed from fleet support status to that of raider, she put to sea at the end of November 1916, manned by a crew of 400 under the command of Korvettenkapitän Karl-August Nerger. Leaving port she carried 458 mines in her after holds (which were to be sown in various places from Cape Town to Auckland), seven 150 mm guns, four 12-inch torpedo tubes, and a variety of smaller armament. In addition she carried a cub, *Wölfchen*, a demountable two-seated float-equipped biplane that was to be used very successfully for reconnaissance.

Escaping the British North Sea dragnet by going around the north of Iceland through Denmark Strait, her first "port of call" was Cape Town, off which she laid 25 mines on 16 January 1917. Interestingly, in approaching that port, she passed — going in the opposite direction but in full view — a troop ship convoy guarded by British cruisers any of which could have blown the *Wolf* out of the water. The mines set that night, along with another small field off Cape Argulhas, soon accounted for three ships (aggregating 17,008) tons that were sunk and two more (totaling 16,244 tons) that were badly wounded but managed to make it into port.

One of the few benefits of having had all friendly merchant marine chased off the seas by the British "distant blockade," was that these mines could be sown almost indiscriminately. Any ship at large on the oceans could be assumed to be either enemy-owned or potentially aiding in their war effort somehow. By this stage of the Great War, the German admiralty had happily leaped to the conclusion that whatever was afloat and at large was fair game. Indeed, at the end of her momentous voyage, Captain Nerger's greatest worry was running afoul of his own country's minefields.

Proceeding around the end of Africa into the Indian Ocean, the plodding vessel continued her voyage, laying another minefield off Colombo and then one off the west Indian port of Bombay. Turning westward, *Wolf* recovered the *Turritella* from her British masters and turned her into another auxiliary. Thirty months earlier that ship had been the *Gutenfels* of the Hansa Line which had been seized in the harbor of Alexandria by the British at the outbreak of the war and had been serving her new masters as a tanker. Back under German control, she was renamed another *Iltis*, given a two-inch gun from the *Wolf*'s inventory, 28 mines and a prize crew headed by Leutnant Brandes. After sowing her mines, this skunk unfortunately encountered the British cruiser HMS *Odin* on 5 March 1917 and had to be scuttled by her own crew. Captain Meadows, the dispossessed British skipper and his entire crew had already been bundled aboard the *Wolf* and quartered in the aft hold, #4, where they were to live in varying degrees of crowding and discomfort until the ship finally returned to Kiel more than a year later. Before the voyage ended, the after holds of the *Wolf* became the prison quarters of some 400 men — as the mines went out, the men took their places. Women taken from their numerous captures were given cabin quarters amidships.

While chasing prizes around the equatorial zone of the Indian Ocean, where her most "profitable" months were spent, these prisoners suffered immensely from the heat, and were only allowed on deck when no other ships were in sight. Even so, they came to dread the ringing crash of the huge, but hinged, plates, used to disguise her gun mountings, as they were loosed to fall against the ship's sides. The prisoners were penned next to the hold containing, at first, upwards of 400 mines, each packed with half a ton of explosive. They learned to watch the action, either through the cracks around their hatchway or via holes left by rivets that popped out under the strain from the ship's guns firing, as the supply of mines gradually dwindled, thankfully to nothing.

In her hit-and-run rampage around the Indian Ocean and off New Zealand and Australia over the next ten months, *Wolf* — continuing her disguise as a peaceful slow-moving tramp steamer — captured or sank another four British steamers aggregating 13,226 tons' capacity. To this was added four American sailing vessels aggregating 2,934 tons, three other sailing vessels for another 5,357 tons, and on 26 September 1917, their best prize, the well-victualed Japanese twin-screw steamer *Hatachi Maru*, of Nippon Yusen Kabushiki, for 6,557 tons. Near the end of their voyage, when off the tip of Africa, the Germans were again fortunate in capturing a Spanish collier of 4,648 tons. In the meantime, the mines *Wolf* had set off the east coast of Australia and elsewhere had put another 56,152 tons out of the war.

An interesting sidelight to the sinkings by mines set in Australian waters was the intensity with which local ANZAC officials denied the possibility that any German vessel might have been operating this far from the Fatherland. The explosions which sank three ships in the Tasman Sea were all blamed on "Communist" agents who had managed to place time bombs in the ships' holds before they left port.

Captain Nerger's superb seamanship and bold good fortune even attracted the admiration, however grudging, of a crew member of the captured Australian ship, *Wairuna*, Roy Alexander, who later wrote a fine account of his experiences, *The Cruise of the Raider Wolf*.[13] More important for the morale within the Fatherland, when *Wolf* returned to Kiel on 24 February 1918, after her epic 64,000-mile voyage, many warships of the German High Seas Fleet were lined up to receive her. All members of the crew received Iron Crosses, Nerger received a "Pour le Mérite" and great publicity was given to the ship's successful voyage and safe return.

That return, however, would not have been possible without the fortuitous capture, and retention, of the Spanish collier *Igotz Mendi* (Spain was a neutral nation), whose cargo of 7,000 tons of coal gave the Wolf fuel to complete the voyage from off Cape Argulhas to Kiel. The refueling process turned out to be a risky venture. Seeking to find calm waters in the anchorage of Trinidad Island, Nerger learned from his careful listening to the wireless[14] that the island was now occupied by a Brazilian radio station and accompanying militia. With Brazil now at war with Germany, he was forced to transfer coal while at sea. In the open sea south of Trinidad, the two ships were lashed together amid the rolling waves and several hundred tons laboriously transferred. However, despite numerous fenders between the tossing ships, a number of the hull plates on both craft were dented, rivets popped, and the collier's bridge was severely damaged. One crew member was crushed to death during this process. A second refueling, another 2,000 miles to the north, was no easier on the two ships, but the transfer was sufficient to keep the slow-moving *Wolf* going the rest of the way home.

Toward the end of the voyage, the damage resulting from the refueling impacts caused leakage at the rate of some 40 tons of water per hour. When the ship's pumps became temporarily clogged, there was a period of severe panic as water rose over the knees of the stokers in the boiler room. Sluggishness induced by this problem compounded the ship's loss of speed due to the year's growth of weeds and barnacles that fouled her bottom. Rated at her departure as using 60 tons of coal per day at ten knots, and only 35 at a more economical eight knots, she was now using 60 tons just to move along at a bare five knots.

However, upon successfully eluding the British for 14 months at sea and again upon his midwinter return by way of Iceland, Nerger found his ship held outside the harbor of Kiel for a week; fresh food was supplied to his crew and prisoners to alleviate the severe impact of scurvy which was affecting almost everyone aboard, the prisoners the worst. In addition, a horde of dock workers was hustled aboard to repair the damage of her long cruise, including that which had been inflicted by the refueling process. Adorned with a bright coat of paint, Wolf was finally deemed fit to be saluted by the massed bands on every ship she passed as she made her way to a place of honor next to the anchorage of the flagship, SMS *Bayern*.

❖ ❖ ❖

The freighter *Güben* had been built at the Neptunwerft yards in Rostock in 1914 for the German-Australian line. However, with the start of the war, Germany's overseas trade vanished (as foreseen by First Lord Churchill) and she never got anywhere near Australia. Converted late in 1915 to a well-armed raider along the lines laid down by Oberleutnant Wolf, she was commissioned as SMS *Greif* (2) on 23 January 1916 and sent to sea a few weeks later. Her career was short and not very sweet. Before finding her way to the open sea, the condor got involved in a fight with two British armed cruisers, both larger than she. While HMS *Alcantara* was the first to be sunk, she was soon followed to the bottom of the shallow North Sea by the *Greif*. Of her ten officers and 130-man crew, half the officers, including Fregattenkapitän Rudolph Tietze,[15] and 92 of the crew went down with their ship. The balance spent the rest of the war in an English prisoner-of-war camp.

There never was a third wave of surface raiders. U-boats were more "productive."

PART SIX

20

The Last Gasp

She was launched from Blohm and Voss in 1910 as *Cap Finisterre*, named for a geographic landmark in the northwest Spanish province of Galicia akin to Land's End in Cornwall, and designed for the Hamburg to South America service, which she entered on 8 August of the following year. This was the first of a five-ship series (*Cap Trafalgar* being the second) which were intended to bring some of the same measure of swift service and comfort to the Europe–South American run that Ballin and Weygand's ships had been bringing for 20 years to the passage between Europe and North America. Hardly a speedster, her quadruple expansion reciprocating engines could drive her at a top rate of only 16½ knots. She was almost a dead-in-the-water plodder by comparison with the Cunard liner *Mauretania*. But her 1,389 passengers (served by a crew of 339) could enjoy numerous sophisticated amenities, including a built-in, tiled swimming pool, on the two-week trip down the ocean to her final destination at Buenos Aires. The "Cap" sisters all made stops at various intermediate European ports such as Rotterdam, Antwerp, Boulogne, Le Havre, Corunna, Vigo and Lisbon; in midocean at Madeira and Las Palmas; and in South America at Recife, Bahia, Victoria, Rio de Janeiro, Santos, Paranagua, Sao Francisco, Rio Grande, and Montevideo.

Although listed as a stand-by auxiliary cruiser for any forthcoming war, *Cap Finisterre* was never fitted out for such duty. The outbreak of the Great War found her at home in Hamburg, where she remained peacefully

Cap Finisterre in 1911, long before her Pearl Harbor visit. Hamburg-Süd.

tied up "for the duration." Four years later the undamaged 14,500-GRT ship was among the spoils of war, and in July of 1920 she ended up assigned to the Japanese government as war reparations. It was difficult to see how the Japanese had suffered very much by way of losses from German depredations in the Great War — only three of their ships were sunk. Nevertheless, they ended up part of the "Allies" and got in on the division of spoils both in this kind of asset and in territorial gains. It was the Japanese seizure of Tsingtao which gave them the toehold in China that led, by a logical daisy chain, to their war against the United States a generation later.

The *Cap*'s civilian life after 1921 included ownership by Toyo Kisen of Tokyo which renamed her *Taiyo Maru*. With her registered tonnage refigured slightly downward to 14,457 she entered the transpacific trade between Yokohama and San Francisco. In 1926 Toyo Kisen was merged into Nippon Yusen Kaisha (NYK). Thereafter, in 1934, *Taiyo Maru*— still the largest and most luxurious member of the Japanese merchant marine — was refitted with new, oilfired boilers which increased her speed to 19 knots.

When an increasingly icy chill came over Japanese-American relations as the land of the Rising Sun began to intrude ever more deeply into the Chinese mainland, transpacific trade with the United States slowed; it was almost at a halt by 1939. A brief thaw set in in late 1940, when the enormous quantity of scrap steel removed from various elevated railroad lines in the major cities of the eastern United States (Boston's Atlantic Avenue and New York's Third Avenue) was shipped to Japan. With this thaw there appeared hope in America that Japan's burgeoning "Greater East Asia Co-prosperity Sphere" might exist compatibly and peacefully with the rest of the world, and *Taiyo Maru* was sent on a supposed trading voyage to Honolulu. Her real duties in that harbor, however, were to confirm and enhance the observations that had been made for more than a year by Takeo Yoshikawa, a 29-year-old naval intelligence agent attached to the local Japanese consulate. For the past six months his sole function had been to note the comings and goings of the major elements of the American Pacific Fleet and the schedule of deployments at the other military base facilities on Oahu.

Also in on the "observing game" for Consul General Nagao Kita, though not very effective at it, was a transplanted German, Bernard Julius Otto Kühn, who had been resident in Hawaii since 1936. After the events of 7 December 1941, Kühn did not last long as a "sleeping" enemy agent; he was arrested two days after the sneak attack and, along with all the rest of the consular staff, bundled aboard a U.S. Coast Guard vessel and taken to the mainland. At first interned with other Nisei at a camp in northern Arizona, the Japanese consular staff was finally exchanged for Americans held in Japan. But Yoshikawa, despite having operated under another name while engaged in his Hawaiian mission, lived for many years in Japan in fear and hiding, unhonored and distrusted by all.

Since 1939, the Commander-in-Chief of the Japanese Navy had been Isoroku Yamamoto, a veteran of the hugely successful Russo-Japanese war of 1904–5 that brought the Land of the Rising Sun onto the world stage with a resounding thump. He was now 57 years of age, a man with extensive experience in American ways, and determined on a plan that was designed to stun the American nation. His scheme envisaged a weakened and humble United States brought to the bargaining table and compelled to allow the Japanese to proceed unhindered with their plan for domination of all "East Asia."

The implementation of Yamamoto's plan did knock several capital ships out of action, some of them permanently, and surely had a major impact on the United States, but instead of bringing on an attitude of fear and a desire for conciliation, the attack suddenly awoke the heretofore "sleeping giant" in a unanimous feeling of outrage. After the Battle of

Midway, the fierce determination of Americans to avenge the treacherous insult and injury soon turned the Pacific Ocean into an American lake and made even interisland shipping in Japan subject to considerable risk.

Taiyo Maru had left Yokohama for Honolulu in early October 1941. Aboard, but in civilian attire, were three Japanese naval officers assigned to make detailed observations along the planned route for Yamamoto's task force, and, more importantly, to verify that Yoshikawa's voluminous data were correct. While ostensibly loading and unloading cargo, *Taiyo Maru* spent five days, midmonth in October, tied up in Honolulu, during which time intermediaries from the consulate carried Yoshikawa's detailed schedules, sketches and materiel counts to the ship. When, at last, the visiting naval officers were satisfied that the spy's accumulated information was accurate, the 31-year-old ship left Honolulu for home at the end of the month.

The Japanese High Command's order for Kido Butai, the code name for the Pearl Harbor attack, was issued on 5 November, while Yoshikawa, still operating under the pseudonym of Tadashi Norimura, continued to send further updates home by coded radio messages. Fatefully, but to no avail, the spy was able to report that the three aircraft carriers of the Pacific Fleet, complete with destroyer and cruiser escorts, had left their base for points unknown on 5 December. The absence of the carriers from the destruction that ensued at Pearl Harbor was critical to the subsequent Battle of Midway, less than six months later, in which the Japanese Navy was effectively reduced to its prior position of inferiority to that of the United States.[1] As well as being the turning point of the war against Japan, the Battle of Midway was the ultimate proof that command of the air above it was essential to command of the sea.

Five months after the fateful Japanese attack on Pearl Harbor, on 8 May 1942, the American submarine, USS *Grenadier*, was on her second voyage out of Pearl Harbor and operating 85 miles off Nagasaki on the west coast of Kyushu. *Taiyo Maru* had long since safely returned from her Hawaiian reconnaissance venture and was now assigned to transport duties between the port of Mutsu at the north of Honshu to the recently overrun island of Luzon. She carried a manifest of 1360 souls, including numerous technicians, scientists, economists and industrial experts, who had been assigned the task of bringing the rich resources of these newly acquired territories into prompt utility for the Japanese war production effort, which was already showing serious signs of strain. The aging vessel made it safely down the Sea of Japan, but then two of the *Grenadier*'s torpedoes struck her squarely amidships and over half (817) of those onboard were drowned. The sinking of this one relatively old ship reportedly did more damage to the Japanese leadership morale than the subsequent shooting down of Admiral Yamamoto's plane or the sinking of the huge new battleship, *Yamato*, two years later.

Thus it was that a German-built Hilfskreuzer, never used as such and given to a one-time enemy of the Fatherland after the Great War, met her end while serving a friend of the Fatherland in the sequel conflict.

❖ ❖ ❖

Not including the damage done at Pearl Harbor, between them all, the Kaiser's Hilfskreuzer sank a total of 96 enemy merchant ships with an aggregate registered tonnage of 379,158. They sent another seven ships (24,906 GRT) home as prizes, and released five to carry prisoners to neutral ports. In addition they set mines which sank an additional 19 merchant ships and two major enemy warships. The lessons learned were valuable, for in the sequel conflict a generation later, Hitler's Hilfskreuzer (none of which were famous name vessels) sank 657,801 tons of enemy shipping — almost twice the tonnage of the Great War — and sent home 30 prizes aggregating 158,362 tons' capacity.

In the Second World War, Der Führer did not repeat the one giant mistake which finally lost the first great conflict for the Kaiser, in the Bavarian contingent of whose army Adolf Hitler had served. Though the German merchant fleet was considerably smaller than it had been a generation earlier, on 1 September 1939, none of it was left stranded in the initially neutral safety of an American port.

Appendix

The major vessels of the German merchant marine derived their names from a variety of sources—classical, colonial, hometown, ports of call, Imperial royalty, Teutonic heroes. There was no consistent pattern except with the East African and Woermann Lines: the one used titles of rank throughout; the other based its nomenclature purely on internal company influences, having started in the mid–1800s as a family concern trading to the Cameroons. In the main text, the derivations of names are given for those ships featured. In this appendix, other than those which are self-explanatory, we supply much of the same information for all the lesser known passenger vessels of German ownership in commission as of 1 August 1914. H = HAPAG; N = NDL; S = Hamburg-Süd; G = Gdynia-Amerika; W = Woermann; D = Deutsche Ost Afrika, most of which played no great part in *Der Erste Weltkrieg*. With the numerous renamings that went on as a result of changes in ownership (Kosmos Lines, for instance, was acquired in its entirety by HAPAG prior to 1910) it is sometimes hard to follow the fates of ships. Where we are not sure of anything, we have left it blank.

Owner	Name of Ship	Year Built	Gross Reg Tons	Location on 8-3-14	Year of Demise
N	**Aachen** (Rhineland city—Aix-la-Chapelle to French)				
		1895	3,833	Bremerhaven	1915
	Sunk off Cape Jutland while serving as a fleet auxiliary				

Owner	Name of Ship	Year Built	Gross Reg Tons	Location on 8-3-14	Year of Demise
H	**Abessinia** (German for Ethiopia)				
		1900	5,753	Hamburg	1921
	Stranded in the Red Sea				
D	**Admiral**				
		1905	6,298	Overseas	
	Seized in Delagua Bay				
W	**Adolph Woermann**				
		1906	6,355	Rotterdam	1938
	Reparations to Britain, 1919				
H	**Alesia** (small town in southern France where Caesar captured Vercingetorix)				
		1896	5,167	Rangoon	1926
H	**Alexandria** (city of Egypt)				
		1900	5,656	Hamburg	1936
S	**Amazonas** (river of central Brazil)				
		1890	2,950	Hamburg	1915
	Torpedoed off Em's Germany				
H	**Amerika** (see Chapter 14)				
		1905	22,225	Hoboken	1958
H	**Antonina** (small city of southern Brazil)				
		1898	4,010	Tampico	1960
	Taken over by Mexico, 1917; sold back to HAPAG				
H	**Arabia**				
		1896	5,456	Syracuse	1924
	Seized by Italy, 1915				
H	**Aragonia** (province of Spain)				
		1897	5,446	Hamburg	1923
H	**Arcadia** (generic mythological name for lovely place)				
		1896	5,456	Norfolk	1926
	Seized by United States in 1917				
H	**Armenia**				
		1896	5,471	Hoboken	1927
H	**Artemisia** (Aegean gulf off Thermopylae)				
		1901	5,739	Hamburg	1930
H	**Athesia** (ancient name for segment of Greece)				
		1899	5,751	Callao	1932
	Seized by Peru, and sunk off the coast				
S	**Bahia Belgrano** (see Belgrano)				
		1897	4,817		
S	**Bahia Blanca** (city and bay of Argentina)				
		1912	9,349		scuttled 1940
	Sold to Argentina in 1918				

Owner	Name of Ship	Year Built	Gross Reg Tons	Location on 8-3-14	Year of Demise
S	**Bahia Castillo** (Ramon, president of Argentina)				
		1913	9,949		wrecked 31 July 1944
	Seized by Brazil, 1917				
N	**Barbarossa** (see Chapter 13)				
		1896	10,984	Hoboken	1924
H	**Batavia** (see Chapter 9)				
		1899	11,464	Hamburg	1924
S	**Belgrano** (South American general)				
		1888	2,616		
	Sold to Woermann; seized by Brazil in 1917				
H	**Belgravia** (2) (district of London)				
		1907	6,648	Hamburg	
	Became *Wolf* (2)				
N	**Berlin** (see Chapter 9)				
		1908	17,324	Trondheim	1931
	To White Star line as *Arabic*				
H	**Bermuda** (Mid-Atlantic island)				
		1898	7,027	Hamburg	1932
H	**Bethania** (city of South Africa)				
		1899	7,548	At Sea	1944
	Captured by HMS *Essex*; reparations to Japan; torpedoed by USS *Drum*				
S	**Bilbao** (city of Spain)				
		1905	4,798	Hamburg	1932
	Surrendered to England, 1919				
H	**Bismarck** (see Chapter 14)				
		1913–22	56,950	Hamburg	1940
	Reparations to Britain as *Berengaria*				
H	**Blücher** (see Chapter 13)				
		1901	12,334	Hamburg	1929
	Reparations to France in 1923				
N	**Bonn** (university city of Rhineland)				
		1895	3,969	Odessa	1920
	Seized by Russia; stranded in Bosporus				
N	**Borkum** (North Sea island of Germany)				
		1896	5,642	Genoa	1917
	Sunk as SS *Asti* by *U-93*				
H	**Bosnia**				
		1899	9,683	Hamburg	1924
	Reparations to Britain; burned in Red Sea				
N	**Brandenburg** (segment of Prussia)				
		1901	7,532	At Sea	1924
	Seized by USA, as USS *Hecuba*				

Owner	Name of Ship	Year Built	Gross Reg Tons	Location on 8-3-14	Year of Demise
N	**Bremen** (2) (see Chapter 13)				
		1896	11,570	Bremerhaven	1929
	Reparations to USA; scrapped as SS *King Alexander*				
N	**Bremen** (3) (see Chapter 10)				
		1900	10,826	Hoboken	1923
N	**Breslau** (city of Germany)				
		1901	7,524	New Orleans	1948
	Seized as USS *Larkspur*				
H	**Brisgavia**				
		1899	6,550	Hamburg	1934
S	**Buenos Aires**				
		1912	9,180	Hamburg	1936
	Reparations to France				
H	**Bulgaria** (see Chapter 15)				
		1898	11,440	Baltimore	1924
	Seized as USS *Hercules*				
N	**Bülow** (German chancellor)				
		1906	8,980	Bremerhaven	1951
	Scrapped as SS *Nyassa*				
D	**Burgermeister**				
		1902	5,945	Hamburg	1934
	Reparations to France				
S	**Cap Arcona**				
		1907	9,832	Hamburg	1938
	Reparations to France in 1920				
S	**Cap Blanco**				
		1903	7,523	Hamburg	1920
	Reparations to Britain; burned out				
S	**Cap Finisterre** (see Chapter 20)				
		1911	14,503	Hamburg	1942
S	**Cap Ortegal**				
		1903	7,818	Hamburg	1932
	Reparations to France, 1919				
S	**Cap Polonio**				
		1914	20,157	Hamburg	1935
	Reparations to Britain; sold back to Süd in 1921				
S	**Cap Roca**				
		1900	5,786		
	Seized by Brazil, 1917				
S	**Cap Trafalgar** (see Chapter 6)				
		1913	18,710	Buenos Aires	1914

Owner	Name of Ship	Year Built	Gross Reg Tons	Location on 8-3-14	Year of Demise
S	**Cap Verde**				
		1900	5,909	Hamburg	
	Reparations to Britain; sold back to Süd in 1921				
S	**Cap Vilano**				
		1906	9,467	Pernambuco	1940
	Reparations to France; bombed and sunk at Le Havre				
N	**Cassel** (German-born English financier)				
		1901	7,543	Bremerhaven	1926
	Reparations to France				
H	**Cincinnati** (see Chapter 15)				
		1908	16,339	Boston	1918
H	**Cleveland** (see Chapter 15)				
		1908	16,971	Hamburg	1933
N	**Coburg** (city of Thuringia)				
		1908	6,750	Rio de Janeiro	
	Reparations to Brazil; in service 1990 as Pocone				
N	**Columbus**				
		1914	34,356	Bremerhaven	1936
	Reparations to Britain as SS *Homeric*				
H	**Corcovado** (Chilean volcano)				
		1907	8,374	Istanbul	1934
	Reparations to Portugal, 1919				
S	**Corrientes** (river of Argentina)				
		1894	3,720	Bahia	1936
	Seized by Brazil, 1917				
N	**Crefeld** (site of Prussian victory over Russians in 1758)				
		1895	3,829	At Sea	1932
	Tender for SMS *Karlsruhe*; stranded as *Espana IV*				
N	**Derfflinger** (Baron Georg von, Prussian general of 17th Century)				
		1907	9,144	Port Said	1932
	Reparations to Britain; sold back to NDL in 1923				
H	**Deutschland** (see Chapter 17 and as *Kaiserin Auguste Victoria*)				
		1898	16,502	Hamburg	1925
N	**Dresden** (2) (principal city of Saxony)				
		1914	14,690	Bremerhaven	1916
	Sunk in Baltic by Russian navy				
W	**Eduard Woermann**				
		1903	5,642		
N	**Eisenach** (city of Thuringia)				
		1908	6,757	Pernambuco	1962
	Reparations to Brazil; scrapped as SS *Santaren*				

Owner	Name of Ship	Year Built	Gross Reg Tons	Location on 8-3-14	Year of Demise
W	**Eleanore Woermann**	1902	4,642	At Sea	1915
	Sunk by British after supplying Admiral Spee				
N	**Erlanger** (city of Thuringia)	1901	5,285	Bremerhaven	1917
	Sunk by mine				
W	**Erna Woermann**	1902	5,580		
D	**Feldmarshall**	1903	6,101		
N	**Frankfurt (2)** (major city of Rhineland)	1899	7,431	Bremerhaven	1931
	Reparations to Britain; scrapped as SS *Servistar*				
W	**Frieda Woermann** (sold to HAPAG as *Belgrano*)				
N	**Friedrich der Grosse** (see Chapter 13)	1896	10,771	Hoboken	1919
H	**Fürst Bismarck** (German chancellor)	1905	8,323	Hamburg	1935
	Renamed as *Friedrichsruh*				
H	**Fürst Bülow** (German chancellor)	1910	7,638	Hamburg	1934
	Reparations to Britain; sold back to HAPAG in 1921				
H	**Galicia** (province of Spain)	1904	6,146	Antofagasta	1933
D	**General**	1910	8,063	Hamburg	1936
	Reparations to France				
H	**General Belgrano** (Manuel, hero of Argentine independence)	1913	10,056	Hamburg	1932
	Reparations to Britain; sold back to HAPAG in 1926				
N	**George Washington** (see Chapter 14)	1908	25,570	Hoboken	1951
H	**Georgia** (district of Russia)	1891	3,143	New York	1917
	Sold in 1915 and torpedoed as SS *E. F. Green*				
W	**Gertrud Woermann**	1907	6,456	Bahia	1943
	Seized by Brazil; beached after collision				
N	**Gneisenau** (German military hero of Napoleonic wars)	190	8,081	Valparaiso	1943
	Reparations to Italy; sunk by U-boat				

Owner	Name of Ship	Year Built	Gross Reg Tons	Location on 8-3-14	Year of Demise
N	**Göben** (August von, Prussian general of 19th century)				
		1906	8,800	Vigo	1931
	Reparations to France as *Rousillon*				
H	**Gothia** (Latin term for much of north Germany)				
		1884	2,433	Barcelona	1923
H	**Graf Waldersee** (see Chapter 16)				
		1898	13,102	Hamburg	1922
H	**Granada** (2) (city of Spain)				
		1906	6,751	Barcelona	1931
	Reparations to Britain; back to HAPAG in 1922				
N	**Grosse Kurfürst** (see Chapter 13)				
		1900	13,245	Hoboken	1937
H	**Habsburg** (hamlet of Aargau, Switzerland; ruling family of Austria-Hungary)				
		1906	6,437	Hamburg	1921
	Scrapped as *Teutonia* (4)				
H	**Hamburg** (see Chapter 13)				
		1899	10,552	Hoboken	1928
N	**Hannover** (2) (city of central Germany)				
		1900	7,305	Bremerhaven	1932
	Reparations to Britain; sold back to NDL in 1921				
W	**Hans Woermann**				
		1900	4,059	At Sea	1917
	Captured by British; later torpedoed				
N	**Helgoland** (German-held island of North Sea)				
		1896	5,666	Plymouth	1915
	Seized as HMS *Polyanna*; torpedoed				
W	**Henry Woermann**				
		1011	6,062	Bahia	
	Seized by Brazil in 1917				
D	**Herzog** (German "duke")				
		1896	4,946		
W	**Hilda Woermann**				
		1914	9,300	Hamburg	1941
	Captured at sea by British in 1940; torpedoed off Vigo				
N	**Hohenstauffen** (German royal house)				
		1906	6,489	Rio de Janeiro	1964
	Reparations to Brazil; scrapped as SS *Cayuba*				
H	**Imperator** (see Chapter 14)				
		1912	51,969	Hamburg	1938
N	**Kaiser Wilhelm II** (see Chapter 12)				
		1902	19,361	Hoboken	1940

Owner	Name of Ship	Year Built	Gross Reg Tons	Location on 8-3-14	Year of Demise
N	**Kaiser Wilhelm der Grosse** (see Chapter 5)				
		1897	14,349	Bremerhaven	1914
H	**Kaiserin Auguste Victoria** (see Chapter 17)				
		1905	24,581	Hamburg	1931
H	**Kiatschou** (alternative name for Tsingtao) (see as *Prinzess Alice*) (see Chapter 13)				
D	**Kigoma** (settlement on Lake Tanganyika				
		1914	8,156	At Sea	1934
	Reparations to Britain; sold to HAPAG in 1922 as SS *Toledo*				
N	**Kleist** (von Nollendorf, a Bohemian general in Napoleonic wars)				
		1907	8,959	Bremerhaven	
	Reparations to Japan as Yoshimo Maru				
N	**Köln** (Rhineland city — Cologne to French)				
		1899	7,409	Boston	1923
	Seized as USS *Amphion*				
D	**König** (German "king")				
		1896	5,043		1915
	Sunk by British at Dar-es-Salaam				
N	**König Albert** (see Chapter 13)				
		1899	10,484	Genoa	1924
H	**König Friedrich Augustus** (a.k.a. Frederick III of Prussia)				
		1906	9,462	Hamburg	1933
	Reparations to Britain; to CPR in 1921				
H	**König Wilhelm II** (King of Prussia)				
		1907	9,410	New York	1947
	Seized as USS *Madawaska*				
N	**Königin Luise** (wife of Frederick William III, mother of Der Grosse; see Chapter 13)				
		1896	10,771	Bremerhaven	1924
D	**Kronprinz**				
		1900	5,689		
N	**Kronprinz Wilhelm** (see Chapter 7)				
		1901	14,908	Hoboken	1924
	Seized as USS *Mount Vernon*				
H	**Kronprinzessin Cecilie** (see Chapter 10)				
		1905	8,689	Falmouth	1926
	Seized as HMS *Princess*				
N	**Kronprinzessin Cecilie** (see Chapters 10 and 11)				
		1906	19,503	Bar Harbor	1940
S	**La Plata** (major estuary of South America)				
		1898	4,032	Hamburg	1924
	Reparations to Britain; to HAPAG in 1922				

Owner	Name of Ship	Year Built	Gross Reg Tons	Location on 8-3-14	Year of Demise
G	**Latvia** (district, then of Russia)				
		1908	8,596	Gydnia	
	Reparations to Japan as *Fuso Maru*; sunk in World War II				
N	**Lützow** (city of Mecklenburg)				
		1908	8,826	Suez	1932
	Seized; sold back to NDL in 1923				
N	**Main (2)** (see Chapter 15)				
		1900	10,067	Bremerhaven	1925
	Reparations to France				
D	**Markgraf** (military lord — boundary keeper)				
		1893	3,680		1915
	Destroyed at Tanganyika by British				
H	**Moltke** (see Chapter 13)				
		1901	12,335	Hamburg	1925
	Reparations to Italy for Lloyd Sabaudo				
H	**Navarra** (medieval kingdom with capital at Pamplona)				
		1905	5,779	At Sea	1914
	Auxiliary for *Kronprinz Wilhelm*; sunk in La Plata				
N	**Neckar** (river of central Germany to Rhine)				
		1900	9,835	New Orleans	1928
	Seized as USS *Antigone*				
H	**Nitokris** (ancient desert city of Egypt)				
		1906	6,150	Coronel	1932
	Reparations to Britain; sold back to HAPAG in 1926				
N	**Norderne** (German island of North Sea)				
		1896	5,497	Bremerhaven	1916
	Sunk by mine while auxiliary				
S	**Patagonia** (district of Argentina)				
		1890	2,975	Buenos Aires	1933
	Interned; sold to Chile; wrecked on 4 October				
H	**Patricia** (see Chapter 15)				
		1899	13,424	Hamburg	1924
	Reparations to Britain's Ellerman Line				
H	**Pennsylvania** (see Chapter 15)				
		1896	13,333	Hoboken	1924
H	**Pisa** (city of central Italy)				
		1896	4,959	Hoboken	1934
	Seized as USS *Ascutney*				
G	**Polonia** (Latinized name for Poland)				
		1910	7,890		1939
D	**Präsident**				
		1900	3,335		1914
	Sunk by British				

Owner	Name of Ship	Year Built	Gross Reg Tons	Location on 8-3-14	Year of Demise
H	**President Grant** (see Chapter 15)				
		1907	18,072	Hoboken	1952
H	**President Lincoln** (see Chapter 15)				
		1907	18,162	Hoboken	1918
S	**Presidente Mitre** (Bartholeme, president of Argentina)				
		1894	8,832		1956
H	**Pretoria** (see Chapter 16)				
		1897	13,234	Hamburg	1921
	Reparations to Britain				
H	**Prinz Adalbert** (brother of Crown Prince Wilhelm				
		1902	6,030	At Sea	1917
	Captured, 1914; torpedoed 6 September				
H	**Prinz Augustus Wilhelm** (brother of Crown Prince Wilhelm)				
		1902	4,733	Colombia	1920
	Scuttled 1917 off coast of Brazil				
H	**Prinz Eitel Friedrich**				
		1902	4,650	Hoboken	1955
	Seized as USS *Otsego*; sold to USSR in 1945				
N	**Prinz Eitel Friedrich** (see Chapter 8)				
		1904	8,797	Tsingtao	1927
	Seized as USS *De Kalb*; returned to NDL in 1921				
N	**Prinz Friedrich Wilhelm** (see Chapter 15)				
		1908	17,082	Kiel	1930
N	**Prinz Heinrich** (brother of Kaiser Wilhelm II)				
		1894	6,636	Oporto	
	Seized by Portugal				
H	**Prinz Joachim** (brother of Crown Prince Wilhelm)				
		1903	4,760	Hoboken	1933
	Seized as USS *Moccasin*				
N	**Prinz Ludwig** (14th Century prince of Brandenburg)				
		1906	9,687	Bremerhaven	1925
	Reparations to Britain, as SS *Orcastle*				
H	**Prinz Oscar** (brother of Crown Prince Wilhelm)				
		1902	6,026	Philadelphia	1928
	Seized as USS *Orion*				
D	**Prinz Regent**				
		1903		Hamburg	1932
	Reparations to France				
N	**Prinz Regent Luitpold** (of Anhalt-Dessau, "Der Alte Dessauer")				
		1894	6,595	Genoa	
	Seized as *Pietro Calvi*				
N	**Prinz Sigismund** (son of Prince Heinrich, cousin of Crown Prince Wilhelm)				
		1902	3,302	Sydney	
	Seized as SS *Bambra*				

Owner	Name of Ship	Year Built	Gross Reg Tons	Location on 8-3-14	Year of Demise
H	**Prinz Sigismund** (consort of Queen Maria of Hungary)	1902	4,689	Colon	1958
	Seized as USS *Gorges*; sold to USSR in 1941				
N	**Prinz Waldemar** (brother of Prince Sigismund)	1903	3,227	Honolulu	
	Seized as USS *Wacouta*				
N	**Prinzess Alice** (cousin of Crown Prince Wilhelm) (see Chapter 13)	1900	10,911	At sea	1930
	Auxiliary to SMS *Emden*				
N	**Prinzess Irene** (wife of Prince Heinrich) (see Chapter 13)	1900	10,881	Hoboken	1932
D	**Prinzessin**	1905	6,387	Hamburg	1933
	Reparations to France				
W	**Professor Woermann**	1912	6,079	Hamburg	1956
	Reparations to British as *Professor*				
G	**Pulaski** (Polish-American patriot)	1912	6,516		1949
S	**Rei de Portugal**	1889	8,236		
	Sold to Prince Line				
H	**Rhaetia** (2) (canton of Switzerland)	1904	6,600	Philadelphia	1924
	Seized as USS *Black Hawk*				
N	**Rhein** (see Chapter 16)	1899	10,058	Hoboken	1928
	Seized as USS *Susquehanna*				
H	**Rhenania** (3) (Latin form of Rhineland)	1904	6,455	Naples	1915
	Seized by Italy; sunk by mine				
H	**Rhodopis** (city on Greek Island of Rhodes)	1906	7,056		1932
	Built for Kosmos Line by Blohn & Voss				
S	**Rio Grande** (river of North America)	1904	4,456		
	Seized by Brazil, 1917				
S	**Rio Negro** (river of South America)	1905	4,699		1933
	Reparations to Britain; purchased by Ellerman Line, 1920				
N	**Roon** (Albert von, Prussian Minister of War)	1903	8,022	Bremerhaven	1925
	Reparations to Greece as *Konstantinopolis*				

Owner	Name of Ship	Year Built	Gross Reg Tons	Location on 8-3-14	Year of Demise
S	**Rosario** (city of Argentina)				
		1913	6,079		
	Became SS *Buenos Aires*				
H	**Rugia** (2) (Latin name for eastern Germany)				
		1905	6,598	Emden	1933
	Reparations to England; sold back to HAPAG in 1921				
S	**San Nicholas**				
		1897	4,739	Rio de Janeiro	
	Seized by Brazil, 1917; still in service in 1957				
S	**Santa Barbara**				
		1908	3,763		1950
	Seized by Portugal, 1916				
S	**Santa Elena**				
		1907	7,473		
S	**Santa Fe**				
		1903	4,477	Antwerp	1932
	Seized in port; sold back to Süd in 1921				
S	**Santa Ines**				
		1914	5,261		1940
	Became *Rio de Janeiro*; torpedoed 9 April				
S	**Santa Maria**				
		1907	7,401	Hamburg	1932
	Reparations to Britain, sold back to Süd in 1922				
N	**Scharnhorst** (Prussian general and writer)				
		1904	8,131	Bremerhaven	1934
	Reparations to France as *La Bourdonnais*				
N	**Schleswig** (northern province of Germany)				
		1903	6,955	Bremerhaven	1932
	Reparations to France as *General Duchesne*				
N	**Seydlitz** (Friedrich Wilhelm von, 18th century Prussian cavalry commander)				
		1903	7,942	Sydney	1933
	Seized, 1914; returned to NDL in 1921				
N	**Sierra Cordoba** (mountain range of central Argentina)				
		1913	8,226	Callao	1942
	Reparations to Peru; bombed & sunk on 9 January as SS *Ruth Alexander*				
N	**Sierra Nevada** (mountain range of southernmost Spain)				
		1913	8,235	Brazil	1943
	Torpedoed as SS *Baye*				
N	**Sierra Salvada** (mountain range of Spain)				
		1913	8,227	Brazil	1955
	Seized, 1917				

Owner	Name of Ship	Year Built	Gross Reg Tons	Location on 8-3-14	Year of Demise
N	**Sierra Ventana** (minor mountain range of Argentina)				
		1913	8,396	Bremerhaven	1940
	Reparations to France as *Alba*				
H	**Swakopmund** (city of German Southwest Africa)				
		1903	5,611	Rotterdam	1930
	Was an earlier *Professor Woermann*				
D	**Tabora** (city of west central Tanzania)				
		1912			1916
	Destroyed by HMS *Hyacinth* at Dar-es-Salaam				
S	**Tijuca** (peak near Rio de Janeiro)				
		1899	4,801	Bahia	1942
	Seized by Brazil; torpedoed 15 August				
H	**Tirpitz** (German Grand Admiral)				
		1914	21,833	Hamburg	1952
	Reparations to England				
H	**Vaterland** (see Chapter 14)				
		1912	54,282	Hoboken	1938
N	**Willehad** (8th century bishop of Bremen)				
		1894	4,761	Boston	1924
	Seized for use as POW ship in New London as USS *Wyandotte*				
D	**Windhuk** (city of German Southwest Africa)				
		1905	6,365		
	Reparations to Italy				
N	**Wittekind** (9th century Westphalian military chieftain)				
		1894	4,755	Boston	1924
	Seized as USS *Iroquois*; became SS *Freedom* in 1919				
N	**Würzburg** (city of northeast Germany)				
		1900	5,085	Lisbon	1921
	Seized by Portugal				
N	**Yorck** (German name for English city)				
		1906	8,976	Bremerhaven	1933
	Retained by NDL after war				
H	**Ypiranga** (location near São Paulo where Brazilian independence was declared)				
		1908	8,309	Hamburg	1950
	Reparations to England as SS *Assyria*				
N	**Zeppelin** (German advocate of lighter-than-air craft)				
		1914	14,588	Bremerhaven	1934
	U.S. Navy transport; back to NDL in 1927; grounded and capsized off Norway				

Notes

PART ONE

1. Bell (1868–1949), Vice-President of the Reichstag and later to hold several important positions in the Weimar Republic, was not an original designee; he replaced the ailing Postmaster General, Johann Giesberts (1865–1938). Müller (1876–1931) was the Foreign Minister.

2. It is worth considering — in seeking to find ultimate blame for the "spark" of the war — that the Dual Monarchy had received several warnings, even from Serbia, that the Archduke's "good-will" visit to Bosnia-Herzegovina might not be advisable. Or everyone could have listened to the words of Chancellor Bismarck who said that "some foolish thing" in the Balkans would ignite the next war.

3. Repeatedly romanced to provide cannon fodder for the battlegrounds of Europe, Japan's leaders wisely concentrated on taking over all the German possessions in the Far East and Pacific Ocean.

4. Much of England's manpower of military age was devoted to the manning of largely inactive capital naval vessels. Canada had a higher fatality rate than the parent country's, 1 in 57; India's, in contrast, was barely 1 in 10,000.

5. Page 220, *Memoirs of Count Witte*, by Abraham Yarmolinsky: Doubleday, 1921.

6. On 19 November 1918, Vice Admiral Ludwig Reuter led a 50-kilometer-long procession of warships — already relieved of all ammunition — from Wilhelmshaven to various British ports, ending at Scapa Flow at the northerly tip of Scotland.

7. Queen Victoria, whose numerous offspring married into all the royal

houses of importance in Europe, was grandmother to both Kaiser Wilhelm II and King George V.

8. Both these names, honoring Prussian heroes, would be reapplied to more powerful German naval vessels in World War II.

9. At the one-sided battle off Coronel, where Admiral "Kit" Cradock lost two warships, over 1,500 British seamen, and his own life.

10. On 20 September 1914.

11. Churchill, *The World Crisis, 1911–1914*, New York, 1924, page 208.

12. Manual on the Conduct of War.

13. This is a political office, akin to the American Secretary of the Navy. The First Sea Lord would be comparable to the professional Chief of Naval Operations.

14. After 4 August 1914, only the Baltic Sea was open to German shipping; British submarines also operated there.

15. Churchill, Appendix "C," *The World Crisis, 1911–1914*, New York, 1924.

16. For the British, the Great War was reluctantly entered into on 4 August 1914, two days after it had begun for the Belgians and French. Their "cease fire and withdraw" ultimatum to the German government had never been taken seriously in Berlin, and expired at midnight, 3 August.

17. *Scharnhorst* and *Gneisenau*, though built in different yards, were sister ships. Four-stacked, heavy cruisers, capable of speeds up to 23.5 knots, they carried eight 200mm (8-inch) guns as their major armament. Both were lost to His Majesty's battle cruisers *Invincible* and *Inflexible* in the battle off the Falkland Islands on 8 December 1914, along with the light cruisers *Nürnberg* and *Leipzig*.

18. *Königsberg*, namesake of the class with *Nürnberg*, was built at the imperial yards of Kiel in 1906–7 at a cost of almost 5.5 million marks. At the end of October 1914, she was blocked in the mouth of the Great Ruaha River of East Africa and scuttled there the following 11 July.

19. *Dresden* and *Emden* were sister ships, laid down as light cruisers in 1906. Carrying ten 105mm guns plus lesser armament, they were capable of speeds up to 25 knots. *Dresden* was scuttled off Mas a Tierra, Chile, on 14 March 1915, after fleeing from superior British cruisers. *Emden* was beached at North Cocos Island on 9 November 1914, after a losing battle with the much heavier Australian cruiser, *Sydney*.

20. Churchill, *The World Crisis, 1911–1914*, New York, 1924, page 307.

21. In later years and under a different ownership, the most famous employee of these yards was one Lech Walesa.

22. *Prinz Eitel Friedrich* had been built in the smaller Reihersteig yards at Hamburg.

23. The United States had also embarked on a frenzied ship-construction program. The program even included such unorthodox procedures as making ships of cast concrete; they did not work very well.

24. Grey (1862–1933) was descended from the famous Earl Grey, sponsor of Britain's landmark "Reform Bill" of 1832. A Liberal member of Parliament, he was under-secretary in the Foreign Office 1892–95 and Foreign Secretary for ten years after 1906. He retired in 1916 because of failing eyesight.

25. The heirs of Alfred Krupp, the "Kanonenkönig" of Essen, were probably somewhat more significant.

26. In 1917 the ship, *Cleveland*, was sold to some Swedish interests pursuant to this belated authorization. However, delivery could not be made and the Allies seized the ship in 1918 while she was still tied up at Hamburg.

27. Theobald von Bethmann-Hollweg (1856–1921) served as Chancellor after the resignation of von Bülow in July 1909. He was forced to resign seven years later by Hindenburg and Ludendorff, by then the de facto rulers of Germany, because he sought to achieve a negotiated peace as American entry into the war was seen as meaning ultimate defeat for the Fatherland.

28. The Austrian merchant marine and navy were "small potatoes" compared with those of Germany.

29. In this "optimistic" prediction the normally astute Ballin was considerably off the mark. When the Great War ended, Austria lost its prime port of Trieste and its naval base at Pola; it was now a landlocked nation with no merchant marine at all.

30. This was a reference to the unrestricted submarine warfare against the Allies, the results of which finally brought the United States into the war.

31. In this matter he was aided, as was Franklin Roosevelt in his much more evident affliction, by a compliant press corps.

32. This text was the official written version, and was published three weeks later from the castle of Amerongen, near Utrecht, where the Kaiser had taken refuge. The urge to rule, however, never left him. In 1935, after 17 years of exile, he tried to engineer a deal with Adolf Hitler that would let him return to Germany as some sort of titular head of state. All *Der Führer* ever gave him, though, was a full military funeral after his death on 5 June 1941.

33. Both HAPAG and NDL were publishing advertisements in major American newspapers, promoting their sailings for three months hence, right up until 1 August.

34. By the war's end, American troops filled almost one quarter of the Western Front line and more were arriving daily.

35. The mathematician will note that this arithmetic is both rounded off and makes some assumptions: allowing for repairs and turnaround time, the *Kronprinzessin* made a round trip in about four weeks; the 767 makes six round trips per week.

36. This was the heaviest gun that could be served manually.

PART TWO

1. "Prince of Grapeshot." A mildly pejorative nickname earned in 1848 because of the vigor with which his troops put down an insurrection that year.

2. *Bismarck*'s captain was laboring under der Führer's order never to surrender his ship. Meanwhile, 2,500 miles to the east 21-year-old Gottfried von Bismarck, whose uncle, another Otto, was ambassador to Italy, was trapped at

Stalingrad where his unit was fighting cold, starvation, lice, typhus and with no ammunition until finally overwhelmed as well.

3. *Lucania* had, in turn, taken the record from the Inman liner, *City of Paris*, which had held the title, with a speed of just over 20 knots, since 1889.

4. The disadvantage of having no radio apparatus had just been widely brought home when the first mate of the Oceanic Company's *Mariposa*, William Watson, had to row 87 miles to shore at Monterey, California, to report that his ship had run out of fuel.

5. Reymann (1872–1948) subsequently spent some time as a prisoner of war, but was exchanged and became Chief of Staff to the Baltic Station and, in 1921, President of the Navy Peace Commission. He retired with the rank of Vizeadmiral but lived on to see another world subjugation of Germany, dying on 10 July 1948.

6. There were four German colonies in Africa at the start of the Great War: Togo, which became French after the war and independent in 1960; Kamerun, which followed the same path; German Southwest Africa, which became a British protectorate and then independent as Namibia in 1990; and the major outpost of German East Africa, which also became British as Tanganyika and then independent as Tanzania (with Zanzibar) in 1961.

7. Now in England, Guglielmo Marconi's great contribution to the use of radio was evolving directional antennae, both for transmission and reception. His skills gave the British a great leg up over the Germans on intelligence gathering.

8. The latter was captured in the West Indies by British cruisers a few weeks later.

9. Buller (1873–1960) came from a family with naval tradition and connections. His father was Admiral Sir Alexander Buller, and he had served seven years as flag lieutenant to the famous First Sea Lord, "Jackie" Fisher. He had served on both the battleships *Camperdown* and *Victoria*, fortunately prior to their notable collision in June 1893. In 1919, Buller married Lady Hermione Stuart, the only daughter of the 17th Earl of Moray. Two years later he was made commander of the royal yachts and retired with the rank of admiral in 1931.

10. As of 2001, Hamburg-Süd was still alive and well.

11. Students of history will recall that the sympathetic folk of Uruguay were also called upon to provide shelter to the German "pocket battleship," *Admiral Graf Spee*, a generation later. Their second act of generous neutrality came out no better for their guests than did this first.

12. Besides other "friendly" ports, these included such places "overseas" as Aden, Auckland, Bermuda, Cape Town, Colombo, Esquimalt, Gibraltar, Halifax, Hong Kong, Malta, Perth, Singapore, Suez, Sydney, and Trinidad (Caribbean).

13. On this crossing, *Carmania* was carrying some $10,000,000 in gold bullion to help sustain the shaky foundations of some British financial houses.

14. Ironically, and somewhat in recompense, in one of the last acts of the war, the British battleship, *Britannia*, was torpedoed and sunk off Cape Trafalgar on 10 November 1918.

15. One of the famous German marching songs of the period ends with the words: "Wir fahren gegen England"—"We sail against England."

16. Gallieni (1849–1916) was a much underappreciated hero of World War I. Having refused the position of commander-in-chief, he retired from active duty in April of 1914, but was recalled in August to command the "Army of Paris." After his efforts won the First Battle of the Marne, he was made Minister of War and in 1921 was posthumously created a Marshal of France.

17. Speck von Sternberg was a professional diplomat who had served five years as military attaché in Washington during the second Cleveland administration. He was appointed to the ambassadorship in 1903, and served in it until his death five years later.

18. Thierfelder (1883–1941) was a native of Rostock. After his internment during the war years he served as port captain at Haugesund and as a staff officer to what was left of the German Navy.

19. Churchill's maternal grandfather was the New York financier, Leonard Jerome.

20. Winston Spencer Churchill, *The World Crisis, 1911–1914, New York, 1924*, Appendix "E."

21. HMS *Suffolk*, laid down in the spring of 1901, was the youngest of the *Monmouth* class of "first class" armoured cruisers. Her main armament consisted of 14 six-inch guns and she carried a crew of 678. These British ships were all slower than the newer *Karlsruhe*, but as a compensation they were also much better armed.

22. To this very day, that affinity remains strong; though astronomically appropriate for all of Europe west of Germany, Portugal is the only nation on the continent to conform to Greenwich Mean Time.

23. *Agincourt* had a very convoluted history, having first been built for Brazil. When that nation could not pay for her delivery, she was then resold to the Sultan, who demanded that western-style facilities in the ship's heads be replaced with those more traditional in his land. Before arriving in time for the Battle of Jutland, *Agincourt*'s plumbing had to be changed once again.

24. As of this date, the First Lord was unaware of the fate of the *Karlsruhe*, and *Dresden* was still at large in the Pacific.

25. Winston Spencer Churchill, *The World Crisis 1916–1918*, Vol II, New York, 1927, p 158.

26. The leaky and useless Russian barkentine, *Pitan*, had been stopped but allowed to proceed.

27. These were German-built sister ships of the Barbarossa Class *Grosse Kurfürst* and *Friedrich der Grosse*.

28. The French honorary "de" is comparable to the "von" in many Teutonic names, meaning "of" or "from."

29. Taken over from the Japanese in later years, Tsingtao was also headquarters for the United States naval forces in the western Pacific after the conclusion of World War II.

30. Thierichens was later interned in the United States for the duration of the war, and then placed on the German Naval retired list.

31. The *Choising* was fortunate to be at liberty. Before the war was ended there were 45 German ships interned in the Netherlands East Indies and 72 in

Portuguese harbors. There was also a total of 99 German ships interned in American-controlled ports of which 62 pertained to HAPAG.

32. This story is well told in Mücke's little volume, "The Ayesha," translated into English and published in Boston in 1917 by Ritter & Company.

33. HAPAG's much smaller ship of the same name was already legally interned at Hoboken.

34. Churchill, *The World Crisis 1911–1914*, p. 326.

35. Pfundheller, who died on Christmas Day 1940, had been an administrative officer in the Reichmarineamt and later retired as a Vizeadmiral.

PART THREE

1. In later years, the United States Shipping Board rated her speed at 24 knots.

2. On her second westward crossing (3,145 miles) under Captain Polack, the *Kronprinzessin* made the run at an average speed of 23.31 knots and had one day of 603 miles.

3. "Erhard has suffered an attack of catarrh of the bladder; Siegfried."

4. Richter had been the original skipper of the *Kronprinzessin* in 1907 and Högemann until mid–1913.

5. Andrew Jackson Barchfield, medical doctor and politician, represented the 32nd District of Pennsylvania from 1905 to 1917. German-born Richard Bartholdt represented the 10th District of Missouri from 1893 to 1915 — he had just declined election to a twelfth term. Governor Charles Miller of Delaware, only part way into his four-year term, was also aboard.

6. Probably the most affluent and influential was Samuel Newhouse (1853–1930), a mining magnate and financier of Utah and New York, not to be confused with the media magnate of a later generation.

7. For the gold coins, the actual bills of lading indicated the following:

To Paris:	Goldman, Sachs & Co.	$ 1,076,634
	Heidelbach, Ickelheimer & Co.	1,584,000
	National City Bank	2,104,254
To London:	Guaranty Trust Co.	4,942,937
	National City Bank	1,061,719
		$10,769,544

8. Blair, who had married Florence Osborne Jennings 23 years earlier, also belonged to the Union Club, the National Golf Links, the Racquet & Tennis Club, the Riding Club, the Pilgrims, and the Sons of the Revolution. In addition, he was a director of several railroads.

9. Quoted (in translation) from page 220 of "Unser Feld ist die Welt"—"Our Field Is the World"—a commemorative history of HAPAG-Lloyd.

10. The United States was followed into the European war by: Panama and Cuba on 7 April; Siam on 22 July; Liberia on 4 August; China on 14 August; Brazil on 26 October; and Guatemala, Nicaragua, Haiti and Honduras in the late spring of 1918.

11. Hale (1848–1934) was appointed by President Theodore Roosevelt for the Federal District of Maine in 1902. A native of Turner, Maine, he had served two terms in the U.S. House of Representatives for the Portland area. In his recounting of recent events, Hale made no attempt to pick sides, analyze reasons, or attach blame — in the later words of television's Sgt. Friday: "Just the facts…"

12. The attorneys for North German Lloyd included John Munro Woolsey (1877–1945) a distinguished authority on Admiralty law who was later elevated by President Hoover to the Federal Bench, where he became most noted for his decision in regard to James Joyce's controversial novel, *Ulysses*.

13. Here, and throughout his findings, Judge Hale employed an alternative form of spelling for Serbia that has been totally superseded in modern usage.

14. Southeast of Belgrade, this had been the capital of Serbia from 1878 to 1901.

15. The Socialists, however, scheduled a demonstration on 28 July, against any war.

16. The sudden outbreak of war inconvenienced everyone. The famous Boston Symphony Orchestra, led from 1912 to 1918 by the German conductor, Karl Muck (1859–1940), had to postpone its opening and cancel its western tour because of the detention in Europe of its leader and several other key members.

17. "Independent and perpetual" Belgian neutrality had been guaranteed by the 1839 Treaty of London, to which the signatories were: Austria, Britain, France, Prussia and Russia. On 3 August German Chancellor Bethmann/Hollweg admitted that Germany had done "a wrong" which he promised would be rectified as soon as France was subdued.

18. Illustrative of the incompetence within the Russian hierarchy, Sukhomlinov was reported by a German commentator to have stated with some pride that "I have not read a military manual for the last twenty-five years." Jilinsky, chief of the Russian General Staff was described by his contemporary, General Sazonov, in the latter's memoires (*Fateful Years*, New York, 1928; page 286) even less complimentary terms: "It was very difficult to make him work, but to get him to tell the truth was well-nigh impossible."

19. On 30 July, the French railways mobilized 4,278 trains, solely for the carriage of regulars and reservists of the Army. On 27 July, Vice-Admiral Augustin de Lapeyrère, Commander-in-Chief of the French Navy, had convened a war counsel of all his principal subordinates.

20. Prince Alexander, who had been educated in Russia, was in fact the regent for his ailing father, King Peter, who had been elected on 15 June 1903.

21. On 28 July, Austrian Foreign Minister Leopold von Berchtold published the following statement: "The Royal Government of Servia not having replied in a satisfactory manner to the note remitted to it by the Austro-Hungarian Minister in Belgrade on 23 July, 1914, the Imperial and Royal Government finds itself compelled to proceed to safeguard its rights and interests and to have recourse for this purpose to force of arms. Austria-Hungary considers itself, therefore, from this moment in a state of war with Servia."

22. There were stated to be more than 200,000 eligible Austro-Hungarian reservists in the United States. Many of them had booked passage on the *Vaterland*

(due to sail on 1 August) to return home. The fine print of the decree stated that this amnesty only covered those who returned at once to their military duties.

23. The rapidity with which the Russians were able to mobilize came as quite a shock to the German High Command. Their famous Schlieffen Plan assumed that Russia would take at least 100 days to get her massive manpower fully ready for war. To meet the unexpectedly rapid assembly of the Czar's army, several divisions that had been earmarked for the right wing of the drive against France were hurriedly entrained for the Eastern Front. In effect, the Russians thus allowed the French to win the crucial first Battle of the Marne.

24. Consols, regarded as the soundest of investments, were perpetual interest-bearing bonds issued by the British government as early as 1751.

25. During the 20 years prior to the outbreak of the Great War, Manchester was the regular summer domicile of up to a dozen diplomats.

26. There were two dissents to the majority decision, from Justices Mahlon Pitney and John Hessin Clarke, who found themselves in agreement with the majority of the Circuit Court.

27. In July 1929, the newest North German Lloyd *Bremen* (fourth of that name), returned the title to Germany, having made the same transatlantic run at 27.92 knots.

28. NDL had a total of 27 ships in United States' ports on 7 August 1914, not counting the *Kronprinz Wilhelm* and *Prinz Eitel Friedrich* that came along a few months later.

29. This was the second steamship *Bremen*, whose story appears in Chapter 9. The first ship of this name had opened NDL's service to New York on 19 June 1858.

30. The order was formally abolished by command of Napoléon in 1809, but survived in Austria as a purely religious group.

31. Palasciano (1815–91) was a Neapolitan medical doctor who achieved fame as a captain in the Bourbon army during the battle of Messina. His refusal to obey an order *not* to give aid to wounded enemy soldiers made him a hero to the Risorgimento forces and the International Red Cross.

32. Pocahontas, daughter of the great chief Powhatan, dropped her personal name of Matoika and was given the Christian name Rebecca at the time of her marriage to John Rolfe.

33. The story has it that the president of Cunard told King George V that he was going to name the latest "largest ship in the world" after "Britain's greatest queen," having in mind George's grandmother, Victoria. The King thereupon replied that he was sure that his wife, Her Highness, Queen Mary (of Teck), would be very pleased.

34. This ship was 16,000 tons larger than the Cunard liner, *Olympic*, and is not to be confused with a somewhat contemporary Belgian-registered vessel, *Vaderland*, which was taken over by the White Star line just before the start of the war, renamed *Southland*, and torpedoed by *U-70* some 140 miles off Donegal's Tory Island on 4 June 1917.

35. Eighty or so feet less than the 200 feet which is about the average for the English Channel.

36. *Tasso* was the loser in this occurrence, coming close to sinking; the NDL ship lost only some paint.

37. Denmark officially sat out the Great War; but with her relative weakness and close proximity to Germany, she was forced to maintain a high degree of cordiality toward her enormous and powerful neighbor.

38. A strong political ally of Sir John Macdonald, Canada's founding prime minister, Sir Wilfrid (1841–1919) had been a strong proponent of trade reciprocity with the United States and had served as prime minister from 1896 to 1911.

39. American Admiral Chester Nimitz, a hero of the sequel conflict, once explained why his ships were traditionally described as being of female gender — "because it costs so much to keep them in paint and powder."

40. From *Daheim* of 15 April, 1899, Vol XXXV, #29.

41. As of mid–June 1920, the United States Shipping Board had more than 250 ships idle in New York or Hampton Roads.

42. After the war, the more luxurious *Imperator* made three trips to bring 28,036 of those men back home.

PART FOUR

1. The Canadian Pacific has inspired more attention from historians than most transportation companies. This author has a dozen different and complementary volumes on this topic, and has even written one — *The Great Glacier and Its House*, 1984.

PART FIVE

1. The title "graf" translates into English as "count"; a Burggraf, however, also has title to a castle. This Burggraf had been navigation officer on the pre–Dreadnaught battleship *Posen* and an aide-de-camp to the Kaiser. He was placed on the retired list as a rear admiral at the start of the Second World War and died in 1956. Some of his offspring, however, served under Hitler, notably in the campaign against Russia in 1942.

2. Winston Churchill had resigned this post on 21 May 1915, after the failure of the Dardanelles Campaign and was now at the front in France. The Earl of Balfour had to handle the news.

3. Actually, the largest of these ships, *Appam*, at 7,781 tons, was used to take off the crews of the other vessels, then dispatched to a neutral port in Spain where she was interned for the duration.

4. One of these ships, the 3,300 ton *Westburn*, was laden with prisoners and sent to Santa Cruz de Teneriffe, in the Canary Islands, and sunk there after delivering her human cargo.

5. Wolf (1880–1920) was a native of Breslau and no relative of the Oberleutnant.

6. Luckner (1886–1966), who became a sail training officer on the *Niobe*

after the Great War, achieved much subsequent fame after his retirement for his world tour of 1937–39 in his yacht, *Sea Devil*, about which he published two books. See also Lowell Thomas's *Count Luckner, the Sea Devil*, published in New York in 1927.

7. Named for the Commander of Napoleon's Imperial Guard at Waterloo.

8. This was an eminently appropriate name, inasmuch as the Crown Princess had just presented her husband with their youngest child, also named Cecilie.

9. Knorr had been a naval attaché in both Tokyo and Washington and had then been given command of the cruiser, SMS *Breslau*.

10. As in the Second World War, the German steel industry was very dependent on the high-quality magnetite iron ore shipped south from Kiruna. As long as the Swedes kept the ore coming, it was deemed better policy not to antagonize them.

11. HAPAG's first ship of this name was six years older and is more fully discussed in Chapter 15.

12. After this voyage Hermann (1881–1927) was made chief of naval reconnaissance forces, but retired at the end of 1919.

13. Yale University Press, 1939.

14. From the moment she left Kiel, until her return to its safe harbor, some fifteen months later, Nerger never used his radio transmitter. To do so would have surely given his position away and brought his voyage to a swift end. The Germans had finally learned.

15. Tietze, aged 40, was one of the older skippers of these raiders. He had previously been on the Admiralty staff and was commander of the pre–Dreadnaught battleship SMS *Wörth*.

PART SIX

1. The Washington Treaty of 1922 on the limitation of naval armaments had specified a ratio of capital ships of three for Japan, to five each for the United States and Great Britain, to 1.67 each for France and Italy.

Index